J. B. Priestley – The Dramatist

Gareth Lloyd Evans

J. B. Priestley – The Dramatist

HEINEMANN : LONDON

William Heinemann Ltd
LONDON MELBOURNE TORONTO
CAPE TOWN AUCKLAND

First published 1964

Printed in Great Britain
by Bookprint Limited
Kingswood, Surrey

Contents

For Barbara

and my Mother

and the memory of my Father

INTRODUCTION

The work of J. B. Priestley spans five decades in time, and the novel, drama, criticism, essay, journalism and broadcasting in scope. His name has occupied a prominent place in the emotional and intellectual turbulence of twentieth-century social and political life. At one time, during the second world war, he seemed to be all reasonable men's epitome; at others, he has seemed to be the self-conscious conscience of society. He has been reviled, then admired; lauded, then ignored. Throughout, there has persisted the steadfast image (with its half-mocking studiedness) of the pipe-smoking realist. Like a chubby rock he has seemed capable both of withstanding the waves and, when it pleased him, of commanding them to stand off. Whenever there has been the need for the exertion of common sense, the image, and sometimes the presence, of Priestley, has been called upon. Also, when society has seen the need for a whipping-block, the same has occasionally happened. He has been ubiquitous in his creative activity and in his influence, but the price he has had to pay, as an artist, for all his activities, is that of being known by many and really understood by few.

In an age of specialisation the man whose intellectual net is cast wide is often regarded with suspicion. But the merits of specialisation, though no doubt admirable in the precise world of science and technology, do not necessarily have any potency for art. The evidence of literary history is against the Godhead of specialisation. Shakespeare, Johnson, Shelley, Arnold, Dickens and Eliot speak for the ubiquitous man of letters. But the modern academic critic, himself often a product of a constraining specialisation, sometimes mistakes dedication to a narrow field of activity for quality. The ceaseless and wide activity of Priestley has caused him to be judged by some as a Jack of all trades and a master of none. For others, his very ability to climb so regularly into the best-seller class is itself indicative of a partial talent. But, again, the evidence of history is against this notion of popularity as necessarily the stigma of the second-rate.

The commercial success of some of Priestley's plays, especially in the 1930s has not brought with it any systematic critical examination of his plays. There has been a surprising critical neglect of a dramatist whose plays are performed in more countries of the world than those of any other living English dramatist. Similarly, his own critical writings on the drama and theatre have not, in this country, been the subject of more than cursory examination.

Priestley's plays have about them, on the page, the implied smell and fabric of theatre itself. They are written less out of the head, as it were, than out of the head and heart together which both know and feel for the actuality of performance. He has always engaged himself with theatre in an active sense, and the content and form of his plays can only be properly evaluated in the context of rehearsal and performance. They demand a response which must constantly involve both their literary content and their theatrical reality. The latter, unfortunately, is a context not always by any means available, and in my analysis of many of the plays I am conscious of its lack. It is, therefore, worth emphasising that many of my judgements have had to be based on 'performances in the head', the disadvantages of which may perhaps be only too clear.

This book does not attempt a detailed survey and analysis of the whole of the dramatic work of Priestley. In general, it takes its themes from the three collected volumes of Priestley's plays, which are conveniently divisable into 'Time-plays', 'Comedies' and 'Sociological plays'. In some degree the book is intended as a companion to these volumes.

Its main intention, however, is to try to provide some indications of the dominant qualities of Priestley as a dramatist – his strengths and his weaknesses. In attempting this, it is obvious that subjective evaluation will be dominant. Thus, offence may be caused to some who find their 'favourite play' cursorily dealt with or merely mentioned, and to others who feel that undue attention has been paid to plays they would wish to dismiss with a word. Subjectivity works both ways – for the critic and for the reader.

David Hughes's general study of Priestley the writer has been a great source of imaginative stimulation, and I owe a debt to many people who, in conversation and, in the case of Mr J. C. Trewin, in correspondence, have helped and encouraged. But, above all, my wife must have my greatest thanks. She has screwed my courage to the sticking post, uprooted from the manuscript more faults than it even now shows, and deserves better for her labours.

Stratford-upon-Avon, 1964

PART ONE

CHAPTER ONE

The Man and His Imagination

Priestley's essays and novels are full of references to, and asides about, the theatre. He gives a constant impression that, even in his imaginative writing, he is never far away, in his inner mind, from a world of footlights, greasepaint, and the old fourpenny balcony on a Saturday night. The word 'magic' is never absent for long from his writing: 'What then was the compulsion, the force that hurled me towards these barriers? It was the ancient witchery of the work itself, the eternal fascination of the Theatre'.

Even in the harsher moments, which he has often experienced, when money has frustrated a scheme, or a play has turned sour early, the deep under-swell of the romantic captive man can still be heard: 'I am not too fond of the metropolitan theatre world, with its smart hangers-on, its mysterious financial gentlemen, its supper-room exhibitionists, its You were marvellous, darling, nonsense'.

There are two extremes to Priestley's life in the theatre – the one which is emotionally vibrant, cautiously loving, sometimes boyish in its enthusiasm, and the other which often fumes and stamps, is frustrated, and which often seems upon the point of rejecting this most fickle mistress. But the two extremes are held in balance by a constant obsession – the vulnerability of the drug-addict even when, for a time, hard practice is whispering the word 'reject' in his ear. There is no tradition of theatre-work or addiction in Priestley's lineage. His autobiographies and his talk make it clear that it is not heredity which infected him with this particular fever. The autobiographies relate very clearly a not uncommon growth of this association with the world of theatre. The accounts are similar in theme and emotional contour to those of many who grew up or were youthfully adult in the late 'nineties and the Edwardian era, when neither money nor distance seemed an insuperable barrier to theatre-going. The availability of a variety of theatre experience dominates the accounts of so many of the afficionados of the theatre in the early twentieth century. Whether it was Battersea or Bradford they could easily get there:

> Bradford then had two theatres and two music-halls, all under our patronage. I was especially fond of the fourpenny balcony at the Empire – not the cheapest seats, for there was a twopenny gallery behind us – where I forgot my discomfort. . . . the expert 'packers' treated us like sardines – looking down on Grock and Little Tich and W. C. Fields and Jimmy Learmouth.

Even the more austere sensibilities of T. S. Eliot are roused by the memories and meanings of the rich and varied theatre-world into which Priestley was so easily enticed: 'In the Music-Hall comedians they [the lower class] find the expression and dignity of their own lives'. The emphasis here, and in Priestley's own accounts of his first experience of theatre, is on the Music Hall, and on the relationship of this form to its noisy class-conscious audience. All Priestley's reminiscences begin with Music Hall, and its effects have never entirely disappeared either from his own plays or from his theoretical writing about theatre. For Priestley, drama is, in the richest sense of the word, 'entertainment', and the cue to the richness which the word implies for him is his own joy at seeing Little Tich and the others. Priestley has never subscribed to the notion of drama being merely therapeutic, educational or even polemical, although those who have taken his later 'message' plays more stringently than he himself intended, have thought otherwise. Bluntly, the starting-point for Priestley now, and in the early days, was entertainment. It is the delight in the experience of theatre of all kinds which contains for him as dramatist the realities of the relationship between the art and its society. Magic is one thing certainly, but the magic is for him under the constant surveillance of that part of him which sees the theatre as that point where man is at his most alive, whether he be actor, playwright, or audience: 'If I wanted to make people feel deeply I should use the drama. You can create a quality of emotion in the theatre beyond any you can achieve in another medium'.

The Edwardian music-hall was, uniquely, a place where the rabidly sectarian class-consciousness (certainly in the cheaper areas of the house) found a ready counterpart in the earthy extrovertism of the performers who usually identified themselves with the 'lower orders' of the audience. Priestley's sense of the relationship of theatre to society was moulded in this democratic melting pot. The magic of theatre and the sense of its human dimensions were created together in Priestley. Originally the 'magic' was one in which 'the actors were ... almost visitors from outer space', and this blended with a notion that took time to grow into full consciousness: 'You can create a quality of emotion in the theatre beyond any you can achieve in another medium'.

His absorption in the theatre was then, at first, romantic – the practicalities came later. He revelled in what he experienced in the galleries, he wanted to write for theatre, to write about it, and to act in it. He records an early *œuvre projeté* which was to be a series of sketches about theatre called *Moorton Sketches – at the Music Hall;* he also recollects writing dialogues in dramatic form with titles like *Youth Smoking Russian Cigarette* and *Man With Calabash Pipe*. He was stage-struck enough to want to act, and he joined the local Playgoers' Society in Bradford. It was, however, many years before he fulfilled the apogée of his desires – to act on the professional stage. For ten 'glorious but tiring days' he took over at short notice, the part of Henry Ormonroyd, the bucolic photographer of *When We Are Married* at the St. Martin's theatre. He was well over forty when this happened, and he was thirty-nine before his first play was written and produced on the professional stage.

A criticism often levelled at him which is readily given a cheap punning gimmickry by the phrase 'Jack of all trades', is that he has thinned his talent by attempting too much in too many literary forms. He has admitted that he has probably written too much, and also that his output is qualitatively uneven. But it is too simple an equation to assume that his restless activity is the result of an egomaniac compulsion to see himself in print, or of a demagogic belief that all he has written is badly needed by a waiting world. He finds it difficult to envisage his readers:

> I cannot even imagine them. Millions and millions of my novels have been sold, in many different languages all over the world, yet I have never been able to imagine who read them, and often, setting aside friends and acquaintances, I have felt that nobody was reading them.

That this is not arrogant acceptance of a dimly appreciated inevitability is shown in his doubtful words about his own novel-writing:

> The danger of this hasty topical novel-writing is that while taking so wide an aim you may hit nothing except your own reputation, failing to give your readers a story that satisfies them and equally failing to convert them to your point of view. I was not aware of this danger at the time, but, tempted, I fell, and more than once.

The reasons for his varied and large output are complicated, and their expression is made more difficult by the fact that Priestley himself is conscious of the criticisms levelled at him, and has been at some pains to answer them with honesty while, at the same time, openly resenting their implication.

The gregariousness of his emotions and intelligence has always directed him to pursue the satisfaction of an intense curiosity about people and, at the same time, an insatiable lust to communicate, either on the page or via the voice, has prompted him to try and share the excitement which his adventurous mind has experienced. This is the core of the matter – it is natural to this man to search, savour and share. But certainly, up to the 1930s he wrote with a ferocity of pace because he had deliberately chosen the career of writing and wished to justify the choice. But of equal weight was the necessity to keep the wolf from the door of his young family. Having turned down Quiller-Couch's suggestion of a lectureship at Cambridge, he moved to London in 1922 with a capital of less than fifty pounds. From 1922 to 1930 he wrote novels, essays, and reviews; he read for publishers. He was very certainly, very conscientiously and very deliberately, a journeyman. It needs to be remembered that, in this variety of work, he performed nothing that was unique either to his own generation or the one immediately preceding him. Shaw, Symons, Edward Thomas and many others of the literary generations surrounding Priestley did no more and no less than write what they could, when and where they could.

So, at first sight, the reasons for the ubiquity of his pen seem equally balanced between the urges of his personality and the economic necessities of a chosen career. But the slightest acquaintance with Priestley immediately suggests that this balance is made delicate by a number of other factors. One of these factors is involved in the image for which he, in part, has been responsible, which has been projected on his public – that of the bluff realist, the pipe-smoking super-confident Northerner. In fact he is very cosmopolitan in taste and habit, and has spent by far the greater part of his life in the southern part of these islands. But the image is only skin-deep. There exists in Priestley the unexpected quality of a lack of self-confidence:

> What was behind all this hopping from novels to plays to autobiographical-descriptive books? Possibly a fundamental lack of what I appeared superficially to have in abundance – self-confidence. Perhaps I was afraid of committing myself to any one thing. Perhaps I hopped about so that I made a difficult target.

This is the older man speaking, and its tentative hindsight may suggest to some a kind of special pleading. He admits that he was not conscious of a lack of self-confidence in his early years – a statement which would seem to reinforce the charge of special pleading. But one is strongly inclined to dismiss the charge for a number of reasons, not the least of them being the unequivocal sequel to the above remarks:

> When I was in my middle teens, certain that I would never be a wool-merchant, but not sure if I would be a writer, an actor, or a musician, my father sensibly warned me more than once that I might be a Jack of all trades, master of none. Even as early as 1924 when he died, he would have admitted that he had been wrong. But sometimes now I think he might have been right.

His father represented for him an iron source of moral and physical courage and truth. It must have been hard to countenance the possibility that he might have been right, particularly since, as Priestley makes clear in his conversation and in his autobiographies, to some extent the dynamic to be a writer was given fuel by a radical spirit: 'The older I get the better I understand the part played in my life and writing by early influences. Politically and socially I am a radical; culturally I am a conservative. I really belong to the avant-garde of the 1880s – say 1886, the date of Fauré's second piano quartet'.

It is in the heady honesty of the personal presence of Priestley, however, that the truth of these assertions of his can alone be tested. His bluntness is never bludgeoning and is used more often than not to elicit fact and truth than to assert or impress. His decisiveness of opinion is only peremptory when he has fools at hand, and is always open to the countering point-of-view. His provocativeness is never rude except when he has arrogance to contend with, and it is more often than not intended more catalystically than otherwise. His humour is rarely malicious and proceeds more from an earnest good-fellowship than a desire to be cleverly witty. His response to praise is embarrassingly gracious, but flattery withers in his presence. Above all he has not lost a certain kind of rare innocence which can make him excited about a book he is writing or reading or a person or place he has become acquainted with. He is far from being a plaster-saint and he has in good measure the most common human failings of occasional irascibility and prejudice in small matters. But the most intense impression derived from the man is that of a civilised and caring human being, the complexity of whose personality hides behind the plain face of a genial realist. Part of this complexity is induced by the absence of a militant self-confidence in a pattern of mind and emotions which constantly urges him to take up the pen on behalf of anything which is just, true, and exciting.

The impact of person on person in the shifting relationships of our social and intellectual world is perhaps the least acceptable evidence to support a contention. But a proliferation of such evidence cannot be totally ignored, and this evidence exists in abundance in the largely unrecorded words of many friends and acquaintances. It all amounts to a refutation of the old image of Priestley – an image which cracks open with the sudden realisation that here is a fundamentally shy man who is as good a listener as he is a talker.

In this context the reasons for his largesse of writing are given an additional depth. The main movement is between the extremes of internal compulsion and external impulse. The balance is always delicate, for as soon as the personal and emotional seems to be the main weight, some practical matter is detected and the balance begins to shift in the other direction.

Priestley believes writing to be essentially a craft. His own writing habits, and the nature of his intelligence and imagination will not admit of the concept of waiting upon inspiration. If he had waited longer with a good deal of his writing it would certainly have been the better for it, but he might have gone a little hungrier each day: 'Perhaps I made too early a start, not giving them [i.e. ideas] time to act properly as catalysts of creation'.

The craftsman in Priestley cannot accept the time-using notion of the visitation of inspiration from some outer source, though the poet in him most strongly accepts the idea of a mysterious power within the imagination which subtly informs, illuminates and eventually bodies forth the ideas and the emotions. But, for him, this process must be granted the right environment in which to dispose itself. The environment is made up of the workroom, the desk, the blank paper, the pencilling hand and the chronometer – the latter being a warning rather than a dictator. Given these conditions, Priestley maintains that it is the duty of the writer to explore form and the means of communication, although for him personally the idea of duty is bound up with the emotion of delight. Except in odd snatches of verse which appear in some of his plays Priestley's exploration of literary forms has halted at the frontiers of poetry. Here there is yet again a misunderstanding which ranges from outright opinions that he has 'no poetry in him' to Eric Bentley's assertion that he has deliberately exploited a low-tensioned conception of art making, quite consciously, a specific and planned appeal to the lowest common denominator of sensibility: 'The man who, being a small artist, knows he might be a great entertainer, the man whose seriousness is all too easily compromised by his knowledge that he will reach a broader public if he is not too serious'.

It is possible to counter the inference of this judgement with the naïve statement that Priestley is a lover of poetry and serious music and painting. His tastes in poetry are more satisfied by the tough intellectual lyricism of Donne and Yeats than by what Bentley might perhaps expect – a wallowing in the shallows of minor verse. But to state that he reads and enjoys poetry, is sensitively knowledgeable about painting, is no real answer to the charge that, as writer, he has no seriousness and no poetry in him. To say that a writer has no poetry in him suggests several possibilities– that he literally does not write in a poetically verbal medium; that he lacks the kind of imagination which transcends the merely facile reporting of events, situations and characters, whatever form he may be using; that he has no scale (implied or explicit in his work) of moral and aesthetic values which may be said to lift his vision beyond the shifting, conventionalised and expedient values of day to day society.

On the first count Priestley stands condemned – little of his published work is in a poetic form. On the second count he may very certainly be acquitted. His book on *The English Comic Characters* alone reverberates with an acutely controlled sensitivity which reveals the comic characters in depth, and is as much aware of their symbolic as of their realistic value. The third charge – that his values are ordinary and attached too firmly to the desire to appeal to the lowest common denominator of his public requires closer examination.

Intellectually he seems at times to shy away from, rather than not be possessed of, that staying power which carries ideas beyond a certain point. He sometimes puts an infuriating full-stop to a flow of thought, or will bend it, as it were, back on itself at the precise point where it requires body and fulfilment. His *Literature and Western Man*, remarkable for its clear exposition, and the vivid rightness of so many of its judgements, is flawed by an occasional closing of the author's inner eye and ear either to the inevitable movement of his argument or to its possible development. The section on T. S. Eliot, for example, has a number of seminal phrases and paragraphs which give the impression not so much that Priestley is only capable of half-truths, but is reluctant emotionally to proceed to the full truth. Thus, he writes: 'A major poet in this age has to do for himself what society will no longer do for him; he has to create a foundation and framework of some sort, a world within the world, for his poetry'.

He proceeds to state that had Eliot remained in America he might have been able to do all this, but believes that Eliot's failure is that:

> He accepted, whatever he may have thought of it privately, the British Establishment – the dole system, the refusal, until the last minute, to challenge the dictatorships, all the humbug and cant, the politically manipulated snobberies, the hard-faced industrialists and financiers. . . . No doubt Eliot disliked many of these things; but he had to accept them: a man cannot ask to join a nation in order to become one of its most distinguished rebels.

And, finally, he declares:

> But Eliot was trapped in his acceptance. The exquisite instrument went murmuring through metaphysical quartettes; there was chilly and arid praise of chilly and arid authors, bone saluting bone; there were cautious notes towards definitions of culture; but the poetry did not ring out, the prose speak out. A major poet in a bad time should make powerful enemies.

Either of the first two of these three quotations in themselves cry out for expansion, but, partly because Priestley fails to do this, the third seems almost ludicrously illogical. One cannot demand that a poet should create a world within a world and then take Eliot to task for his 'metaphysical quartettes': one cannot lay down that a man cannot join another nation to become one of its most distinguished rebels, and make as its bedfellow the further dictum that a major poet in hard times should make enemies. And, indeed, for all Eliot's quaint flirtations with the Akensides of literature, there are far fewer 'chilly and arid authors' in Eliot's critical canon than Priestley implies. The suspicion grows that Priestley is less in the process of contradicting himself wittingly than that, having perceived clearly certain features of Eliot's work and position in the twentieth century, he suddenly side-steps into a sparring posture because the 'world within a world' of Eliot's poetry is far from his taste.

On Yeats however, who, he also declares, 'created a world within a world' in his poetic imagination, Priestley is impressively logical and critically fecund. This is perhaps because he finds in Yeats something which is absent in Eliot, something which may be termed a 'persona'. Priestley seems impatient with those who have not caught their fingers in the door-jambs of their society and set their own minds alight by a kind of spontaneous or apparently spontaneous combustion. Whereas in the section on Eliot the words 'arid' and 'chilly' fall like buckets from a cemetery wall, for Yeats, Priestley reserves a tocsin, writing of his 'passionate plain speech', his 'heightened and heroic life'. In these two phrases Priestley has identified for himself the persona of the man and the artist. Where Priestley cannot find for himself intellectual and emotional blood (and 'sincerity' which he believes Eliot to have in abundance, is not enough); where he cannot find committed artist and man in a tense counterpoise, then the charity of his fundamental fairness stops short. The result seems either illogical, unfinished or prejudiced; it is, in fact, often a kind of fierce sadness or regret – his section on Eliot ends thus: 'His technical mastery deserves all the praise it has received; he will have some stature even when all his influence has gone; but he would have been a greater poet if he had stayed at home, by the great rivers than ran through his boyhood'. And one would have to remember the fierce honesty of Priestley's attitude to his own work to realise that the last sentence is no sneer but a sigh.

But this characteristic of Priestley's is far more intermittent both in *Literature and Western Man*, and elsewhere in his work, than some of his critics might admit. Nevertheless it is present sufficiently frequently to give a certain colouring, not only to his critical works, but also to his plays and novels, the full nature of which remains to be discussed. It is remarkable that those who condemn its presence as evidence of either a prejudiced or limited mind have failed to note its most compelling counterpart in his work. This consists of a glowing precision of judgement which appears in paragraph after paragraph of his critical work; it bespeaks the man who, though he may not write poetry, has, in that sense in which a mind may be said to be poetical when its conclusions are just and its communication imaginative, a poetic imagination. Thus of Robert Frost's poetry he writes that much of it 'appears to have the rhythm and tone of cautious conversation, spoken out of the side of the mouth by a man not looking at you'.

Of Maxwell Anderson who suffered 'from not writing prose and never arriving at poetry'.

Of two romantic poets: 'Southey had character without genius, and Coleridge had genius without character'.

Of a third, Byron:

> It was as if one of Rousseau's day-dreams came to life. Byron had every qualification for the role of leading man in the drama of the Romantic Age. He was a prolific, impassioned and glorious poet; he was an aristocrat and as beautiful as Apollo; he was misunderstood and abused by his fellow-countrymen; he was wickedly amorous, a satanic philanderer, though capable – or so a million women dreamed – of being reformed by the love of a good woman; when weary of brittle gaiety and debauchery, he retired, a solitary exile, to various picturesque places, and there, wrapped in a cloak, with the clear-cut, pale, sad

face of a young Lucifer, he composed immortal stanzas to the ocean, the mountains, thunder-and-lightning.

Many of his judgements have, at a lower intellectual tension, but with the additional verve of descriptive imagery, the quality of inevitability and of the immaculate common sense of Dr Johnson. Certain phrases in John Bailey's book on Johnson can be applied with precision to Priestley's critical make-up. 'A man with an eager interest in all the business and pleasure of life. . . . In his writings as in his talk, he was not afraid to be seen as what he actually was. . . . He is not only a supreme master of common sense; he is a supreme master of the language of common sense'. In the preface to his Shakespeare, Johnson wrote:

> It is impossible for an expositor not to write too little for some, and too much for others . . . I have indeed disappointed no opinion more than my own; yet I have endeavoured to perform my task with no slight solicitude. Not a single passage in the whole work has appeared to me corrupt which I have not attempted to restore or obscure which I have not endeavoured to illustrate. In many I have failed, like others, and from many, after all my efforts, I have retreated, and confessed the repulse. I have not passed over with affected superiority what is equally difficult to the reader and to myself, but where I could not instruct him have confessed my ignorance. I might easily have accumulated a mass of seeming learning upon easy scenes; but it ought not to be imputed to negligence that, where nothing was necessary, nothing has been done, or that, where others have said enough, I have said no more.

In *Rain Upon Godshill* Priestley writes:

> To write fifteen hundred easily-understood words, in a crisp dogmatic style, about the relations between men and women, the importance of education, the growing fear in the world, the nature of happiness, the problem of Time, or your fundamental beliefs, is to be compelled to take stock of such thought as you

> possess, hastily to reduce your mind to some kind of order, and to put yourself to a rather searching test. I am, of course, assuming that you are trying to be sincere and are not turning out hokum at so much a paragraph. Making allowance for the large slap-dash method, as necessary to a journalist as it is to a poster artist, you must please grant me sincerity. I am not as certain of anything as I appear to be in a newspaper article, or for that matter in a book, but that does not mean I am faking, but only that the medium of communication demands a crisp dogmatic style.

The parallels of tone and self-consciousness in these statements are very close. A certain pride, a desire to be believed, a sense of writing as craft, all lie upon the surface of these urgent apologias. But, more than this, there is surely the sense that we are in the presence of two men whose professionalism does not seem to rest upon an isolated pinnacle. It might be said that, in the matter of criticism, both Priestley and Johnson are imbued with a certain spirit of amateurism. This is nowadays so often a pejorative word that is not easy to redefine it in terms which do not run the danger of special pleading. The meaning may perhaps be best expressed by the dictionary definition itself–from which contemporary usage has absented itself. The amateur is one who 'is fond of, one who cultivates a thing, as a pastime'. The implication is clear – that however skilled the cultivating might be, the impulse which governs it has its source in a delight, an excitement, perhaps even a lust, which refuses to be cooled and ossified by formalisation or vocationalism. Both Johnson and Priestley express sharp condemnation of those scholars who, they allege, are victims of a joyless and wisdomless turning away from the facts of existence. Johnson's:

> Deign on the passing world to turn thine eyes,
> And pause awhile from Letters to be wise.

is echoed in Priestley's broadside on 'text-book thinkers': 'It is these little men who produce the "nothing but" accounts of this life, robbing it of all mystery and wonder'.

They both rejoice in the condemnation of those 'mere antiquarians' who are 'rugged beings', although for Priestley, for 'antiquarians' one should read 'Professors of Eng. Lit.'.

There are few living writers whom it would be possible to imagine writing the letter to Lord Chesterfield, but Priestley would be one of them. Perhaps Wesker and Osborne would equal him in the anger generated, but neither would come as close to Johnson as Priestley in the deployment of a scornful and merciless common sense.

Johnson and Priestley represent a particular species of wrter who may very obviously be regarded as symbolic of the English Spirit. They embody a tacit urge to rebellion without violence, are suspicious of cold professionalism, have faith in the processes of 'common sense', and reveal an overt sentimentality which is both an earnest of their pleasurable experience of living and a desire to be accepted by their fellow-men.

With no intention of implying a qualitative equality in Johnson and Priestley, it may be said that they share this status of unique Englishness. The proof of it lies perhaps in the simple fact that neither has ever been regarded only as a 'man of literature'. Their strongest admirers and sternest critics tacitly accept both as being in the nature of institutions. Pejoratively used this word implies narrowness of vision, prejudice, superficiality of thought and feeling. Admiringly used, it implies unsullied sensibleness, catholicity of taste, thought and feeling, together with the belief that they who are institutions, are guardians of, and spokesmen for, that vague entity called 'English culture', and that vaguer one called 'the public conscience'. As always, the truth lies in an essence which is the result of an amalgamation of these extremes; but the extremes are as implacably represented in Priestley's writing, as in Johnson's.

In his polemical writings about this country, and the flaws which he finds, Priestley is often at pains to show that his criticism springs from love not hate. When this happens, his sentimentality reduces his prose to a *thé-dansant* flippancy:

Nobody has praised more enthusiastically than I have the

diamond light of the Arizona desert, but it never catches at my heart as a certain light in England does, the light of a fine morning in June when every piece of leaf or blossom in the foreground is sharply vivid, but beyond them everything is gradually shading and melting away into what is in the far background nothing but an exquisite green tenderness. I say that this occasional English light is not merely magnificent, like the one that you see nearly every morning in the American South-West; it is heart-breakingly beautiful, turning earth and air into music. No wonder we have such poets.

But, relieved of the need to wear his love on an embattled sleeve, Priestley writes like a careful painter, with an eye for relationships within a wide canvas, but above all with his emotional responses dictated by what is being looked at and not by what seems to be, as in the passage above, an imposed feeling:

There, far below, is the knobbly backbone of England, the Pennine range. At first, the whole dark length of it, from the Peak to Cross Fell, is visible. Then the Derbyshire hills and the Cumberland Fells disappear, for you are descending, somewhere about the middle of the range, where the high moorland thrusts itself between the woollen mills of Yorkshire and the cotton mills of Lancashire. Great winds blow over miles and miles of ling and bog and black rock, and the curlews still go crying in that empty air as they did before the Romans came. There is a glitter of water here and there, from the moorland tarns that are now called reservoirs. In summer you could wander here all day, listening to the larks, and never meet a soul.

In his reflective writing on the English character he reveals again these extremes. His perceptiveness in distinguishing wit from humour is striking:

Thus we have standards, but not standards that are exactly known and acknowledged. Where all is known and acknowledged, one set of ideas ruling every mind, there may be wit in plenty – you may see it working like the guillotine – but there will be little humour, the mind must be free to play to be humorous.

Yet he can be loose to the point of inconsequentiality:

And then the people. Because they are my own people I prefer them to all others. But not all the English. We have some types that I detest above all others. But the ordinary folk here seem to me the nicest in the world. No people are more fundamentally decent and kind. Perhaps the Scandinavians and Dutch are just as decent and kind, but they seem to me somewhat duller folk without the odd twist of character and humour that colour the English common people.

It is not that the sentiment cannot be admired, but that its manner of expression and its curiously non-sequitur flavour makes it seem banal and half-true. It cannot be over-emphasised that when the less happy extreme is to the fore in Priestley's writing, the impression is that it is a combination of urgency and a desire to be perfectly understood which is the main cause. Priestley's concern for the basic virtues of individual freedom, right of comment and civilised standards of behaviour, his loathing of cant, duplicity and inequality, have made him, ironically, his own worst enemy. The truth is that, certainly in a political context, he has often been misunderstood, accused of arrogance, stubbornness and of addressing himself to the lowest common denominator. His support of minority organisations like C.N.D., his strictures of politicians, made him, particularly after the war, the recipient of much abuse. He has been called many things in the attempt to label him, but no one has come closer to the truth than himself with his own phrase 'cantankerous radical'.

Lone wolf best describes what has always been Priestley's stance in political matters. If, by choice, he has often found himself drawn to the wilderness of the Arizona desert, he has, because of his temperament, often found himself driven back into a less attractive political wilderness, although 'political' is a word that formalises what, in him, is unformalistic. He belongs to no political party though the caste of his mind and feelings would obviously incline him towards a liberal socialism. All men are political men insofar as they think of themselves within the pattern of an organised society, and this, in an acute sense, is the way in which Priestley thinks of himself. But it is one thing to be political in this sense, and another to be so within the formalised terms of a party organisation. In this latter context Priestley may be said to be the most 'un-political' man since, from his first writings to his last, he has shown himself an enemy of any organised movement which either reveals itself to be, or is, ipso facto, a disavower of personal liberty, personal honesty and public welfare. The perfect state is implied in this *cri du coeur:*

> A man is a member of a community, and the fact that he is a member of a community immensely enlarges his stature and increases his opportunities.... But as well as being a member of a community a man is also a person, a unique individual, and it is in fact the business of the community not simply to glorify itself but to produce better persons, to enrich its individual sphere.... And most of us feel that the vast and complicated paraphernalia of contemporary life, all the politics and economics and sociology, all the ministries and conferences and communities, all the production and distribution and transport, exist to serve, to nourish, to guard, to create opportunities for these moments of pure liberty, this fulfilment of the dream, which may be just a family sitting round a fire, two lovers whispering in the dark, a man staying up to finish a pipe.

What is expressed in the final sentence above in tones which some might shy away from for their undertones of sentimentality, emerges elsewhere in harder forms:

> 'we should not look for individual liberty in our economic life, which after all belongs to the community, but should find it in our cultural and personal life...'

> '... a truly democratic state should consist of a few real states-

men and several million politically-minded citizens, and not of a thousand politicians and several million sheep'.

The image of the family by the fire, the whispering lovers, and the man staying up to finish his pipe has a deeper perspective in Priestley's psychology than the manner of its expression would suggest. There is a curiously primitive quality in his imagination which lies like a dark sky behind a good deal of his political thinking and writing. Time and time again, in the midst of his invective against politicians, against 'admass', advertising, and the many other lunatic irritants of life, Priestley returns to these dark quarters of his mind where he seems to find not only some kind of personal peace, but also the true magical germ of the ideal human existence. The word 'primitive' here has two connotations, first, as a description of his basic conception of the best political organisation, and second of his notions of the relationship of man to his total environment. The first connotation concerns Priestley's repeated evocation of the life of the family as the ideal blueprint for the best political organisation. The family or small intimate group which exists happily for the good and prosperity both of itself as a unit, and its individual members, emerges in his essays, his novels and his plays. In *Time and the Conways* and *The Linden Tree* the sense of family identity is very powerful and, when the closed magical circle is broken, the sense of grieved loss is equally potent. In *Bright Day* (significantly Priestley's favourite among his novels) the image acquires a deeper meaning and is a microcosm, one may say, of the Priestleyan concept of the perfect state. Here happiness, kindness, thoughtfulness and civilised pursuits are presented with a clear and emotionally rich validity. But equally, the power of the novel is sustained by the constant sense that the circle is a delicate construction at the mercy of the defaulting of one of its members, and of the harsh intrusion from outside of jealousy, power, envy and death. Hughes calls it Priestley's 'deepest and most mature contribution to the experimental science of living'. This makes it sound cooler than it is, but is nevertheless an accurate description of the inevitable effect that it has on the reader. *The Good Companions*, and *They Came to a*

City are, in form, projections from the basic concept of the family circle as the seminal organisation for the perfect state. It is not enough to say that the concept is often sentimentally communicated, giving the impression of a comfortable retreat for the exhausted man of affairs who begins to grow a weary of this world. It is often expressed thus, and as such it may reflect Priestley's personal idyll – the 'Shangri la' which childhood happiness and the nostalgic memories of family create and tremulously nurture in the adult mind. But equally often the concept is communicated with a clarity and emotional propriety which takes it beyond the realm of personal fancy and into that of political and human reality:

> We come out of the nursery – and begin to grow up ... I know what our problem is. It isn't how to produce a few brilliantly gifted individuals, how to procure for one small class the utmost luxury and refinement, how to give enormous power to a few groups, how to produce two or three colossal monuments of art or learning. Modern man is essentially co-operative and communal man. What we do best – and better than men have ever done in earlier ages – is never something that an individual can do but always something that men have to create together. ... Either the earth must soon be the miserable grave of our species or it must be at last our home, where men can live at peace and can work for other men's happiness.

Priestley, the man, may indeed look upon the idea of family from behind the rose-tinted hues of nostalgic memory, but the political Priestley has no illusions about the family of man or, more pertinently, about the need to think of family in the largest sense as completely all-inclusive, and not in nationalistic terms. Referring to a letter from a Dutchman, he writes:

> He had been over here recently, and, as a friend of ours, he was worried. There was not, he said, the ghost of a plan, no general enthusiasm for a better way of living, but everywhere an apathy. He found our people kind and courteous, but – I give

> his own phrase – 'extremely uneducated, indifferent to almost everything but sport'. . . . I could not disagree with it, though I knew as a visitor he had seen the worst of us, for the best of our life is always hidden away from casual inspection. We are a people who live better in private than in public. But I doubt if we live very well any more in private.

This was written not during the self-conscious heart-searching atmosphere of 1964, but in 1939.

And in *Faraway* he writes:

> I owe a lot to England. But I owe still more to the world. I'm all for English people being English, and French people being French, and Chinese being Chinese. I loathe cosmopolitan people, who haven't any roots anywhere. But all that's just fun. . . . There are some things too big and too serious to be national. They belong to mankind itself. All the things that are really important don't acknowledge any sort of frontier.

His conception of the family of man is primitive in the sense that the starting-off point for organised man is the herd instinct. It is the best of this instinct that Priestley seeks to keep and nurture, while realising the impurities both of man himself and of any organisation that man is likely to evolve.

But his sense of family is also primitive in that it is surrounded by a feeling of primal wonder. The circle is, for him, whether it be the small one of the family, or the large one of nationality, indeed charmed. It is at this point in his personality that the seeking, sometimes wayward intelligence and feeling about mankind meets the sense of wonder, that Priestley, the artist, exists.

Priestley responds spontaneously and emotionally to human beings and situations. Indeed, he gives the impression that the rational part of him is a carefully nurtured compensation for spontaneity – as if he were afraid of the consequences of total immersion. But the qualities to which he responds should not be underestimated. The starting-point is the word 'magic' which he uses so frequently in his writings. Its meaning for him often implies an aura which, both in his novels and his plays, surrounds the family or closely-knit group. Even in *Dangerous Corner* (written for basically practical reasons) there is a surrounding atmosphere – in this case a sinister air which seems to infect the characters so that they are forced to speak and act in certain ways. In *Time and the Conways* the aura created is more characteristic. Even the stage-directions specify its presence:

> *There is a party at the Conways, this autumn evening of 1919 (but we cannot see it, only hear it). All we can see at first is the light from the hall coming through the curtained archway on the right of the room, and a little red firelight on the other side. But we can hear young voices chattering and laughing and singing, the sharp little explosion of a cracker or two, and a piano playing popular music of the period.*

The direction '*we cannot see it, only hear it*' distances the scene, giving it, despite the fact that we are able to recognise the details of a party to hand, a sense of mysterious remoteness.

At the end of Act One, Kay is left alone on stage, and the direction is:

> *The room is not in darkness because light is coming in from the hall. Kay goes to the window and opens the curtains, so that when she sits on the window-seat, her head is silvered in moonlight. Very still she listens to the music, and seems to stare not AT but INTO something, and as the song goes soaring away, the curtain creeps down.*

Here the atmosphere of mystery is concentrated upon a single character, and the actress is given a clear direction to suggest identification with something that exists outside normal experience.

The direction that the curtain should '*creep down*' is unusual. The implication is that the moment should imperceptibly fade and not be expunged by a swirl of red velvet.

The final stage direction of the play reads:

> *The moonlight at the window shows us Alan looking at her earnestly,*

> *and we just catch her answering smile, as the song swells out a little. And then the lights begin to fade, and very soon the three girls are no more than ghosts and all the room is dark, but the moonlight – and the faces of Kay and Alan – still lingers; until at last there is only the faintest glimmer, and the Conways have gone, the curtain is down, and the play over.*

Here the sense of remoteness and of illusion rather than actuality is powerful. The emphasis on the curtain being down and the play being over seems less a direction than a comment on the nature of what we have been seeing.

In this play the constituents of the mysterious aura are in harmony with the movement of the action – in a sense the action is an exemplification of them. Happiness and joy are fleeting, grief and death are close companions to joy; there are certain moments when a few people may apprehend a mystery which only very few are capable of understanding; there are rare moments of close identification between two people – as with Alan and Kay. Ladislaus Löb in his study *Mensch und Gesellschaft bei J. B. Priestley* has shown that the constituents of the magic which surround life, and which appear in the plays with such emotional vibrancy, are expressed in more intellectual terms elsewhere in Priestley's work. In *Midnight on the Desert:* 'I do not understand either the people who will not accept the visible world at all or the people who will accept nothing else. . . . I have always been equally repelled by the idealism that denies matter and the materialism that denies mind'.

In *Rain Upon Godshill* he writes:

> What we must do now . . . is . . . to live . . . not throwing away our science and the mechanistic view of things it necessitates, but retaining them as an instrument of power, a tool against the stubborn earth, while at the same time we live at heart like poets and priests, aware that this is still a magical world moving with wonder and awe through a mystery.

In the play *Dragon's Mouth* this is expressed with unequivocal succinctness: '. . . there's something in us, belonging to another order of being that can't be identified with all this political stuff and its processes'.

The impression of a twin dimension of attitude by Priestley towards human life is clearly shown in these statements. The realist in him is unable to deny the time-grasped facts of the human condition, the romantic in him is unable to deny the aura of mystery around human beings.

But it becomes increasingly clear that whatever precise definition Priestley's intellect is able to make about the human condition in his autobiographies and polemical articles, the artist in him sees this condition very much more against the context of the mystery than against the context of the material facts of the contemporary social world. His remark in *Rain Upon Godshill:* 'I am coming to see that personality is not only one of the supreme realities, but that on any cosmological scale of thinking it is nothing but an illusion . . . the more inward you go, the less Jones is mere Jones, and the more he is also Smith, Brown, Robinson and much else besides', is an implied explanation of the majority of the characters in his plays. He has often been accused of writing a thin naturalism when really his attempt has been to illustrate this belief in the illusion of personality. Many of his characters, certainly the women, lack 'identity' in the sense that they seem mere mechanisms in the intricate engineering of the plot of the play. It is certainly true that, at times, Priestley sacrifices credibility of character to the demands of plot-line, but there are other occasions when the kind of naturalistic credibility that we have come to expect of him is, in fact, not intended. (This is obviously true of the time-plays, but less obviously of the much-underrated *Music At Night*.)

David Hughes rightly declares that in some of his time-plays Priestley finds himself in a dilemma where 'the logic of language is always getting awkwardly in the way and demanding further explanations whenever it attempts to explain something', and he implies that the naturalistic forms which Priestley stubbornly adhered to in the time-plays (a judgement which *Johnson Over Jordan* confutes) present a major problem 'when he tries to reconcile his excursions into the nature of time and the reality of dreams with the solid wooden boards of the naturalistic stage on which he was still determined to stand'. It is not so much naturalistic forms (for Priestley is nothing if not an experimenter with form) that present the problem which Hughes correctly diagnoses, but more the language and the necessity of giving credible 'objective correlatives' in character, so that audiences will not feel that they are being swept into a limbo of mood and symbolism.

The time-plays in particular reveal Priestley carefully adhering to language which has too little poetic reverberation in it, although this is not to say that the totality of effect is not associative. Moreover, though there are many scenes where naturalism is at a premium, he too often compromises his theme to create characters who still bear some resemblance to actuality. All the time-plays may be said to be revelations of heightened states of consciousness involving the awareness of eternity. But this presenting of the relationship of the individual to his consciousness of eternity is not a simple matter of emotional crises on the limitless shores of fathomless oceans. Priestley, in the best of his plays which explore the context of the mystery, is no James Barrie or Sutton Vane. The essential difference between such plays as *Marie Rose*, *Outward Bound* and *I Have Been Here Before* and *Time and the Conways* is that between relentless exploitation of emotionalism and emotional exploration of the mystery of life. One feels that Barrie squandered a fine talent upon unworthy material, while Priestley's whole imaginative being is at full stretch, and his technical virtuosity working with his inspiration:

> My interest in the time riddle is part intellectual, part intuitive. I am intellectually curious like a man faced with some half-deciphered hieroglyphs, and am pricked on, as such a man might be, by an intuitive feeling that here is the grand challenge.

The grand challenge took him into the theatre, to write the most fascinating group of plays of any playwright of the twilit decade which we call the thirties. But, having accepted the challenge of his imagination, to explore in dramatic terms, the banks and shoals of time, he found himself trying to satisfy that urge towards the theatre that had always been part of his make-up. His restless curiosity produced not only the time-plays, but comedies, sociological plays, and slight entertainments. The quality is uneven, but every play is marked by the restlessness of a mind that is never satisfied with what it has just done, and seeks to find not only new themes to explore, but new methods of exploration. But it is in the thirties and in the time-plays that he finds the true heart of his craft and imagination.

CHAPTER TWO

Priestley and the Thirties

It has become the custom to denote recent decades by a descriptive adjective, in an attempt to fix what is taken to be the prevailing or outstanding characteristic. The 'naughty' nineties heralded the process of dubbing, and since then no decade has been immune. The dangers of this procedure are obvious: 'naughty' describes only a small area of the nineties; what in some aspects of the twenties was frivolous or gay was ironically not in others. The thirties have perhaps received a tag least equivocal in its implications – 'the age of anxiety'. Few could cavil at such a description which includes the growing clouds of war, the actualities of Spain and Abyssinia, the slump. It is only when one turns to particular areas of the thirties that it is found that 'anxiety' must give way to some qualification. There is no 'anxiety' in Auden's firm mastery of poetic technique; the pressures of the decade give no hint of having induced a tentative and unsure communication. Even Eliot's sometimes tiresome assertions that 'words slip and slide' are seen to have something of the quality of contrived self-conscious humility.

In the theatre 'anxiety' is a word to be regarded with caution. In one sense the theatre is always 'anxious', always, as Shaw said, 'at a low ebb'. There does not seem, except in one important particular, much justification for applying the word without qualification to the theatre world of the thirties. Certainly at the beginning of the decade, the growth of the cinema seriously affected audiences, and some theatres closed, and certainly, with the diminution of Shaw's presence (despite the artificial insemination of reputation at the Malvern Festival), there was a sense of greatness dissipated, with nothing to take its place. Anxiety, certainly at the beginning of the decade, furrowed the brow of many a financial report on the state of a theatre. But in other respects there was a richness of effort and achievement that, in hindsight, provides a picture of excitement rather than of unrelenting gloom. The emerging genius of Gielgud and Olivier was given the impetus of challenge by the fiery talent of Wolfitt, and the cool precision of Richardson. Edith Evans and Sybil Thorndike were flanked by the careful grace of the young Peggy Ashcroft, and the dark passion of Flora Robson. The theatre was much richer than it had been for many years in the promise of talent and genius and, in one or two cases, its fulfilment.

If touring companies were gradually becoming victims of the cinema, many plays from abroad came into the country, the Old Vic triumphed and a new theatre was built at Stratford-upon-Avon. If Shaw was played out, it seemed towards the end of the decade as if a dramatist of comparable stature might be in embryo in T.S. Eliot. Though theatres closed, younger dramatists experimented, and while such plays as *The Ascent of F6* and *The Dog Beneath the Skin* now seem ungainly and brash, the experiments were made, and there was much writing and talking about the nature of theatre. The amateur movement flourished, and acting schools were able to lay foundations for a prosperity which the war was not able to extinguish. The prognosis of war did not cast a blight upon the enthusiasm manifest in so many aspects of theatre, and in the provinces, which would be most likely to display the worst effects of anxiety, a virility of effort and achievement persisted.

It was in the 1930s that the word 'repertory' began to slough off the pejorative associations that had long been associated with it, and at Liverpool, Birmingham and the newly restored Maddermarket theatre at Norwich, seeds, which had been planted earlier, began to show their survival ability and something of their quality. The spirit of optimism seen at Birmingham under Barry Jackson may stand for the whole world of provincial theatre during the thirties. It was an optimism often beset by the harsh realities of financial difficulty, but it persisted and grew, and gradually brought with it not only a growing recognition of the force of provincial theatre, but also of its potential quality. In 1931 Jackson sent a company to Canada, in 1932 he presented Elmer Rice to the notoriously critically sceptical Birmingham audiences. In the same year at the Malvern Festival he presented *Ralph Roister Doister*. In 1935 his production of *1066 And All That* moved to London. That same year Barry Jackson produced his now famous modern-dress *Hamlet*. The Birmingham theatre may have been exceptional in the extent of its artistic success and fortunate in its administrator, but the kind of spirit, essentially optimistic, which informed this theatre, could have been found elsewhere in the country. Barry Jackson wrote to J. C. Trewin from Malvern in 1938:

> Almost every aspect of classical and modern theatrical art has been attempted. There have been violent fluctuations of response, but in anything that is more or less continuous – and theatres do continue in spite of apathy, financial setbacks and other ills – ups and downs are bound to happen, particularly in an undertaking that depends directly upon the wayward and quite unaccountable vagaries of audiences. The one form of play – and there are exceptions – which has not met with wide approval is tragedy: the professional and working middle-class declare that they meet too much in the daily routine to derive inspiration or satisfaction from it in the theatre. This lack of appreciation for what is deepest and most enduring in dramatic literature is regrettable. . . .
>
> All theatres are life in little, not only in what happens on the stage, but in their actual being, their personnel, their audiences. To prophesy is futile. The past has shown what can be done and augurs well for years ahead, but a sensation of such security as is humanly attainable would be advantageous to the hopes of the directors, the artists, and those who so loyally and regularly appear in the auditorium.

This letter expresses well the traditional caution and the not-to-be-denied optimism of the theatre. If there is a name for this kind of spirit, and hence a name for the kind of theatre which persisted in the thirties it is J. C. Trewin's word 'turbulent'. In the early part of the decade the turbulence was given the quality of violence because of the sharp effects of the cinema, and the reaction to those effects by the theatre itself. It is in fact the persistence of reaction and counter-reaction which makes the word applicable. But the thirties exemplified a turbulence that is in the very nature of theatre. Priestley puts it thus:

> They may paint their faces to take part in a Mystery. And I suspect that it may be some obscure but deep-seated apprehension of this and not simply the glitter and applause, the possibility of easy fame, the erotic atmosphere, the escape through exhibitionism, the whole glamorous bag of tricks, that leads men and women to sacrifice their time, their health, their peace of mind in the service of the theatre.

The whole hierarchy of the theatre world lies in that love-hate relationship with a mistress which makes the situation eternally turbulent; theatre, like New York to the traveller, is always the place you want to get away from, and always the place you want to get back to. Priestley, knowing the risk which, because of the advent of cinema made the turbulence of the early thirties even more violent, deliberately chose to enter the whirlpool, and his own comment on his decision goes to the heart of why, however chaotic and despairing the theatre scene seems to be, there remains an optimistic obsession to be part of it.

> This took me into the thick of it, but for some years I enjoyed being there, working on the production side with friends like Irene Hentschel and Basil Dean and Michael MacOwan, and on the managerial side with other friends like A. D. Peters, J. P. Mitchelhill and Thane Parker. Working with people in the theatre is tricky, especially if you are the author as well, because in there, away from daylight and common sense, everybody knows best. Not being really sure of anything, we all pretend to be absolutely sure about everything. So friendship, as distinct from the false good-fellowship that comes and

goes so quickly, prevents colleagues from turning into so many irritants.

For Priestley in the thirties the opportunity presented itself to work with people of adventure and imagination – like Mitchelhill who had no theatrical tradition in his background, but who felt something perhaps of the gambler's lust: not for gold, but for the risks of the game. Perhaps the truth behind the theatre's continuous existence lies in the fact that it attracts two kinds of gambler and adventurer – the one who is prepared to back his imagination against odds that often seem ludicrous, and the one who is prepared to back his money for a good financial return. Of the first type Barry Jackson is the best example. His note to the Repertory Theatre's programme for 1932, which he sent to J. C. Trewin, and which contained the names Barrie, Philpotts, Shaw, Goldsmith, Zuckmayer, Maugham, Fielding and Heywood, reads: 'An interesting year's work, but quite demented of course. No-one in their right senses would embark upon such a gallimaufrey'.

Priestley and Mitchelhill who entered the theatre in the same spirit of adventure as Barry Jackson, would have agreed that the formation of their own company was something in the nature of a gallimaufrey. But behind this there was the determination not to be involved and trapped by the second type of gambler – the one to whom theatre is a commodity: 'It is this gaming-house atmosphere that makes serious work in the Theatre so difficult in the English-speaking companies'.

Priestley found the theatre of the thirties full of both types of gamblers, and throughout his career in the decade he persisted in having a controlling right in the production of his plays. Priestley lost and gained financially during the thirties, but the driving force which prompted him to put on play after play of his own, and to give aid to younger playwrights and directors was not financial. Bascially what drove him was the possibility of taming and tying down, by the work of his own hands, that magic which had first lured him to the galleries of the theatres of his youth. For him, money represented enough power to ensure his own control of the destiny of his plays. His part in their presentation was nearly always considerable – any aspect of the art of theatre fascinates him, and his committal has often brought down upon his head the charge that he wanted to do everything himself. There is no doubt that some found him difficult to work with, but the detracting instinct which is easily aroused when one sees how much of a part he did play in some of his productions must be modulated by the evidence that his plays and his productions attracted the services of most of the distinguished names of the thirties. In some cases the association with Priestley was repeated several times, notably with Basil Dean, Irene Hentschel, Ralph Richardson, and Michael MacOwan. It is easy to misinterpret the nature of Priestley's close association with the production of his own plays, though this is not to say that it is necessary to condone the principle that an author should be vitally committed to the production of his own plays. He is most certain in his attitude about the place of the author in the theatre:

> We are often asked if dramatists should produce their own plays. I have had to do it more than once but never yet, I believe, at my own request, for unlike some of my colleagues, good experienced men of the theatre too, I hold that it is better if the author of the play leaves its production to somebody else.

He knows his own weakness:

> Moreover – and this certainly applies to me – a dramatist is rarely as patient and tactful at handling players as an experienced producer is, and he is apt, as I know I am, to become bored and irritated and impatient by hearing the speeches he has written and lived with spoken badly over and over again or delivered simply as groups of words when the actors have only half-memorised them.

But he does not claim that his words are sacrosanct: 'Authors are inclined to fall in love with certain scenes, certain speeches that may need to be modified'. But the commitment must be there because for Priestley the prompt copy is the final text.

In the thirties he shared with Emlyn Williams and Noël Coward this characteristic of heavy involvement in the presentation of his plays. Indeed this is a phenomenon which gives the writers of that time their particular quality of being less mere playwrights than composite men, employed, as it were, not by the dictates of the urge to create in words, but by a vast organisation in whose work they might be called upon to perform a variety of tasks.

In Priestley's case the control which he wanted, and his insistence that the prompt copy was the final script, drove him hard into the actualities of the theatre world. The life he led was often only a little short of frantic. All the time he was writing, and interspersed were sessions of casting, of watching rehearsal, of keeping a weather eye on the books and the box office. But it is clear that there was another adhesive which bound him to a world many of whose aspects he found inimical. He hated the nervy falsities of first-night parties, the gay darling impetuosities of the green room and the chosen pub. He loathed the grim-faced commodity men to whom a play was a piece of merchandise and the theatre so much wrapping paper. Yet all this could not and has not robbed him of that original craving for magic and fellowship. His relations with certain players was warm, with Richardson particularly: 'That we remained friends, as indeed we are still, is partly explained by the fact that we have common interests outside the Theatre, for he is not all actor, just as I am not all author. And each of us thinks the other a fine fellow – but a bit cracked'.

It is the sense of warmth and fellowship in a community which is devoted to the creation of magic that may explain something of the lure theatre has for him. If he was no innocent abroad in the grim realities of theatre economics in the thirties, there was, and is still, a curious innocence in his attitude towards the 'players' and what they can do: 'I only wonder when at least some part of our minds will be able to travel in time, to recapture the past that has not really vanished at all, to see the old velvet curtains rising and falling again, to applaud once more the brave players'. The sense of belonging to a troupe of brave fellows is very strong in Priestley's emotional make-up. It is essentially one with his vision of life as a mixture of the exciting and sad, ephemeral and eternal. It is at once sentimental and practical, since it allows him the self-indulgence of being emotional about a world that he knows to be hard and ruthless, once he has become part of it.

But there can be no doubt that Priestley was often over-sensitive to criticism in the thirties. In fact he engaged in far less public wrangling with critics than some other playwrights, but when his nerves were touched he was often to be seen wearing his heart upon his sleeve. He was on good terms with Agate and has remained on friendly terms with Ivor Brown, despite the fact that the former did not always spare him the full measure of his oddly sinuous sarcasm. They had several good-tempered brushes, but the most telling encounter is published in Agate's *Ego* in letters whose theme goes deep into the heart of Priestley's persistent feeling that he was misunderstood. The letters were exchanged in 1945 but their subject matter relates closely to the thirties, and particularly to *Johnson Over Jordan*. The general reception of the play had greatly disappointed him and this, coupled with the fact that the run was short, created a bitterness which still rankles to some extent. The repeated note of the criticism of the play was that it was so full of devices that it lacked cohesion and that it derived slavishly from German expressionistic drama. Priestley in *Margin Released* has not changed his explanation, which he gave in the thirties, of his intentions in the play: 'I took such dramatic technique as I possessed as far as it would go, using the most objective form there is for material that was entirely and deeply subjective'.

In April 1945 he wrote in *The Observer* of the hostility which he felt the older dramatic critics displayed to experimental work: 'They forget that an art, if it is to remain vital and engrossing, must avoid falling into routine. Writers must be for ever making fresh efforts, and so must dramatic critics'. This stung Agate to look up the records of his own comments on various experimental plays, and to remind Priestley of the many favourable judgements he had made of such plays as *Time and the Conways*, *I Have Been Here Before*, *The Dance of Death*, *Thunder Rock*. He added that the reason for his dislike of *Johnson Over Jordan* was 'not because the presentation was new, but because, while pretending to be new, it was, or seemed to me to be, a mish-mash of *Outward Bound* and *Liliom* done in the demoded Elmer Rice manner'.

This could not have been more precisely calculated to incite a strong defence. After some preliminary skirmishing, in which Priestley allowed himself the luxury of saying: 'I cannot help wondering what you would have said of *The Dance of Death* if I had written it and not Strindberg', and Agate the equal indulgence of declaring: 'About your fourth play, *Desert Highway*, I abstained from seeing this because I felt, rightly or wrongly, that I wasn't going to like it', the battle was seriously joined. It was *Johnson* that lay at the basis of Priestley's ire. Agate's notice had declared that it was a play about death, Priestley maintained that it was a play about life. Agate had declared that there were no fresh ideas in the play, and Priestley countered with 'though they may not have been wildly original (for I make no pretence of being an original thinker, and if I were I would not choose the theatre as my medium), they were ideas, and derived an emotional impact from the way they were presented'. Agate had said that the play was a return to expressionism. Priestley denies this – the object of expressionism 'was to flatten out character, to ignore the individual and concrete instance, and to find drama in the relations of purely symbolic figures'. His object, on the other hand, 'was to show a real man in real relationships, but to do it outside time, to present it all, as in dreams, in a four-dimensional manner'. He admits that some of the production did suggest expressionist manner, but will admit no further involvement in it.

Agate closed the engagement with a note:

> Would all controversies were conducted in this spirit. This is just to thank you for your share in our little bout, and to say that I await all or any of your new plays with the greatest eagerness. I shall bend up every mental as well as corporal agent to the terrible task of giving them careful and critical attention. Delete the word 'terrible'.

These two were well-matched, both able to make the hardest

statements with a grace of wit, neither willing to abandon personal principle but able to give way on detail. But the significance of the encounter is what it reveals of Priestley's mentality. Faced with an adversary he respects, he is prepared to do what perhaps the creative artist should beware of – explain the created work. More pertinently, his defence of the play shows a clear-sighted awareness of its nature. Few readers of the play would now deny that it is by way of an evocation of a man's life, that its thematic movement depends on a series of generalised ideas which are heavily touched with feeling, that its chief character is conceived of much more in realistic than symbolic terms. Indeed the play might have benefited if it had trodden more firmly the expressionistic territory. Priestley has the ability to indicate the nature of his plays with great clarity, though it is admittedly occasionally difficult to disentangle this from the urging of a qualitative pleading, as when he writes to Agate: 'It contains, among other things, in Johnson's long soliloquy about Desire the most careful speech I ever wrote for the theatre. (Morgan singled it out I remember.)'

Priestley's contentions with the critics in the thirties, of which this is a fair example, can be interpreted in several ways. It is possible to point to the extremely personal statements and say that here is a vain man who complains when he does not feel enough attention is being devoted to him, or the wrong attention is being accorded him. It is possible too to say that he doth protest too much about his play being misunderstood, and indulges in over-explanation of intention. Equally it is possible to suggest that, conceiving of himself as a serious artist, and possessed of an insatiable curiosity about, and a care for, his profession, it was inevitable that he should, from time to time, become involved in controversy. This latter view he himself, perhaps naturally, would accept:

> Let me make it clear again what I am complaining about. I do not expect to be praised for everything I do (though I have the usual wistful hopes) but I consider myself a serious artist in the theatre, with a good technical knowledge of its resources, and I have struggled hard to bring experiment to a theatre terribly

lacking in it, and I feel entitled to claim the serious careful consideration of senior critics.

To look back on the dramatic history of the thirties is one of the most nostalgic of operations for the middle-aged, for the simple reason that it lies behind the steel arras of the war years. Behind that arras lies youth and a comparative carefreeness, in front of it exists another world, the world of age, more close-fisted emotionally, more mordant in its reactions. Many of the plays of the thirties create a nostalgia for a past that was wiped out with a thoroughness that leaves few traces outside the emotions and the memory. Some of the thirties' plays remain in the memory only because their titles evoke the perhaps illusory happinesses of another world. They are like old clothes pulled out of the family band-box, a little pathetic with the smell of moth balls, different in size from when we first saw them though fondly one imagines that with a little altering here and there they might again be serviceable. *Cavalcade*, *Private Lives*, *Escape Me Never*, *Dear Octopus*, *Quiet Wedding*, *Storm In a Teacup*, *French Without Tears*, *George and Margaret* – these are some of the chief evokers of nostalgia. Whatever their dominant mood might be they have become part, less of the intellectual growth of the middle aged, than of his emotional memory. They are part of the first coming to grips with the territory of emotional response, and in this sense each of these plays has for many people the quality of being part of their inner secret selves.

But there are other plays of the time which, while they have much of the same broad-based nostalgia of these, have also an extra quality – something of durability in the fabric. *The Barretts of Wimpole Street*, *Murder in the Cathedral*, *Richard of Bordeaux*, *Eden End*, *Love On The Dole*, *Night Must Fall*, *Time and the Conways*, *I Have Been Here Before*, *Johnson Over Jordan*, *The Corn Is Green*, *The Family Reunion*. These plays tease the sensibilities, but they also quicken the intellectual perception of the dramatic legacy of the thirites and, to a certain extent, they have an existence independent of the demands of personal emotionalism. Eliot's two plays not only represent the most successful attempt to clothe drama in poetry, but thematically have the power to set the mind speculating; their success is that Eliot gives literary concepts a theatrical potency. Williams's plays hold their place less by the depth of their characterisation and their themes than by the immaculate sense which they convey of the rightness of their characters in the environment depicted, by the accurate brilliance with which the characters are etched and the rhythmic and evocative strength of the language.

The Barretts of Wimpole Street, though perhaps something of its original cause célèbre atmosphere still governs judgement, takes the eye for its refusal to sentimentalise a situation which it honestly depicts. *Richard of Bordeaux* remains perhaps less for its own merits than for the opportunity it provided John Gielgud. Priestley's plays, like the rest, have a fair share of the contribution made by the thirties to personal emotion, but it is difficult to escape the other qualities of durability which they have. If they cannot speak to today's younger generation, they can speak to an older one, but, more pertinently, the claim might be made that they will continue to speak to the graver ears of those whose youth lies just behind the last bend that was taken. In a generation of playwrights, a surprising number of whom were approaching or had reached middle age in the thirties, Priestley writes most certainly for the generation he had arrived at when he wrote his first play for the theatre. The time-plays which he wrote, and which constitute his chief contribution to the dramatic legacy of the century, reflect a sense of loss which was one of the chief legacies of the first world war to the generations that survived it.

The plays seem to be paying an implicit tribute to, and shedding a tear for, a generation that had disappeared. Priestley's psychological make-up gives a strong impression of a personality that has had to meet the challenges of existence while labouring under the disadvantage of being conscious of missing allies. The elegiac atmosphere which tinges the plays is a projection, one suspects, of his own personal grief that a whole generation of strength was lost to the world, and that the world could never catch up with what was lost. His frequent belligerence often has the flavour of taking up the cudgels on behalf of a dead generation that can no longer fight or answer. The magic of good fellowship which informs his love of theatre, and which informs his plays, is given a keen regretfulness of tone by his personal memories of those closed circles of masculine fellowship that he found in the trenches:

> Nobody, nothing, will shift me from the belief, which I shall take to the grave, that the generation to which I belong, destroyed between 1914 and 1918, was a great generation, marvellous in its promise. This is not self-praise, because those of us who are left know that we are the runts.

The magic of the fellowship of such lost men must have been intense. It was a magic which can mean little to anyone who did not experience it, and might easily be imagined as sentimental by anyone who did not know what happens to the mind and feelings in the presence of the hourly possibility of sudden death. Priestley's claim to permanence relies to some extent on the meaningfulness of the elegiac tones of his time-plays to those who know what a slim thing life is, and to those who are able to look back from the half-way point of their own lives and see the mixed strands of fulfilment and unfulfilment, the unsuspected gaieties and griefs. *Eden End* and *Time and the Conways*, one suspects, are likely to hold their places because they are tied not merely to a particular generation's tragedy but to the essential melodrama of all human life.

Yet there is another sense in which the experience of the lost generation has influenced the plays. The fellowship of the trenches, was, perforce, a masculine one, the generation that was lost was masculine. To a large extent, though not exclusively, the plays take a tonal value from a masculine world which is brusquely straightforward, tight-lipped, disinclined to wear its heart upon its sleeve. For example, the love-relationships in the plays have tenderness, sentiment and irony, but they have nothing of the utter commitment of sexual love. It is not that one demands from plays such as his which are largely concerned with that half-way sector between what we think we are and what we really are, a direct communication of passionate sexual love. But there is hardly even an indirect communication of its existence. Sexual love does not go much further than admiration and shared verbal felicities. The language of masculine fellowship is often a kind of shorthand, as it strives to avoid the rhetoric and associativeness which makes emotional involvement explicit.

Much of the shorthand good-fellowship language of the twenties and thirties derived from the first world war, just as its counterpart in the late forties (more *bragadoccio* with its 'wizard prangs' and 'gone for a Burton') derived from that area of fighting which still had much in it of the intimate personal conflict and comradeship – the war in the air. A rather tight-lipped symbolism characterises the language of deep emotion when it seems necessary that the emotion should not be explicit.

Priestley's language in the thirties preserves much of this shorthand quality. In so doing, it is a direct reflection of the way in which a middle class generation which had gone through the war tried, perhaps unconsciously, to keep up the pretence of hiding its feelings. Priestley more than any other dramatist, except Coward, gives the verbal ghosts of a generation the opportunity to speak again. The sense of the brevity of life, the preciousness of friendship, the facing up to unpleasantness and sorrow, the sudden darts of gaiety – these were the chief emotional heirlooms of the war for people of Priestley's generation. It is these things that he places naturalistically and allows his characters to express in the speech 'natural' to them, alongside his own personal vision of human existence. Thus the plays are thematically bifocal, and the language is often too obviously bifocal. The naturalism of the language of the generation he is writing about often shades into the neutral tones of the dramatist stating his case.

Alan speaks to Kay in *Time and the Conways:*

ALAN: . . . Has all this – been a bit too much for you?

KAY (*ruefully*): Apparently. And I thought I was tough now, Alan. See, I was doing the modern working woman – a cigarette and a whisky and soda . . . no good, though . . . you see, Alan, I've not only been here tonight, I've been remembering other nights, long ago, when we weren't like this. . . .

ALAN: Yes, I know. Those old Christmasses . . . birthday parties. . . .

KAY: Yes, I remembered. I saw all of us then. Myself, too. Oh, silly girl of 1919! Oh, lucky girl!

ALAN: You mustn't mind too much. It's all right, y'know. Like being forty?

KAY: Oh no, Alan, it's hideous and unbearable. Remember what we once were and what we thought we'd be. And now this. And it's all we have, Alan, it's *us*. Every step we've taken – every tick of the clock – making everything worse. If this is all life is, what's the use? Better to die, like Carol, before you find it out, before Time gets to work on you.

Such passages make it easy to conclude that it is the language that is failing to communicate a depth of conception which theme, character and situation demand. The criticism of Priestley that he lacks poetry may be said to stem from an expectation, excited by his themes, that they require poetic language. Priestley's answer to such criticism is characteristically definitive:

> I may be told that I ought to have taken more time, to give every speech a richer flavour. But though I constantly experimented with dramatic form, I was still working within the tradition of English realism. Too much enrichment of speech would have destroyed this realism. An English audience would have begun to ask who I thought these people were. Not being Irish or American, I had at least to lull all suspicion by starting with a familiar thin, flat idiom, before I began cheating. An English dramatist has the hardest task of all. He has to make scenes out of people who don't want to make a scene.

But this is only definitive in tone, and if one is prepared to accept the premises upon which it is made. It is difficult to understand what Priestley means by 'the tradition of English realism' insofar as it puts a premium on the use of 'enrichment of speech'. The character of Falstaff, of whose nature Priestley has a deep understanding, is the most precise example of the realist's method of dealing with matters as they are, and it is equally precisely the 'enrichment' of his language which reinforces the sense of Falstaff's actuality. But in Priestley's use of the word 'enrichment' there is a tell-tale significance. The word suggests an 'adding to' an already existent verbal pattern, a garnishing of staple diet. His implied contention that English audiences have to be 'cheated' into accepting an idiom, by lulling them first into the apparently familiar, and then leading them into the unfamiliar, smacks of the same kind of attitude which prompted Eliot to declare that poetry in drama must make its effects without an audience being aware that it is poetry that they are listening to. The kind of 'cheating' that Priestley is a master of, and rarely fails in achieving, is that in which character *seems* to be a mere natural being existing in a mere ordinariness of environment, but who is found eventually to have become more than himself in an environment and in situations that are different in dimension from what they seem. But the word 'cheating' implies a theatrical manipulation of tricks of the trade, and indeed in some of his more cursorily written entertainments Priestley does little more than pull off conjuring trick after trick. But, in his time-plays particularly, his technical accomplishment is matched by a subtle thematic richness which derives from a deeply held attitude towards the nature of life.

Priestley's time-plays seem, in fact, to be written out of a philosophy of life and, unlike the work of any of his contemporaries save Eliot, they are dramatic expressions of the inner life of the man and not mere exercises in the art of entertaining. All the more to be deplored therefore is Priestley's wayward refusal to tax the imaginations of his audiences with language that matches the themes of the plays. In fine, Priestley, in several of his plays, has made scenes out of people who don't want to make a scene, and he has palpably made of many of his characters non-naturalistic agents; yet he refuses to go the whole way and to accept that a heightened form of character creation demands a form of speech which 'co-exists' with the double-dimension which he gives them. The critical concensus in the thirties about his most experimental plays *Johnson Over Jordan* and *Music At Night* is summed up by Ashley Dukes's comment on the latter play: 'The criticism that he chooses a poet's subject and handles it in prosaic fashion is one that more than ever holds good'.

This is a judgement that rankles with Priestley, but the intermittent anger which informs his attitude towards the critics is given some justification when one reads reviews such as that of Alan Dent of *Johnson Over Jordan* in which he talked of the 'stark insensibility' of the play, and added, after the most cursory examination of the play: 'Years after we may possibly call by the same name the tedium we have experienced at this new play of Mr Priestley'. In the thirties there was no valid justification for either ignoring him or dismissing him in such terms as Alan Dent's. *The Times*, even though on occasion it was hard put to it to be favourably disposed to particular plays, was remarkably consistent in its acceptance of Priestley as a dramatist whose work was always worth serious consideration. *The Times*, more consistently than any other newspaper, saw what Priestley has so often insisted upon: that much of his work was experimental for him. Of *Johnson Over Jordan* it reported: 'A struggling courageous play, an experiment exciting even in its failures'.

Ashley Dukes, the English Editor of the American *Theatre Arts Monthly* gave perhaps a more careful eye to Priestley's plays than any of the reviewers on either side of the Atlantic. He, while finding *Music At Night* not to his taste, never retracted from an opinion that Priestley's work in general was of great potency. Although he wrote of *Music At Night:*

> No description could exaggerate the ordinariness of this batch, scarcely to be called a group, of human beings. An evening in their company on the plane of realist convention would be just terrible. On the other plane of fantasy, speaking their inmost thoughts aloud and revealing their entire being as they respond to works of music that they make no pretence of understanding, they are exciting from the stage point of view because of their unexpectedness, but they have no compelling power.

He nevertheless believed of *Johnson Over Jordan:* 'There is no occasion to revise the judgement that Priestley is the writer of the *Everyman* of our time'.

The general consensus on Priestley in the thirties was that he was always exciting, but that he remained promising. There were excesses of critical opinion on his plays, ranging from Agate's ecstatic review of *Dangerous Corner* to Dent's dismissive comments on *Johnson Over Jordan*. Priestley's brushes with the critics were never initiated by the belief that they had no right to opinion, but from the feeling that he was being misunderstood. It is misunderstanding that rouses his ire more than disagreement.

PART TWO

c*

CHAPTER THREE

Time and Priestley

Time and the artist are both allies and enemies, and it is out of their paradoxical relationship that some of the greatest works of man have been wrought. The artist, grasping part intuitively at the awesome reality of eternity while the present-tense brushes past him, is in touch with the most potent material in his task of showing men to themselves. Time and eternity call the changes by which mankind is measured, and it is still the artist rather than the scientist who is able to show the measurements most potently to the greatest number of mankind. Armed with the evocative dimensions of eternity the artist can, as yet, outbid the scientist whose language has not yet learnt the traffic of common speech. The scientist has yet to find a means to carry his discovery into the realms of common experience. For the moment the artist still holds the greatest number of keys to the doors of man's imagination.

Time is the artist's ally in the sense that, as a basic theme in art, it has *a priori* a property of awe and mystery. But, more than this, its presence in a work of art provides a double poignancy – that which attaches to the idea of the brevity of life, and that which attaches to the vulnerability of the artist himself, to life's ravages. The poignancy of a good deal of art lies in the long-held proposition that the artist, and those whom his work concerns, are mutable, but that, in a sense, the work itself is immutable. This has been the burden, either directly or indirectly, of much English poetry which has, in decade after decade, flung itself in a slightly melodramatic posture of sacrifice into the teeth of time and eternity. Shakespeare, in his grimly sweet evocations of the ravages of time and in his brave defiances where he challenges time to expunge what his art has made undying, is, nevertheless, self-conscious and self-pitying to a degree.

Keats, whose images of a fleeting and bitter-sweet present tense held within them an implicit desire to freeze the present-tense into a perpetual unchanging state, is no less affecting and no less self-conscious. These two poets represent a ubiquitous attitude which, until the end of the nineteenth century, may be said to have been (particularly in lyric poetry) tacitly accepted. The image of the typical pre-twentieth-century poet has much in it of wry heroism – which some like Keats and Shelley were deeply conscious of – as he stands upon the ramparts trying to fight off the inevitable with words that would reach out into the silences beyond his own span. The keen awareness of time and eternity and the very nature of lyric poetry have an affinity. Lyric poetry has to do with that which is intensely felt, here and now – the immediate sensuous experience; to this extent, like the passage of time itself, the experience is swift. But the communication of that experience in the lyric poem is in words whose associations and sounds are contrived by the poet to achieve a quality of timeless beauty and relevance; to this extent the lyric poem is an impersonation of eternity. The poet and his experiences are the slaves of time, but he attempts to make his work the heir of eternity.

Up to the twentieth century lyric poetry held a virtual monopoly of this notion. Novelists displayed little of this obsession with their own status and the status of their art in the context of time and eternity; the dramatists were likewise unpreoccupied. In both cases the reason may be that, certainly in England, the poet came to occupy in the popular mind a position of rarefied loneliness – by the romantic period the conception of poet as anguished, isolated creator, was firmly established. But the dramatist and the novelist in this country, whatever other villifications have been directed at them, have always been accepted by the popular mind as being in a closer contact with their surrounding society – a non-lonely, more 'artisan' status. Loneliness and a preoccupation with time and eternity seem often to go hand in hand.

But in the twentieth century there came about an impingement on art of an inquisitive scientific attitude towards the problems of time, its meaning, and man's relation to it. The artist, no less than the professional scientist, the amateur, and eventually the layman, flew into this inquisition with the bewildered tenacity of the moth to the flame. The work of Einstein and Eddington did not reduce the aura of mystery surrounding the nature of time. In fact, by implication, it increased the mystery by destroying the old and long-held notions of time as a fixed unending line along which the individual moved, creating, through his present-tense consciousness unlimited additions to the past, and proceeding to his own limited future. The personal future diminished as his present tense moved along the fixed line, and eternity lay beyond a constantly receding horizon. Einstein and others put doubts in the way of this mechanistic conception of the nature of time and opened the way for more subtle theories. So far as the artist was concerned, the disruption of the old conceptions tended to make him less emotionally aware of time, and to make him more conscious of how now the new concepts might be manipulated in and for creative writing. Time lost its monopoly as a tremulous additive to the status of art and the artist, but gained in potency as a source from which oblique and multi-dimensioned explorations of the nature of man might be initiated. For the artist the most obvious implication of the work of the scientists was the destruction of the rigidities between time past, present and future in the individual consciousness, and their replacement by a sense of flux, in which the old fixed edges became blurred. Particularly influential was the notion that the 'experience' of time within the individual was valid and not merely eccentric when it was at variance with the mechanistic evidence of chronological time.

Virginia Woolf's 'stream of consciousness', Joyce's manipulation of apparent and experienced time, Maeterlinck's sentimental flirtations with an ever-present eternity, were no mere accidents of artistic imaginations. They grew in a landscape prepared by the scientists, and were given more explicit expressions in some of Wells's novels. It is indeed noticeable that as soon as time lost its traditional rigidity the novelist became involved, sensing, in the new flexibility of definition, that necessary elbow-room for the deployment of his wide-ranging art. The novel, in the early years of the twentieth century, led the way in the exploitation of the new thinking about the mysteries and the problems of time. Poetry remained at first almost untouched, indeed the Georgians clung to the nostalgias of the traditional time-complex. They gave most of the colouring to the persistent image of the late Edwardian and early Georgian eras as a golden afternoon, across whose frontiers sad dark shadows stretched. They were the last group of poets to exploit the old bitter-sweet conception of time and eternity, and the winsome pathos of the fruitless attempt to make time have a stop:

> Oh yet
> Stands the Church clock at ten to three
>
> When small clouds are so silvery white
> Each seems a broken rimmed moon –
> When such things are, this world too soon,
> For me, doth wear the veil of Night.

Although the time-nostalgia has appeared in individual poets since then, it has lost its former emotional hegemony over the lyric poet, and often when it appears, its emotional indulgence is mutated by a harsher wryness or irony:

> Lay your sleeping head my love, human on my faithless arm.
> Time and fevers burn away the beauty from individual children,
> And the grave proves the child ephemeral
>
> The sunlight on the garden hardens and grows cold,
> You cannot cage the minutes within its nets of gold
>
> And I am dumb to tell a weather's wind,
> How time has ticked a heaven round the stars.

Again, the movement of *The Waste Land*, in its image pattern, owes little to the traditional logic of poetic communication. Most readers are conditioned to the expectation of 'beginning, middle and end' in poetry, whatever imaginative excursions the poet may embark upon in the course of his poem. Even in a poem which journeys through time and space, like Marvell's *To His Coy Mistress*, there is a logic in its movement from point to point in the poem. The reader, comfortably, has reference points for his apprehension of the meaning. The poem itself is like a clock and its imagery moves from division to division on the clock-face tacitly confirming that time past, present and future are three entities. *The Waste Land* displays no such clock-face to enable the reader to hold on to his mechanistic conception, and to help him to move logically from one image to another. The meaning of the poem rests almost completely in a complex amalgam of thoughts and emotions which are gathered into a bewildering timelessness. The poem is one of the most obvious, if not the most successful, examples of the way in which certain twentieth century artists have become more conscious of the complexities of time.

Priestley, in his so-called 'time-plays' represents one of the most cogent assaults made upon the problem of time by the prose-writer. He has rejected utterly the old conception that the past is gone irredeemably, that the future is still to come, and that we live in a limited span of present tense from birth to death. The rejection is implicit in his plays, and is dealt with directly in his autobiographies *Midnight On the Desert* and *Rain Upon Godshill*. It is important to understand that though it is possible to abstract a theory of time from his works – sometimes a contradictory one but rarely obscure – he does not write 'out of' a theory. The starting-point is magic – the mystery which surrounds our being here, and which for Priestley is so easily denied by those who have the old chronological view of life: 'There is something in us belonging to another order of being, that can't be identified with all this material stuff and its processes'.

But Priestley, no less than other of his contemporaries, can be seen to be very much in the context of the scientific and quasi-scientific twentieth-century explorations of time. His preoccupation has spanned most of his life, and his latest book *Man and Time* indicates that his passion is not spent.

There are three authors whose influences he acknowledges in his developing views of time. The first was the clergyman E. A. Abbott whose *Flatland* describes a two dimensional world whose citizens have no sensory experience other than length and breadth. When they are visited by a normal three-dimensioned body they cannot recognise it as something which exists at the same *time* as they do. To them this body which has the additional dimension of height appears as a series of surfaces in relation to their Flatland. A ball, for example, would appear to them as a succession of concentric circles, varying in diameter – it would therefore appear to them as a movement in time. Abbott's first inference is that our world could equally consist of more than the normal quota of dimensions but that we are not prepared or equipped to deal with them; his second inference is that any extra dimensions would, if we could perceive them, appear as movements in time.

The second and by far the most seminal influence on Priestley was the work of J. W. Dunne whose catholic mind encompassed the worlds of aerodynamic invention, mathematics and philosophy. His books *An Experiment With Time*, *The Serial Universe*, *The New Immortality*, and *Nothing Dies*, but particularly the first, caught the popular imagination. Their very popularity in fact gave cogency to the judgement by some scientists that the theories were insubstantial, and indeed Dunne's preoccupation with dreams and their meanings suggested to many a personality which only dabbled in scientific matters, and was more attracted by a dubious occultism. Such a judgement ignores the complicated mathematical reasoning which lies behind Dunne's theories and which he is at pains to demonstrate in his books. Indeed only the first part of *An Experiment With Time* is popular in the sense that it is readily understood and deals with matters of common experience, and does so with an excitement which is infectious and stimulating. There can be little doubt that Priestley was attracted to the book by its sheer verve and the atmosphere of mysterious adventure which characterises the first part.

An Experiment With Time attempts to do exactly what it

announces – to conduct an experiment based on individual experiences of dreams to show the complicated nature of time itself and of the individual's experience of time.

Its conclusions, insofar as they are apposite to and utilised in Priestley's work, may be simply stated. First, that in the inchoate structure and content of a dream, what are usually termed past, present and future co-exist and are incapable of being disentangled; second, that the old distinctions between past present and future are meaningless, and that their co-existence is a powerful and valid reality; third, that there exists a *regressus ad infinitum*. The effect of reading the first part of Dunne's book is like that of reading a slightly quaint account of an expedition into the interior of a dark but exciting continent. The expedition is made up of apparently very unlikely members and there is a strong impression of an ad hoc quality not only about the direction which is being taken, but also about the method of travel. Nevertheless, Dunne's account is extremely persuasive and, at times, has an emotional vibrancy about it which strongly suggests utter mystery, intrepid exploring. The atmosphere is maintained by the sheer doggedness of proceeding with equipment and methods which are not specially designed for the adventure:

> And then, what about that curious feeling which everyone has now and then experienced – that sudden, fleeting, disturbing conviction that something which is happening at that moment has happened before.

> I had done nothing but suppose, in hopelessly unscientific fashion for a week or more, and it seemed to me that I might as well complete my sinning. So I took a final wild leap to the wildest supposition of all.

> Was it possible that these phenomena were not abnormal, but normal?

Having reached the point where he concludes that past, present and future exist and can be perceived simultaneously, Dunne is faced with the problem of the next step which, with a daring leap, he takes with his regression theory, which is best described illustratively by Ladislaus Löb:

> I observe an object in front of me. While doing this I am aware of my own observance; therefore there must be in me a second observer who is observing me while I am engaged in observing the object in front of me. The second observer for his part, however, is aware of his own observance which presupposes the existence of a third observer. The conscious mind, according to Dunne, consists of a row of observers, and so ad infinitum. As however the law of the '*regressus ad infinitum*' applies to all things on earth, there must also be an infinite number of dimensions and times (Dunne also supports Abbott's theory that the next highest dimension must always appear as time) each of which contains all previous dimensions and times for ever. The sum of all times represents a real time just as the sum of all observers represents the real Ego. At death Man enters into the fourth dimension where his four-dimensional personality, the sum of all his three-dimensional times on earth, moves towards the fifth dimension. When he dies again he reaches the fifth, sixth, seventh dimension and so on, and each time during this progression a new observer appears.

Thus a new observer is, as it were, unpeeled as each new dimension is achieved, but, more important, this advance from one dimension to another is a new immortality – the infiniteness of time's dimensions ensures immortality.

The third work which made a strong impact on Priestley was Ouspensky's *A New Model of the Universe*. According to Ouspensky, time exists along a circle, with the obvious implication that all the happenings of an individual's life are repeatable. The initial theoretical possibility therefore is that each person relives his life an infinite number of times. This boring prospect is mitigated however by Ouspensky in his 'spiral' theory which suggests that higher intelligences are able to move upward in a spiral movement until they reach a point where they are on a different and higher track of existence. Lower intelligences – criminals and lunatics – correspondingly move in a descending spiral until they are finally and utterly eradicated. So far as the higher intelligences are concerned there are two factors which lend excitement to the possibility of moving in an upward spiral. First, under certain circumstances, hindsight is possible, so that although moving on a higher track than formerly an individual may catch glimpses of a former and lower circular track upon which he has travelled. Second, certain people (the word 'chosen' figures large in Ouspensky), having knowledge of this possibility of hindsight, may be able to interfere in another individual's cycle and to help him to avoid the mistakes, crises and dangers of an event as it looms up again in the repetitive movement of that individual's existence. *I Have Been Here Before* is based specifically upon this 'interference' theory.

The most obvious characteristic of all three of these writers on time is that, emotionally, they imply an immortality without the necessity of a deity, and therefore without the need for a 'faith' combined with religious practice and doctrine. They provide therefore, for the romantic sceptic, the comfort of an eternal life with an apparent scientific justification. More than this they imply not only an infinite number of sentient 'lives', but (certainly in the case of Ouspensky) the implication of a moral structure to the universe and to man's adventures in time. Ouspensky's spirals create a new heaven and a new hell, and give an incentive to the individual to improve his intellectual and emotional sensibilities so that he may move gradually from one time track to another, each time with the possibility of avoiding some of the mishaps and mistakes of a previous circuit. But of all three, Dunne proffers the most exciting evidence, because he avers that there are experiences (in dreams) which we may have in the 'here and now' which 'prove' the existence and the validity of the multi-dimensional nature of human life.

The contraditions, problems and non-sequiturs which a detailed examination of these three writers would reveal (for example why should a descending spiral imply a less worthy and a retracting existence more than an upward one?) are countermanded by their enormous and optimistic emotional appeal. Certainly the flaws which Priestley has found, and his doubts about the *regressus ad infinitum* of Dunne, have not dulled his appetite. In an age of a relentless slackening of systematised religious belief, allied to a blind acceptance of the power of scientific and technological evidence, the emotional needs of even the most intelligently sceptical are often assuaged by such theories. The extent of popular interest in and acceptance of Dunne's *An Experiment With Time* in the 1930s when it ran through two editions and a reprint, was extraordinary. The middle-aged religious sceptic even today will often be found with the name of Dunne on his lips as a palliative to the blank possibility of an utterly definitive termination of consciousness with death.

Yet all three theories, however much they may provide, even without the sanction of general scientific approval, a comforting sense of design and pattern and survival, have an additional magnetism. In structure, content and presentation they suggest a purposeful adventurousness. Dunne's mathematical equations in the second part of his book do nothing to dampen the spirits of the reader who, in the first part, is given the strong conviction that he has been launched into a mystery, but with the comforting sense of order and control about it. The old dreams of the alchemists, and the new dreams of the time-explorers, both enshrine an abiding human craving for controlled exploration into the unknown. Mankind cannot bear very much 'unreality', but it can bear any amount when the journey into the unknown is on a permanent way whose destination is plotted and may have comfortingly been used by his fellow-creatures.

This is the context for Priestley's own absorbing interest in the problem of time. It is important to notice, however, that while the researches of the quasi and the pure scientists helped to destroy the old and relatively simple self-conscious relationship between time, the artist and his art, they helped also to create a new territory of association, not less subtle than the old one, but more subtle and devious. Priestley stands at the very centre of this new world of association, whose first premise is that the individual is no longer a static figure imprisoned in the capsule of a present tense that lasts from birth to death, but can actively journey both backwards and forwards in time. Priestley brought to Dunne and Ouspensky a personality well conditioned to embrace the optimistic adventurousness of their theories, an emotional awareness keyed to the mysterious romanticism which could be prised from them, and a belief in the worth of the human spirit which could be given extra justification by these new intimations of immortality. Furthermore, his unabating curiosity about the technique of writing was given a teasing challenge by the possibility of a multi-dimensioned universe. His use of the time-theories can be conveniently divided into two sectors; the first in which he discusses them (mainly in his autobiographies) and presents his own particular versions of them; the second in his use of them in certain of his plays and novels.

It is typical of Priestley that in his accounts of his own versions there should be a constant implication not only that the concept of a 'new immortality' is exciting and enriching, but that it increases the responsibility of the human being to himself and to his fellows. It is Ouspensky's spiral with its promise of an ascent to a higher dimension, and the consequent onus on the individual to become 'worthy' of an ascent in the spiral, which agrees most with Priestley's belief in the interdependence, and therefore the mutual responsibility, of human beings. His exploration of time in the autobiographies is always an exploration of the needs and responsibilities of the human personality. As a time-traveller Priestley takes the world along with him, and cannot forget the bread and butter functions of body and spirit while he is sipping the heady wine of co-existent past, present and future.

In *Rain Upon Godshill* he begins his exploration with an account of dreams which he has had and others have related to him. It is clear that long before he read Dunne he had become convinced that there was a purposeful meaning in dreams which was not only exciting and capable of investigation, but which was vitally connected with the nature of the human personality. The flavour of some of the dreams recounted ranges from the bizarre to the mundane, and Priestley's account of his belief in their importance has about it as much of excited faith as of sober reason. The paragraph in which he announces their importance is typical of this enlivening, if sometimes disconcerting, mixture:

> I could not dismiss my own dreams like that. They left too deep an impression. It was as if these other people had never done any real dreaming themselves. With a certain air of pride, people would announce that they never remembered dreaming. To me it was as if they had announced proudly that they had never seen great mountains or the sea. They had, I felt, only half-lived. There was a whole world into which they had not entered. And it was not, I began to see, a tiny spectral world of fleeting terrors or vanities. Never from the first did dreams appear to me to be nothing but an idle fantastication of my waking life. They were always more than that. Soon I felt that they were an accompaniment, in some other sphere, to my waking life, having much the same relation to it that the exquisite and tragic tunes for the piano have to the vocal parts in the songs of Hugo Wolf. But just as a Wolf song is the voice and the piano, so our real life is our waking hours plus our dreams.

In his account of various types of dreams Priestley stresses that few people are aware of the catholicity of types in their dreaming lives. For himself he distinguishes four types; the fantastic (often ludicrous, sometimes sinister); a transference type when he seems to be dreaming some other personalities' life; the supra-real type in which a glimpse is caught of some new order of reality, and the 'clear wise dream' in which he is conscious of a new and superior kind of experience. In this farrago which he describes, it is remarkable how successful Priestley is in steering clear of the occult, both in its meaning of experiences beyond the range of ordinary knowledge, and its more popular denotion of mumbo-jumbo spirit-calling. Throughout the account Priestley clearly emphasises that the experiences he is writing of are not abnormal or even unusual, but are, if we choose to give attention to them, completions of our existence. They are the proverbial two thirds of the iceberg which, because they lie in the translucent darkness of water, are often not heeded. To support this he quotes from Jung for whom he has always had a profound regard:

> The view that dreams are merely imaginary fulfilments of suppressed wishes has long ago been superseded. It is certainly true that there are dreams which embody suppressed wishes and fears, but what is there which the dream cannot on occasion embody? Dreams may give expression to ineluctable truths, to philosophical pronouncements, illusions, wild fantasies, memories, plans, anticipations, irrational experiences, even telepathic visions.

Thus Priestley's intuition, his experience of dreams, and the authority of Jung lie behind his first conclusion – that our dream life is as meaningful a part of our existence as is that which we call our conscious working life. His second conclusion, pulled out from the different types of dreams he has had, and again from Jung, is that dreams are not experiences or imaginary fulfilments of one thing only (suppressed wishes or fears), but that they may give expression to a host of things, of which Jung's list gives only an indication. His third conclusion is that dreams are a clue not only to our inward nature as individuals, but to the nature of life itself. It is with these two assumptions that Priestley comes closer to the connection he is later to develop between dreams and time. One overall implied conclusion of his speculations needs, however, to be stressed. He is at pains to make it clear that he does not dream 'autobiographically', but that he quite often does dream 'biographically' – dreaming another man's life. He refers to these dreams as chapters drawn at random from other people's life stories. 'It is as if the wires of experience were crossed.' One such dream he found particularly disturbing:

> One night last year I dreamed myself into some foreign city and though I had no name and did not know what I looked like, I felt I was a younger and smaller man, really somebody else, a student or something of that kind; and I crept into a room where there were a number of tiny models of some

> military or naval invention; and I had just taken one of these from the table when two uniformed officers rushed in, and as I was running out of the opposite doorway one of them fired several times at me, wounding me severely, and as I staggered into the street I could feel my life ebbing away. I was actually wounded during the War but not in this fashion, and have never in waking existence felt my life fast ebbing away. But that moment in the dream had a terrible reality, and I do not believe I could invent that vast throbbing gush of weakness. No doubt most of the dream was my own invention, though I am not given to melodrama of this kind, but I will swear that that swaying progress from the office into the street and the blind weakness that washed over me there were somebody's last moments and that my consciousness had relived them.

The meaning of this dream for him is dramatic: 'We may all have to relive a great deal before we have done, just as if we were the new needles dropped into the records, for ever revolving, of universal human experience'.

The 'universal human experience' is the factor that links his conception of the value of dreams to his speculations on the mysteries of time. Priestley cannot find a simple orthodox explanation of time any more convincing than of dreams. 'The conventional view of it still seems to me as absurdly narrow as it is unrewarding.' He cannot accept coincidence as an explanation of precognition and prediction, and this he illustrates with another dream in which time itself is puzzlingly involved:

> I had gone up to my wife's room after lunch, to see if she was ready to go out, and found her sleeping. I sat in an arm-chair near the bed to wait, and then began to doze. I saw her open her eyes, smile slowly, rub her eyes, yawn and stretch, and then sit up. I stared hard, and the room gave a little quiver, and then I was wide awake and saw that she was still sleeping. Within a minute or so, however, she opened her eyes, smiled slowly, rubbed her eyes, yawned and stretched, and thensat up, just as I had seen her do in my tiny dream a few moments before.

> If anybody wishes to cry 'Coincidence' I shall not be angry, for I realise that the movements of a person waking up are limited; but I can only say that at the time I was convinced that the order of the movements was exactly the same and that I certainly felt I had seen the same thing twice.

He brushes aside the obvious objections to this dream as an example of 'time-travelling', and one has the impression that no amount of alternative explanations are likely to shake what amounts to a kind of faith in transcendental meanings:

> My own opinion is that it happened just as I have told it and that the only explanation is that the secondary self, discovered in sleep when the primary self no longer concentrates on the narrow moment, has a wider *Now* than the ordinary waking self, there is more in its present, and so it could observe my wife coming out of her sleep. Note that this is not really seeing the future if you accept this division of selves. It is the secondary self seeing its present, some of which happens to be in the primary self's future.

This second self which is similar to Dunne's 'observer' is more potently described by Priestley than by Dunne, because the latter is bound by the need for scientific evidence, and possibly because he is not happy with the implications of one observer forcing him to the acceptance of an infinite series of observers. Priestley detects Dunne's uncertainty:

> You will notice that all time-travellers, who find themselves with some freedom of movement along the fourth dimension, can observe but not interfere. (Although Dunne does grapple with this problem of interference, he makes it easier for himself elsewhere by always referring to us as *Observers*.) Once we escape from this little narrow *Now* we are really audience, and even if we should be on the scene we are still audience. There is only one point at which we can interfere, as Dunne shows us, and that is at the *Now* point in what he calls Time One. But this

interference, which must come from that part of the self not enmeshed in Time One, or – to use Dunne's term – some higher Observer, can change the future. Now this has always seemed to me the weakest part of Dunne's argument. (Though I boggle at the regress too, for an *infinity* of times turning into dimensions of space is unthinkable. I feel in my very bones that this is a complicated universe but not as crazily complicated as all that. Something has gone wrong here.) It is like saying the future is there, all nicely shaped and coloured and ready to be put into the newspapers, diaries and history books, but nevertheless is not really there because it is being changed by our interference, madly re-shaped and re-coloured every month or so.

Priestley is less interested in a scientific justification of any theory than in attempting to express his own comprehension, in his bones, and along his bloodstream, of a mystery. There are two aspects of the mystery he is particularly concerned to be clear about. The first is what he calls 'the problem of actualisation', and the second is the problem of 'personality and the soul'. Both of these intrigue him not only for their implication, but because he is conscious of the way in which they affect the basis upon which he creates artistically. There is perhaps no better definition of his time-plays than the sentence in *Rain Upon Godshill* which introduces his speculations upon the problem of 'actualisation'. '[Which] is really the business of bringing events which already have their being in what I believe to be the more enduring and fundamental world of our feeling, imagination and will, into the world of material form.' For him the problem is that of clothing in material terms those parts of life which are hidden away in the 'feelings, imagination and will', and those parts which lie in the darker territories of dreams:

Why do we say 'only a dream'? If we regard a dream as a mere grotesque little shadow of experience, it is obvious why we say 'only'. But I for one, as I have shown, cannot accept that point of view. If a man's dreams should offer him a richness and complexity of experience that he does not know in working life, he ought to put them first.

The implications of this for his plays remains to be discussed, but what now requires emphasis is Priestley's complete acceptance of the validity of the 'inner life'. If it is true that the idea of the family represents the ideal of Priestley's conception of human relations, it is equally true that for him there remains a tremendous validity in the inner experience of the family's component parts – valid so long as the individual realises not only the richness of the dimensions that lie behind the Now, but the responsibilities that such recognition lays upon him.

The second mystery concerns the nature of personality. Priestley is not a Christian, and his retraction from Christianity is, one suspects, less the result of the question of Deity, as the matter of the nature of the individual personality and soul. He cannot believe with the Christians that 'with everybody there comes into existence an immortal soul which may have begun last Tuesday'. He proposes that the possible alternative – that an immortal soul exists before birth – is more reasonable and that it is equally 'reasonable' to assume that the soul has not arbitrarily linked itself to a particular set of physical and mental characteristics but has acquired them for purposes of its own. 'The outward Jones is but a sign and symbol of the everlasting Jones.'

The inevitable conclusion of such a premise is that the whole reality of what we call Jones is not the man we see and hear, the man who catches the train, who loves, eats and sleeps, but includes the Jones who also exists in the long hinterland, the fourth dimensional hinterland, of the soul. But Priestley, while accepting this, cannot at the same time abandon his belief that 'personality is not only not one of the supreme realities, but that on any cosmological scale of thinking it is nothing but an illusion'. The clue to an explanation of this apparent contradiction between the intense validity of Jones with his hinterland of soul, and the illusion of personality lies in Priestley's third type of dream in which he is convinced that he is dreaming the reality of another man's life. One recalls with a sickening *frisson* his own dream of another man's 'last' moments: 'What is wrong [in Dunne] is the suggestion of a steady growth, a thickening and colouring of individuality. Now I feel that the more inward you go, the less Jones is mere Jones, and the more he is also Smith, Brown, Robinson and much else besides'.

The conclusion is plain. There is a universal impersonal consciousness which each individual calls upon, or which is visited upon him, or from which he takes his colouring, at times more potently than others. Priestley's evidence for its existence is again based largely on his own personal experience, and the feel of truth in his own bloodstream:

> There are moments of which you can say . . . 'I was most wonderfully stirred' or 'I was in ecstasy'. But really you produce the personal pronoun to give the feeling a time-and-place reference, for you do not really feel that there was any 'I' but only 'stirred' or 'ecstasy'.
>
> 'What we call personality is a vehicle or one small focal point of a universal consciousness.'

It would be easy to dismiss Priestley's notions of dreams and time as the subjective whistlings in the dark of a frightened man to convince himself that in the viewless winds of time and space he and humanity mean something. But to do this is also to dismiss the basis for the heart and mind searchings not only of many puzzled laymen but also the profoundest philosophers. The search for explanation, for pattern, for meaning, wherever it is found, presupposes a desire to ennoble man into the condition of meaningfulness among the cold stars. There is nothing in Priestley's excited searchings which does anything but give man an importance which he may not in fact have, but which most men crave to have. And indeed who is there yet to say Priestley nay? To accuse him of providing an unjustified comfort is to beg the question. Equally to accuse him of a sort of Model T Ford mysticism, even allowing that he does seem at times to draw too *spirituelle* a conclusion from flimsy evidence, takes no account of the fact that he never allows himself to remain for long an aery cosmos-wanderer. Again to accuse him of desiring the best of both worlds – desiring to be romantic spirit as well as robust realist – is to simplify the issue. The tenor of most of his creative work, whatever its quality, involves both the reality of the working world and the reality of the unknown world of the fourth dimension:

> Eternal life is always a new heightened experience of Here and Now . . . all moments of noble living, the ecstasy of love, the compassion and understanding that enters into every genuine personal relationship, the creation and rapt appreciation of great art, the adventures of the mind among significant ideas, even an amazed wondering about ourselves, all demand this unknown dimension, this timeless being. Every greatly heightened state of consciousness involves eternity.

Thus life, as it is lived, may be ennobled by the acceptance and recognition of the mystery. But even more: all Priestley's political and sociological premises and polemics which are flung into the day-to-day bustle of contemporary society spring from his belief that the universal consciousness from which we project should be a mirror of the kind of society which we should create. If Jones is one with the universe he must learn to be one with the earth.

There is more than a suggestion in Priestley of that species of imagination which yearns towards action, and which cannot feel justified until it has related its visions to the actualities of living. In this sense he is possessed of that romantic tone which is observable in Shelley and Ruskin, but more particularly in William Morris. They all are inhabited by an imagination whose antennae reach not only into artistic creativity but into the affairs of the world. Fundamentally this type of romanticism is optimistic – the cynic might say self-deluding – since its premise is not only the worthwhileness of human existence but the certainty of its perfectability. The more precise parallel with Priestley is Morris who had a shrewder head for the heights and gulfs of his society than had Ruskin or Shelley. Priestley has not made furniture or woven tapestry but he, no less than Morris, has a vision of man's place in the universe and a hard awareness of how that place must be reflected in man's living. Morris's:

> To what a heaven the earth might grow
> If fear beneath the earth were laid,
> If hope failed not, nor love decayed.

has an echoing note in Priestley's:

> We're not in Paradise, and we have no right to expect to be. People fall out of love, children die, there are bestial wars, and everywhere there's ugliness and pain and misery, just as everywhere the sun goes down and the night comes. But people also fall in love, as we've done, and children grow up happily, wars come to an end or are avoided, bits of ugliness disappear – and it's our job not to whine that these things exist but to help them out of the world, and people have fun together, help each other in need, try to soften pain and drive away misery.

The optimistic, no less than the pessimistic, imagination inclines to an overstatement of its point of view, and its communication tends to be tremulous when its intention is really to convey a sense of urgency. Priestley, no less than Morris, is often a victim of his own beliefs in that his vision of what we must aspire to, in his plays and novels, is often couched in words which have lost their heads and remember only their hearts.

Priestley's reply to such a criticism would be that the affairs of man have much more to do with the heart than the head, and that he cannot tolerate the clipping of angels' or man's potential wings by the harsh knife of philosophy which has no place in the seething mystery of life. One might accept this, were there not at times an embarrassing failure in Priestley to give his words sufficient blood to sustain their passionate message. Sometimes their blood-stream is thinned in his attempts to make clear to the greatest possible number what he means. Thus 'people having fun together' conjures up a vast Battersea Park of organised laughter and enjoyment. There is nothing that Priestley would like less than a twee fun fair, but on the other hand there is equally in him a distaste for the over-intellectualisation of his beliefs. Thus, his failure to strike a balance often earns him the reputation of sentimental superficiality. That this is too hasty a judgement is quickly confirmed in those statements when he forgets to be simple:

> We must wait. Even if we believe that the time of our civilisation is running out fast, like sugar spilled from a torn bag, we must wait. But while we are waiting we can try and think and behave, to some extent, *as if* our society were already beginning to be contained by religion, as if we were certain that Man cannot even remain Man unless he looks beyond himself, as if we were finding our way home again in the universe. We can stop disinheriting ourselves. We can avoid both the *hubris* and the secret desperation of our scientific 'wizards that peep and mutter'. We can challenge the whole de-humanising, depersonalising process, under whatever name it may operate, that is taking the symbolic richness, the dimension in depth, out of men's lives, gradually inducing the anaesthesia that demands violence, crudely horrible effects, to feel anything at all. Instead of wanting to look at the back of the moon, remote from our lives, we can try to look at the back of our own minds. Even this *As If* will do something to bring our outer and inner worlds, now tearing us in two, closer together, more in harmony.

Priestley's acceptance of the fourth dimension and of the universal consciousness is a metaphysic for him which does not abandon the world. Indeed the metaphysic helps to strengthen his strong and instinctive sense of community on earth, and his belief in its power to enrich the individual life. His multitudinous expressions of its nature, directly and indirectly, vary from the banal to the graceful and fecund, his 'evidence' varies from the trivially subjective to the disturbingly inexplicable. If at times he seems an idle dreamer with a shovel in his hand, at others, he is a visionary:

> I dreamt I was standing at the top of a very high tower, alone, looking down upon myriads of birds all flying in one direction; every kind of bird was there, all the birds in the world. It was a noble sight, this vast aerial river of birds. But now in some mysterious fashion the gear was changed, and time speeded up, so that I saw generations of birds, watched them break their shells, flutter into life, mate, weaken, falter and die. Wings grew only to crumble; bodies were sleek and then, in a flash, bled and shrivelled; and death struck everywhere at every second. What was the use of all this blind struggle towards life, this eager trying of wings, this hurried mating, this flight and surge, all this gigantic meaningless biological effort? As I stared down, seeming to see every creature's ignoble little history almost at a glance, I felt sick at heart. It would be better if not one of them, if not one of us all, had been born, if the struggle ceased for ever. I stood on my tower, still alone, desperately unhappy. But now the gear was changed again and time went faster still and it was still rushing by at such a rate, that the birds could not show any movement, but were like an enormous plain sown with feathers. But along this plain, flickering through the bodies themselves, there now passed a sort of white flame, trembling, dancing, then hurrying on; and as soon as I saw it I knew that this white flame was life itself, the very quintessence of being; and then it came to me, in a rocket-burst of ecstasy, that nothing mattered, because nothing else was real, but this quivering and hurrying lambency of being. Birds, men or creatures not yet shaped and coloured, all were of no account except so far as this flame of life travelled through them. It left nothing to mourn over behind it; what I had thought was tragedy was mere emptiness or a shadow show; for now all real feeling was caught and purified and danced on ecstatically with the white flame of life. I had never felt before such deep happiness as I knew at the end of my dream of the tower and the birds, and if I have not kept that

happiness with me, as an inner atmosphere and a sanctuary for the heart, that is because I am a weak and foolish man who allows the mad world to come trampling in, destroying every green shoot of wisdom. Nevertheless I have not been quite the same man since. A dream had come through the multitude of business.

This represents the true and valid heart of Priestley's metaphysic, and in it lies the proof of his belief that the more 'inward you go, the less Jones is mere Jones, and the more he is also Smith, Brown, Robinson, and much else besides'.

CHAPTER FOUR

Time Plays

DANGEROUS CORNER

Priestley's first play was produced in London in 1932. Despite the tremendous attractions that the world of theatre had for him in his youth, he held back from involving himself in its ruck and reel for reasons he has made clear. His first aim in the 1930s was to make enough money to ensure the security of his family, and he felt that this aim could be easily frustrated by involvement in a world which has in it so much of chance and accident: 'In the circumstances of production in the English-speaking Theatre you are compelled to exist in an over-heated atmosphere of dazzling success and shameful flops, you are a wonder man in October, a pretentious clown in March, you are in, you are out'.

More than this Priestley had, and still has, a loathing for the financial 'gaming' which surrounds the West End theatre. He has always insisted on being financially involved in the presentation of his own plays, preferring to have some control rather than be at the mercy of the speculator. There is an odd set of quirks in the history of *Dangerous Corner*. Priestley formed a production company, which, at the very outset of a career on the stage, is perilous enough, but to do it with a play which he admits was written within a week in order to prove to himself that he could write for the stage, adds a touch of the bizarre to the enterprise. Oddity does not stop here, however, because its reception by the daily press was so unfavourable that only Priestley's dogged persistence, backed by favourable comments by Ivor Brown and James Agate, ensured its survival beyond five West End nights. This survival has been astonishingly stubborn – the play has probably been presented in more countries, and has a higher number of performances both amateur and professional than any other play written in the last three decades. But, as if to bear out Priestley's belief in chance and accident, the quirks have yet another aspect. Criticism and appraisal of it has ranged from Audrey Williamson's declaration that it shows a 'mastery of technique in the Ibsen manner' to David Hughes's 'it is better theatre than philosophy', to A. V. Cookman's 'it is perhaps the most ingenious play ever put together'. Despite these somewhat off-centre claims, Priestley himself has no doubts about the play: 'It has never been a favourite of mine, for it seems to me to be merely an ingenious box of tricks'.

The proof of the value of Priestley's own judgement is in Guthrie's account of the rehearsals of the play.

> In the original production none of the actors was over forty and all were experienced and efficient people. In a week they knew the words backwards. In two weeks we all felt we had explored the play's narrow limits of characterisation and philosophy. There was another week before we opened. For three more days we rehearsed, the performance at each run-through becoming slicker but less interesting and more perfunctory. With the author's permission we knocked off until a dress rehearsal on the night before we opened.

As soon as the secret of a box of tricks is discovered, there is no more to be learnt and no more to be done, and Guthrie's words point clearly to two of the most obvious characteristics of the play. It has a geometrical finality in the writing of its characters and plot, and its theme is easily contained within this geometry. There is little which requires either from director or actor that reflectiveness in which character-interpretation or emphasis of mood grows subtly in the period of preparation. Of all Priestley's plays *Dangerous Corner* is most obviously an exercise in the art of construction, yet this alone cannot account for its popularity with audiences nor for the insistent magic of its atmosphere.

Quite simply it is a play which can be seen with pleasure again and again, despite its dependence on a plot whose machinations are easily assimilated. The secret of its attraction is Priestley's masterly intuition of what audiences perennially require from stage-entertainment. The greater part of English audiences has remained relatively unsophisticated despite the proliferation of forms of entertainment and dramatic modes in the twentieth century; despite the siren calls of poetic drama, expressionism, alienism, film, television, theatre in the round, the average theatre-goer takes with him to the theatre a set of built-in reflexes which await a stimulant. It is Priestley's feeling for these reflexes which accounts for his success with *Dangerous Corner*. Basically, the average theatre-goer requires a satisfaction of paradoxical cravings for illusion and reality at the same time. The theatre is regarded by the majority of playgoers as a source of relaxation, entertainment – in the sense of getting away from it all. Yet if an audience feels that it is being pushed too far away from it all, it is inclined to cavil at what it sees because it is 'far-fetched', 'unreal', because 'it couldn't happen'. The desire for the drugging luxury of illusion and, at the same time, the desire for a comforting recognition of apparent reality, dance a simple polka in the mental make-up of audiences. In this they display intuitively an appreciation of the true nature of dramatic presentation, although sometimes they will not allow either illusion or apparent reality enough elbow-room to jostle their imaginations into the fullest experience of a play. They are too often content with a superficial satisfaction of a conventional palate.

Priestley's instinctive knowledge of audience-expectation in general enables him, in play after play, to satisfy the appetites. *Dangerous Corner* is a good example of his knowledge. It is 'real' in its depiction of a not altogether affluent, but comfortable middle-class set who seem to have the conventional virtues of being easy-going, and having social charm. There is nothing extraordinary about them as characters. Freda is handsome and vivacious, Betty is a very pretty young thing, Stanton is 'a man about forty', Robert is in his early thirties, and 'is a good specimen'. And, as if to reinforce the expectation of 'reality', Miss Mockridge, the guest, is 'your own idea of what a smart middle-aged woman novelist should be'. Her dialogue is almost completely characterless, and merely gives the slightest hint of an eccentricity and inquisitiveness which he well knows will reinforce the expectation of the descriptions 'middle-aged' and 'novelist'. This character sits very lightly upon the plot, and is quickly withdrawn after doing her job of helping to bring to the surface the irritants which will gradually poison the easy-going dinner party. But she also fulfils the function of providing the audience with that comfortable and self-congratulatory feeling that they have seen someone they can recognise. They have Miss Mockridge nicely 'taped'.

None of the characters makes anything more than a minimal demand on the audiences' imaginations, and they exist almost entirely by the grace, not of any inward compulsion, but of the intricacies of the plot. They have, in fact, the generalised life of characters who are usually associated with the thriller type of play; the particularities of their personalities only have significance in terms of the actions of the plot, and are revealed in the horizontal dimensions of that action and not by the vertical dimension of an acutely observed individual psychology.

Yet it is insufficient to say that they are therefore mere illustrations of elements in the plot, because there is a technical subtlety in the way their quite mechanistic functions are revealed which raises their status above that of the 'whodunnit' play. This subtlety lies in a factor which is easily overlooked as the excitement of the present-tense action of the play unfolds. It is the unusual extent to which the play depends upon actions performed by the characters prior to the opening of the situation depicted. Almost everything that is shown is a projection of things that are unseen by the audience, and which are reported. The past-tense and reported action are the heart and soul of the dramatic action we see, and it is no mean achievement that tension and expectancy should flourish when its source lies so much in hindsight:

MISS M. (*to Freda*): But I suppose you all miss your brother-in-law. He used to be down here with you too, didn't he?

FREDA (*who obviously does not like this*): You mean Robert's brother, Martin.

MISS M.: Yes, Martin Caplan. I was in America at the time and never quite understood what happened. Something rather dreadful, wasn't it? (*There is a pause and Betty and Olwen look at Freda. Miss M. looks from one to the other.*) Oh, have I dropped a brick? I always am dropping bricks.

FREDA (*very quietly*): No, not at all. It was distressing for us at the time, but it's all right now. Martin shot himself. It happened nearly a year ago – last June, in fact – not here, but at Fallows End, about twenty miles away. He'd taken a cottage there.

This is the first uneasy incursion of the past-tense, which persists in being the palpable dynamic of the present in a way which is much more disturbing than the customary whodunnit, where its function is usually to provide intermittent explanation or clarification of a set of actions rather than to initiate a whole new set of circumstances and attitudes. In any case, in the typical whodunnit, information about the past is usually manipulated by one person – the detective – in his attempts to discover the villain of the piece. In Priestley's play there is no one detective, they are all detectives, and the motivation is not so much to discover a villain as to discover the whole truth about a certain situation.

The impression of the real is maintained by an absolute minimum of naturalistic detail in the visual sense. The radio, the off-stage noises, the ringing door-bells are sparingly used and really constitute a set of startling indications of present-tense happening. There is one naturalistic detail which, however, falls into a different category – the cigarette box, like Danny's hat-box in *Night Must Fall*, is a firm link between past and present. The cigarette box, on face value, bridges the mystery of what happened to Martin and the solution which unfolds with painful relentlessness. But as the action progresses it comes to take on the role of a sinister *deus ex machina* whose malevolence is inescapable.

FREDA: . . . I happened to see the cigarette box at Calthrop's. It was amusing and rather cheap, so I bought it for Martin.

ROBERT: And Calthrop's sent it to Martin, down at Fallows End, so that he never got it until that last Saturday?

FREDA: Yes.

ROBERT: Well, that's that.

GORDON: I'm sorry, Freda, but it's not quite so simple as all that. You mustn't forget that I was with Martin at the cottage that very Saturday morning.

ROBERT: Well, what about it?

GORDON: Well, I was there when the parcel post came, with the letters in the morning. I remember Martin had a parcel of books from Jack Brookfield – I don't forget anything about that morning, and neither would you if you'd been dragged into that hellish inquest as I was. But he didn't have that cigarette box.

FREDA: I suppose it must have arrived by the afternoon post then. What does it matter?

GORDON: It doesn't matter at all, Freda darling, except that at Fallows End parcels are never delivered by the afternoon post.

However real the surface impression of the play is in its obvious intention to naturalise a situation which has all the ingredients of fantastic coincidence, this reality is not obtrusive to the extent that it drowns the other desired element – that of illusion. There are, for example, only five indications of setting in the stage directions – a fireplace, a window, a table on which stands a wireless, a hall from which a telephone call is made, and a presumed dining room from which the voices of men are heard. The play is unusual in that it does not have Priestley's customary detailed instructions about setting. Its first words are: 'The curtain rises on a stage in darkness'.

When the lights are turned on no nicely furnished lounge is provided for us by the author. There is merely a short description of the four women who occupy a now lighted stage. Priestley's naturalism in this play is, in fact, to a large extent assumed by the audience. The details of set that are sparsely mentioned could in fact be spotlighted as they are required and then allowed to fade into a faceless background. The result would be a sort of grim charade in a limbo only alleviated occasionally by firm reminders of palpable living.

The dialogue is itself faceless having the quality of a shorthand which is used by all the characters. There is no individual style of speaking, no personal signature to anything that is said. Each character exists in terms of a formula which is merely stated, never explained. Thus Gordon is a weakling, Stanton a plausible rogue, Betty is not so innocent as she looks, Olwen is in love with Robert, and so on. There is no 'why' about the stances which the characters take up, and apart from the demands of the plot pure and simple, the speeches could be easily transposed. At times the shorthand is so basic that it ludicrously simplifies the realities of human emotion, as in the scene in which Freda, Robert's wife, left alone with Olwen, who loves Robert, tells her that she knows:

(*They speak in quick whispers*)

OLWEN: Have you really known a long time?

FREDA: Yes. More than a year. I've often wanted to say something to you about it.

OLWEN: What would you have said?

FREDA: I don't quite know. Something idiotic. But friendly, very friendly. (*Taking both her hands.*)

OLWEN: And I only guessed about you tonight, Freda. And now it all seems so obvious. I can't think why I never guessed before.

FREDA: Neither can I.

OLWEN: This is quite mad, isn't it?

FREDA: Quite mad. And rapidly getting madder. I don't care. Do you? It's rather a relief.

OLWEN: Yes it is – in a way. But it's rather frightening too. Like being in a car when the brakes are gone.

FREDA: And there are crossroads and corners ahead.

This has the novelette's cosy avoidance of difficulties.

Yet, though the dialogue lacks character, colour and depth, its overall effect conveys the rhythms of tension and relaxation which are true to a situation in which unpleasant truth seems, now on the verge of being easily explained, and now fraught with even more sinister possibilities. Before the departure of the outsider, Miss Mockridge, the dialogue has, in general, a brittle nervous quality as it tries to keep away from her implications which are becoming inescapable. After her departure a rhythm becomes apparent – tension gives place to relative tranquillity, and then is restored by a chance remark or a fresh piece of evidence. This rhythm is in itself successful in establishing the generality that human beings, faced with crises, will grasp at straws to expunge the crises, and it shows how, in the midst of them, the temper of a tense situation will occasionally slacken as the bloodstream runs momentarily a little slower.

FREDA (*emphatically*): If you're in love with somebody, you're in love with them, and they can do all sorts of things, be as mean as hell, and you'll forgive them or just not bother about it. At least some women will.

ROBERT: I don't see you doing it, Freda.

FREDA (*recovering her normal self*): Don't you? But there are a lot of things about me you don't see. But this is what I wanted to say, Olwen. If you thought that Robert had taken that money, then you knew that Martin hadn't?

OLWEN: Yes, I was sure – after I had talked to him that last night – that Martin hadn't taken it.

FREDA (*bitterly*): But you let us all think he had.

OLWEN: I know, I know. But it didn't seem to matter then. It couldn't hurt Martin any more. He wasn't there to be hurt. And I felt I had to keep quiet.

ROBERT: Because of me?

OLWEN: Yes, because of you, Robert.

ROBERT: But Martin *must* have taken it.

OLWEN: No.

ROBERT: That's why he did what he did. He thought he'd be found out. He was terribly nervy – always was, poor chap. And he simply couldn't face it.

OLWEN: No, it wasn't that at all. You *must* believe me. I'm positive that Martin never *touched* that money.

FREDA (*eagerly*): I've always thought it queer that he should. It wasn't Martin's style at all that – doing some sneaky work with a cheque. I knew he could be wild – and rather cruel sometimes. But he couldn't be a cautious little sneak thief. It wasn't his style at all. And he didn't care enough about money.

ROBERT: He spent enough of it. He was badly in debt, you know.

FREDA: Yes, but that's just the point. He didn't mind being in debt. He could cheerfully have gone on being in debt. Money simply didn't matter. Now *you* loathe being in debt. You're entirely different.

David Hughes says of *Dangerous Corner* that 'we probably tend in watching it . . . to take it at its face value. There is nothing wrong in this: Priestley always intends his work to be taken at its face value, without any undue effort on the part of the reader or audience, and he designs his work to show as much of its character as possible on its face. It is often his own fault if he is accused of superficiality'.

This statement is as generally true of Priestley as it is particularly true of *Dangerous Corner*. But the face value of this play does hide a theme which only dimly emerges out of what is a theatrical rather than a dramatic *tour-de-force*. The discovery of truth is Robert Caplan's motive in pursuing his questioning of Martin's death, and his anxious quest for it pervades the minds of even those who are reluctant to seek it, and have most to lose from discovering it. Even Stanton is eventually pulled into the orbit of truth-telling. The emphasis is not on the discovery of a fact or set of facts – that is, what happened to Martin Caplan? – but on the relationship of all the characters to Caplan. That Olwen accidentally shot him becomes almost an irrelevancy, that Stanton, not Martin, stole the money, becomes of secondary importance to what he thought of Martin. In revealing the various relationships to Martin, each character also reveals his true relationship to the others. If the end of the truth-telling is the truth about a dead man whom we never meet, the means become an exercise in the relativity of truth. As Hughes says:

Where human relations are concerned there is no absolute. By rigidly adhering to the truth as we see it, we present the matter in question in an entirely different light from someone else whose particular truth, or standard of truth, may be dependent on emotional circumstances that have nothing in common with our own.

The magic which surrounds this particular tightly-knit group is of a dark hue, and it is made up of the growing compulsions to expunge deception, however painful. Reluctances become temporary, and, in the end they are all trapped in a cloying atmosphere where falsehood dissipates but anguish begins. Priestley does not press the theme home, but its presence is inescapable, and on a few occasions its communication is direct:

GORDON: . . . What would have happened if we'd gone on pretending like hell to be happy together?
BETTY: Nothing.
GORDON (*thinking it out*): No. If we'd gone on pretending long enough, I believe we might have been happy together, sometimes. It often works out like that.
BETTY: Never.
OLWEN: Yes, it does. That's why all this is so wrong really. The real truth is something so deep that you can't get at it this way, and all this half-truth does is to blow everything up. It isn't *civilised*.

In this play, thinly, the theme of the responsibility of the individual as a component part of a group, has its first airing in a Priestley play. 'No man is an island' is its motto.

Time is used entirely as a device. Basically the play preserves the unities of time, place and action, except for the intrusion of the device at the end of Act Three. The play of continuous action has a unique ability to impose upon an audience a feeling of excited expectation and reality which is often denied the play which ignores the unities. The excitement is created by the illusion that what is being seen is being created as we see it, and, since it runs in series with our own pulse beats, its meanderings and conclusion are as much a mystery as our own personal future. Excitement and expectation are capable of sustaining belief in actions which on a cooler appraisal seem contrived and coincidental. *Dangerous Corner* never loses its hold on our expectations and therefore cunningly obscures its contrived action. The time-twist in Act Three in which Priestley simply returns to the beginning of the affair, and provides an alternative and seemingly more happy turn in the events, adds yet another acceptable factor to the audience's experience. The twist adds to immediacy and expectancy the very human ingredient expressed in the words: 'If I'd had my time over again, things would have been different'. But, though the play encourages this illusion, in point of fact the dangerous corner which the characters on their second turn of the circuit successfully negotiate, does not involve any willed or conscious action is the first if not the best example of this.

EDEN END

The affinity between this play and Chekhov's *The Cherry Orchard* has been commented on by Audrey Williamson who claims that it was an 'addiction' to Chekhov which influenced the writing. Priestley is too inquisitive and catholic an experimenter with dramatic forms to become addicted to any writer, though his admiration for *The Cherry Orchard* is great, and there can be little doubt that its poetry is of the stuff from which *Eden End* is created. In writing the play, he experienced an uncommon joy in the task. His note to the published edition suggests that he lived for months in a tranquillity with the characters. He writes:

> I found myself wondering how I came to write this particular play, because everything in it is imagined – I have never known any people like the Kirby family – and I know nothing in my own life that would suggest to me this particular theme of the pathetic prodigal daughter. But it gave me great satisfaction to write it.

On face value *Eden End* is about a Yorkshire doctor's family in the year 1912, as certainly as *The Cherry Orchard* is about a Russian family's problems in the year 1904. The aura which surrounds the action of the former, while it is not so pervasive and intense as the latter, is of that kind which lures criticism into being merely descriptive rather than analytic. Phrases like 'melancholic sadness', 'bitter-sweet', 'autumnal tinge', 'mutability' and 'the still sad music of humanity' which are (with different emotional tensions) applicable to both plays, do no more than describe the general mood which is created in the audience almost imperceptibly through the characters and actions. Both plays have been misunderstood in their time: either by a too-embracing acceptance of this generalised mood, or by an unimaginative and slavish preoccupation with their naturalistic surface. Both plays are, at different tensions, poetic plays. To ignore the rhythm set up between their surface appearance and their allusive background is to commit an error equal in kind, if not in profundity, to that which assumes either that *Twelfth Night* is about people seeking mates, or about a golden romantic Illyria, but that it cannot be about both.

The aura which surrounds the Priestley play and the Chekhov is partly created from a paradox in the status of the action and characters as they are presented to us. It depends for its impact on its inexorable revelation that there is not much time left for the tightly-knit group to retain its sense of one-ness. Yet what is also conveyed is a feeling that what happens exists in a timeless limbo. The actualities of the situation are time-bound, but the valid reality of the characters' consciousness of interdependence in the fragile ebbs and flows of human existence, are preciously timeless. The poetry of both plays lies in the dramatic reconciliation of these apparent irreconcilables. The titles of the plays themselves suggest a location where mutability and immutability poignantly meet. The characters are brought together quite naturally and the problems which assault them in both plays are not only credible, but are faced up to in a credible variety of attitudes.

The almost inconsequential ordinariness of the opening scenes of both plays is echoed again and again:

LOPAKHIN: The train has come, thank God. What's the time?

DOUNYASHA: Nearly two o'clock. (*Blowing out the candle*) It's daylight already.

LOPAKHIN: How many hours late was the train? A couple of hours at least. (*Yawning and stretching himself*) I am a nice one, what a stupid thing to do. I purposely came here in order to go to meet them at the station, and then overslept . . . fell asleep sitting in the chair . . . how annoying . . . You should have woken me up.

WILFRED: I'm getting it, Sarah. I'm getting it.
SARAH: You've been at it long enough.
WILFRED: Now just listen. (*He plays again and she stops in the middle, half-way between doors to listen.*)
WILFRED (*wheeling round*): What do you think of that?
SARAH: It sounds like proper playing – almost.

But there are, equally in both plays, other scenes in which the insulation of the characters from any environment both of time and place, is paramount. Here, the characters are made to stand for more than their surface actions and status would seem to justify. And in both plays memories are employed by characters to hold back the onset of the future, and to assert a poignant gaiety which slips away almost as soon as it is mentioned:

> It's just as I remembered it, only so much smaller. All the time I've been away it's been shrinking and shrinking. Like life. Oh – there's the china castle. Still there. Not broken. All sorts of things can get broken – people can be broken – and yet a thing like this can go on and on.

Both plays, in some details, show a similar deployment of effects, but in the final analysis they part company because the poetry achieved by the one is richer and more inevitably achieved than that of the other. In *The Cherry Orchard* the language is naturalistic in form – it impersonates the inconsequentiality, the fragmented character, of human conversation. The sudden darts of words as the mind or feelings are assaulted by a memory, the brooding statements that come from a slowly built up inner tension, the disconnected excitabilities, the remarks that seem to come from nowhere and go nowhere – all these are mirrored in Chekhov. Yet, all the time, the hearer is conscious that much more is taking place behind the words than is spoken. The poetry of the play is created from the rhythm set up between what seems actual and what lies behind. Even a momentary snatch of conversation has this double focus:

MME RANEVSKY: How does it go? Let me see if I can remember. ... I pot the yellow! I double into the middle pocket!
GAYEV: I go in, off. Once upon a time, sister, we used to sleep in this very room; and now I am fifty-one. Odd, isn't it?
LOPAKHIN: Yes, time is passing.
GAYEV: Eh?
LOPAKHIN: Time, I say, is passing.
GAYEV: There's a smell of cheap scent.
ANYA: I am off to bed. Good night, Mother.

This snatch of dialogue which even the characters themselves only seem to half hear, has a subtle *obbligato* in which Gayev's irritation, Anya's fatigue merge into Lopakhin's serio-comic mood.

In *Eden End* the language is not an impersonation of naturalistic language. As in *Dangerous Corner* the characters speak dialogue which does not penetrate deep into the recesses of their minds and feelings, but reports. In one scene alone Priestley is successful in making language a mirror of the inner man rather than a shorthand transcript. This is the scene between Charles and Wilfred at the beginning of Act Three in which they arrive home tipsy:

CHARLES (*with an air of profundity*): If my old man had been a doctor, a lot of things would have been different – very different. But he wasn't.
WILFRED: What was he – your old man?
CHARLES (*very solemnly*): Nothing, old boy – nothing. Just a bloody English gentleman. But never mind him. (*Sternly, raising glass*) Here's to Dr. Kirby – a noble old fellow.

WILFRED (*raising glass*): Here's to him – good old Dad.

CHARLES (*still solemnly*): Let's sit down.

WILFRED: Yes.

They sit down. Charles lights a cigarette. Wilfred looks rather sleepy.

CHARLES: You know, old boy – we've had a good evening. I told you yesterday – when we first met – I said then 'We can go out – you and I – and have a good evening here.' Didn't I?

WILFRED: You did.

CHARLES: Well, we've had one. What was the name of the fellow that gave us a lift in the trap?

WILFRED: Harper.

CHARLES: Harper. A very nice fellow – Harper. But he was badly screwed, y'know, old boy. He ought to have let us drive.

WILFRED: I met a fellow on the boat coming home called Harper. He came from Manchester and he had a glass eye. I hate glass eyes.

CHARLES: And I hate Manchester. If I'd to choose between a glass eye and Manchester, I'd rather have a glass eye. You meant a glass eye, old boy, didn't you–and not an eye-glass?

WILFRED: Yes, glass eye. . . .

Not only does the language here in itself create the sibilant imprecision of tipsy speech, but what is said conveys the ponderous quasi-logic of the semi-drunk. It may be observed in passing that the unmistakeable tones of Ralph Richardson's rich slur are present in Charles's dialogue.

But in general the rhythm that is created in *Eden End* is too explicit and does not come inevitably from the inner source of character. For example the idea that the house Eden End represents not merely home but also reality to Stella is stated, but there is not conviction in the words that it is also felt:

STELLA: I should have thought I was looking like nothing on earth.

WILFRED: I expect you've had a marvellous time, haven't you?

STELLA: Well, mixed you know.

WILFRED: You'll find it pretty dull here.

STELLA: I shan't. (*Draws a long breath.*) It's heavenly. Even though you have been in Africa and come on leave you can't imagine what it means to me to be back again – home. It's real. Everything's real again.

Sarah re-enters, carrying dress behind her back.

WILFRED: I'm going to give Lilian a hand with your room. Then I'll come down and ask you thousands of questions. (*Hesitates.*) I say, you don't think this moustache looks silly, do you?

The homecoming of Mme Ranevsky and her family has a breathless tension but, more significantly, its double focus is unified:

VARYA: How cold, my hands are numb. Your rooms, Mummy, the white and violet ones, have been left just the same.

MME RANEVSKY: Sweet, darling nursery. . . . I used to sleep here when I was a little child. . . . (*Crying*) I'm behaving like a child even now. . . . (*Kissing her brother, Varya, and then her brother again*) And Varya is just the same, like a nun. And there is Dounyasha. . . . (*Kissing Dounyasha.*)

GAYEV: The train was two hours late. What? A nice state of things.

CHARLOTTA (*to Pischik*): My dog eats nuts too.

PISCHIK (*in surprise*): You don't say so.

They all go out except Anya and Dounyasha.

DOUNYASHA: We've missed you so much. . . .

Takes off Anya's coat and hat.

ANYA: I didn't sleep all the four nights of our journey. . . . And now I feel so chilly.

DOUNYASHA: You went away in Lent, but there was snow then, and frost; but now. My dear (*Laughing, kissing her*). I've missed you so much, my darling, my pet. . . . I must tell you now, I can't wait a moment.

ANYA (*dully*): The same old thing, again?

Time as a concept is imposed in an emotional way upon the characters in *Eden End*, and the changes which it wreaks are stated so explicitly that the emotional responses that are made to it have a dissociated look. It becomes a tremulous additive to the characters and to their reactions to situations. Particularly in its guise of the pathetic fallacy that it can stand still in moments of happiness, this sense of an imposed emotionalism is very strong:

> STELLA: We can't always be arranging ourselves in the world's eye, like goods in a smart shop window. Not that sort of talk at all. Just idle, foolish talk that gets you nowhere, that means nothing and yet can mean everything. It doesn't matter now who we are or how we stand, or anything like that. Just think of the two of us here, in a cosy little room, lost in the moorland rain. We're lost too. There isn't anybody else. Just us. And time's stopped for us.

Farrant's reply is too gallant for words – 'I see. At least I think I do', and the whole moment of happiness seems slavishly contrived – a tight-lipped brightness inhabiting a cliché.

Dr Kirby is used to introduce the concept of the inner observer:

> KIRBY: . . . Have you noticed – or are you too young yet – how one part of us doesn't seem to be responsible for your own character and simply suffers because we have that character? You see yourself *being* yourself, behaving in the old familiar way, and though you may pay and suffer, the real you, the one that watches, doesn't seem to be responsible.

Stella's reply to this is about as gallant and personalised as was Farrant's to her earlier words. She says (*eagerly*): 'Yes, I was thinking about that only to-night. It's true'.

Her response, tritely emotional as it is, minimises the presence of the main theme of the play and lessens the significance of her own relationship to this theme. There is a good deal in her which exemplifies the idea permeating the play, that behind the shadow of personality which 'pays and suffers' a deeper uncommitted self watches. Her reply to the stodgy-minded Farrant who, after giving her one of his lumbering kisses, says, with true British application to practicalities 'Now we've got to talk', is a clear manifestation of the idea in action:

> STELLA: Yes, but not the kind of talk you mean, Geoffrey. No plans, no arrangements, no time-tables, no – 'seeing how we stand'. Nothing like that.

And there is a quiet watching stoicism in the way she accepts situations which are imposed upon her. Her sister's duplicity in inviting Stella's estranged husband to *Eden End* to divert her from Farrant is met with a sudden anger as she pays and suffers, but this quickly disappears. She returns to London with her husband to the old familiar ways, and one senses that there is part of her which accepts because it is only called upon to watch. She uses these phrases – 'It isn't any use being angry with people – like that', and 'We have our lives to get on with, to live them as best we can', and, as she takes a last look at the place which for such a short time represented to her the only reality, 'Good-bye – everything'.

On Stella Priestley exerts, though much less intensely than Chekhov, a double focus, but the two eyepieces are not in alignment; both Stella and the other characters are looked at separately – the attempt to create the credible natural situation and the attempt to create the aura, the extra dimension, are dissociated, and one is left too often irritated by the cliché generalities of the one and the manipulated impression of the other. None of the characters generates more than a predictable reaction to the demands of the plot, except for Stella in her intermittent flashes of insight. The aura that surrounds the play and the characters is imposed with great theatrical delicacy by Priestley, but, in the final analysis, it is seen to emerge from a formula rather than from the inevitabilities of character-creation. The formula is clear – to cast over the play the atmosphere of life's sad ironies, its pathos, its fleeting gaieties. Wilfred, the young colonial officer, is bravely pathetic in his growing up, his penchant to be 'with it', his desperate, romantic anguish. Sarah, the old retainer, is wryly, if shrewdly, pathetic in her past-tense existence. Lilian is to be pitied for her lost chances, her dried up envies. Charles Appleby, the failed actor, is a brave codger as he soldiers on his tipsy path to an everlasting mediocrity. Geoffrey Farrant is irritatingly pitiful in his stolid puritan virtues, and Dr Kirby is commendably gallant in his stoical acceptance of his fate, of his limitations, and in his shrewd dictums. This is an acceptable gallery of types to which the conditioned reflexes of the audience may easily respond. It is noticeable that they are all, in a way, 'lost' characters. There is no doubt that, however thinly they are individualised, they provide a consistent image of the atmosphere of mutability which is the play's chief power.

J. C. Trewin commends the play because 'what Priestley does is suddenly to open a window upon 1912 – for a couple of hours we live in that Northern village – live eagerly and feel keenly'. It is not difficult to agree with his implication that it is our emotions that are aroused, but in the harsher limelight of 1964 it is less easy to believe that the play still has the power to pull us eagerly into the lives of the characters. It may be suspected that in 1934, on its first appearance, their lives viewed through the telescope of the intervening years with in the line of sight a war which made nonsense of these people's lives, they would have seemed very poignant. Now, with the excoriations of another war, with social changes, this poignancy is reduced to a reminiscent glow – a delicate calling up of what was but is no more. Equally, the irony implicit in Dr Kirby's words: 'There's a better world coming, Stella – cleaner, saner, happier. We've only got to turn a corner and it's there', has lost its force because sharper ironies have interposed themselves for us. This sort of irony only maintains its sharpness within the context of character conceived in depth, and this Priestley has denied his characters.

Audrey Williamson describes the placing of *Eden End* in 1912 as a trick of technique. But it is difficult to accept this. A trick of technique is one which, as in *Dangerous Corner*, appears, and palpably appears, with the cunning sleight of a conjuror. The trick has been played in this play, if trick it be, before the play opens, in the decision to place it in 1912. But, in point of fact, its placement in time is absolutely essential to the root of Priestley's intentions. This is the lost generation not of '*entre deux guerres*' but of the period before the first war. Lost, in that its illusory sense of the perfectability of things, of 'a good time coming', is seen to be illusory by the observer and to be stubborn as well. The irony of the play lies less in the stated belief of the doctor that things will be better in the 1930s, but in the audience's constant knowledge that things will never be so good for this family as they are at the time when we see them. It is no theatrical trick that puts the play in 1912, but a quiet irony, the deepest one the play has to offer. The play is dated only if it is accepted as a naturalistic period piece, or if its charm is enquired of too closely. Its over-generality of characterisation, its over-mechanical gradations of mood, its overall dissociation of the surface and depths of characterisation, weaken its force. But it has a strength and charm which lies in its insistent communication of the values of living, and of the small delusions and illusions of being alive.

It is a play which will, one suspects, always catch at the hearts of the middle-aged. Somehow it brings to prominence the existence of that strange watershed between the certainties of youth and the resigned doubts of age.

TIME AND THE CONWAYS

In the middle of Act One of *Time and the Conways* Madge, in reply to a mild protest from Gerald that a socialist government might not be any better than the existing one, cries hotly 'All that's wanted is a little intelligence – and enthusiasm – and decency'. Towards the end of the act her twenty-three-year-old brother Robin, new from the war, flushed with the future, says 'We'll show 'em. This is where the Conways begin'.

Madge, an educated girl of 'advanced' ideas, speaks out of a political context, Robin out of the urgent optimism of youth and a war's ending, but also out of his innate sense of class. David Hughes says:

> It is plain that the problem of the Conways and people like

them was a natural concern for Priestley. Belonging himself to this class, growing up among them at a time when the established order of society kept their values and attitudes strictly in joint, he had discovered with them after the first war that the social revolution, the busy changes afoot in the twenties, were going to knock them harder than anyone else.

The surface action of this play is the depiction that for the Conways and their like the time was rapidly getting out of joint. The year 1919 is not where 'the Conways begin', but where they end. What they display – 'a little intelligence, enthusiasm and decency' – is put on the rack by the new order that spreads around them, and by the strains imposed on their family group by their reactions to it. It is impossible to escape the conclusion that Priestley is writing, in the play, a valediction on the passing of the Conway world – the world of easy orthodoxy, conventional virtues, uncomprehending beyond the present-tense which for them has become frozen in a pre-1914 condition. The younger members talk about a new order, but the strong impression is that they are prepared for a new order only insofar as their own world can remain untouched. When we meet them they are clinging to the principles of a little intelligence: ('Thank goodness I was never so stupid as to stop singing German songs. What have Schubert and Schumann to do with Hindenburg and the Kaiser') and enthusiasm: ('I've got all sorts of plans, y'know, Mother. We've all been talking things over in the mess') and decency: ('You're rather like Mr Warsnip – do you remember him – the cashier at the works? Every New Year's Eve your father used to bring Mr Warsnip here after they'd done all the books at the office, and used to give him some port, and when I went in Mr Warsnip always stood and held his glass like this and say "My respects, Mrs Conway, my deepest respects". And I always wanted to laugh. He's retired now and gone to live in South Devon').

The surface action of the play depicts simply what happens to disenchant and defeat the Conways. Not one of them escapes the ravages of what happens between the easy gaiety and optimism of 1919 and the harsher world of 1937. By then one girl has died, the would-be novelist has become mere journalist, the fiery-eyed Girton socialist is drowned in the vinegar of schoolmistress, the eager R.A.F. boy is a shady cad, and the bright girl he married distracted and impoverished by his neglect. In one sense Alan survives, but only because, in any case, his sights were never set high. In 1919 he works in the town hall, has no pretensions or ambitions; in 1937 he has not changed outwardly though he is shown to have qualities other than the recognised intelligence, enthusiasm and decency. 'Alan never minds being dull. I believe he has tremendous long adventures in his head that nobody knows anything about.' Alan is the dreamer though the town hall clock calls him daily to toil. One other victim – Alan's sister Kay – is also shown to have intimations of another kind of reality beyond the illusory life that the family lead: 'But you feel – at least I do, and I suppose that's what father felt too – you feel, quite suddenly, that it isn't real enough – and you want something to be real'.

Alan stands in a master/pupil relationship to Kay, edging her into an appreciation of the reality she is seeking for: 'But Time doesn't destroy anything. It merely moves us on – in this life – from one peep-hole to the next.'

In edging his sister to at least a dim comprehension of another kind of reality Alan pushes the play into another dramatic dimension which at first surrounds its naturalism in an almost imperceptible mist. Priestley's 'natural concern' for the class represented by the Conways is not merely expressed in the bitter events which occur, but through his vision of these events through another dimension which lies behind everyday reality. This vision gives his concern a characteristically sad irony – the Conways' illusions are not the only result of a changing world, but of their failure to apprehend the existence of any other dimensions to their lives than the ones they live with. Hughes says it is 'not a question of dredging up some human material to be exploited in a time-prank'. The justification of this assertion lies largely in how far Priestley is able to express the idea of a social fall and to give it meaning in the non-naturalistic context of his time-theory.

This theory is a simple derivation from Dunne, but it is exploited characteristically by Priestley to 'naturalise' it within the common experience of the characters. One of its elements is expressed by Kay: 'You feel quite suddenly that it isn't real enough – and you want something to be real'. This is the desire of the dreamer, the simple visionary, to see something more behind the non-sequiturs of a present-tense existence. Madge, Kay's sister, represents the earthbound, time-crested creature:

> This life you don't see – call it the Colleyfield common-room if that amuses you – is my real life. It represents exactly the sort of person I am now, and what you and Alan and Mother remember – and trust Mother not to forget anything foolish and embarrassing – is no longer of any importance at all.

Madge's idea of another dimension to life does not take her beyond the confines of the everyday. She is only different in that she thinks of 'real' life as something which she as an individual recognises and accepts but whose meaning for her is hidden even from those close to her. But she is time-bound – her reality does not cross the frontiers of the personality as it exists in this world.

It is Alan who expresses most clearly the antithesis to this – the Priestley version of Dunne:

> No . . . it's hard to explain . . . suddenly like this . . . there's a book I'll lend you – read it in the train. But the point is, now, at this moment, or any moment, we're only a cross-section of our real selves. What we *really* are is the whole stretch of ourselves, all our time, and when we come to the end of this life, all those selves, all our time, will be – *us* – the real you, the real me. And then perhaps we'll find ourselves in another time, which is only another kind of dream.

This suggests the long hinterland behind that part of us that is revealed to and in the world and in his knowledge of its existence Alan is quiescent and content. This is the reality that Kay has to learn, and which she has puzzling glimpses of throughout the play. The core of the play's deployment of this idea is in Act Two where, in the accustomed Dunne fashion, a character 'dreams' the future – this is Kay. From the time she awakens at the beginning of Act Three when she is once more restored to the time of the action of Act One, she has intermittent and disturbing memories of this dream which has constituted the whole of Act Two. Audrey Williamson states that it is a play 'of family life given a new agony and twist by its construction . . . after a happy first act at a twenty-first birthday party just after the first world war, switched us on twenty years to show us the ravages of time, and then back again, as violently, into the optimism of the earlier period'. This judgement ignores the essential quality of the play which is not that we are subjected to an obvious theatrical trick, but that we are shown a double dimension of human life. We are not 'violently' switched back to the optimism of the earlier period in Act Three. In a sense we do not go back at all, since Act Two is another dimension of Act One and Act Three carries on the naturalistic action of Act One. Act Two is the world of the Conways seen through the preternatural experience of one character – Kay.

The transition from the sense of actuality and immediacy of Act One to the dream of Act Two is smooth, and a good deal of responsibility (perhaps too much) is placed on Kay to imply at the end of the first act that she is staring alone into the heart of a mystery – that mystery is the prophetic vision of Act Two: '. . . *very still, she listens to the music, and seems to stare not at but into something, and as the song goes soaring away, the curtain creeps down*'.

In Act Two, when we discover, through Kay, 'what happens' to the Conway family, she is as much a victim of the ravages of time as the rest of the family; she is disenchanted in a family circle which is broken, bitter and querulous. But even as a victim she is still struggling to find a different reality behind the grim picture. When she awakes from her dream of the future (and the first lines of Act Three make it clear that it is an awakening from a dream) it is to find Alan, the one who has 'adventures in the head', greeting her. The whole of Act Three, though it returns atmospherically to the superficial social optimism of Act One, is tainted for us with the relics of Kay's dream. She is now a participant in a present-tense action, but she is puzzled by the memories of visitations from a world elsewhere. Priestley's success in Act Three is that he preserves on the surface the thin gaiety of Act One but taints it with the sorrows and regrets that we, through Kay's dream, know to be under the surface. As Hughes says: 'The emotional satisfaction lies in the fact that we know what will happen and must breathlessly wait for our knowledge to be confirmed, as though listening impatiently for certain exquisite changes of key or sweet progressions in a familiar passage of music'. Priestley does not disappoint us:

HAZEL: . . . Too ordinary at home. On a yacht or the terrace at Monte Carlo or a Pacific Island. Marvellous!

CAROL: That would be using up too many things at once. Greedy stuff!

HAZEL (*coolly*): I *am* greedy.

CAROL: I should think so. (*To the other two.*) Yesterday morning she was in the bath, reading *Greenmantle* and eating nut-milk chocolate.

KAY (*who has been thinking*): No, it wouldn't be too ordinary, falling in love at home here. It would be best, I think. Suppose you were suddenly unhappy. It would be awful to be desperately unhappy and in love miles away in a strange house . . . (*Suddenly stops, shivers.*)

CAROL: Kay, what's the matter?

KAY: Nothing.

CAROL: Then it must have been a goose walking over your grave.

Kay abruptly turns away from them, going towards the window. Hazel looks at her – as the other two do – then raises her eyebrows at Carol, who shakes her head sternly. Mrs C. enters and looks cheerfully at the sight of the tea.

MRS C. (*cheerfully*): Now then, let's have some tea and be nice and cosy together. Where's Robin?

HAZEL: Spooning with Joan in the dining-room.

MRS C: Oh! – hasn't Joan gone yet? I really think she might

leave us to ourselves now. After all, it's the first time we've all been together in this house for – how long? It must be at least three years. I'll pour out. Come on, Kay. What's the matter?

CAROL (*in tremendous whisper, seriously*): Sh! it's a *Mood*.

But Kay returns, looking rather strained. Her mother looks at her carefully, smiling. Kay manages an answering smile.

MRS C: That's better, darling. What a funny child you are, aren't you?

KAY: Not really, Mother. Where's Madge?

ALAN: She went upstairs.

MRS C: Go up, dear, and tell her we're all in here, with some tea, and ask her – very nicely, dear, specially from me – to come down.

HAZEL (*muttering, rather*): I'll bet she doesn't.

Alan goes out. Mrs C. begins pouring out tea.

MRS C: This is just like old times, isn't it? And we seem to have waited so long. I ought to tell fortunes again – to-night.

HAZEL (*eagerly*): Oh – yes – Mother, do.

KAY (*rather sharply*): No!

MRS C: Kay! Really! Have you had too much excitement to-day?

It cannot be overemphasised, in judging how far Priestley has been successful in welding actuality and the realities behind it, that Kay represents a centrality which is involved in both. Like the wry Fool of Shakespeare she is caught up in the swirl of events as they happen, and is as much a victim of them as the whipped, scorned, and rejected Fool. But, equally, she is the agent of a vision whose point of view lies outside the action. Her composite function corresponds to the dual nature of the action. She is part of that Conway world – that middle-class family of 1919 clinging to illusion as it decays, but she does not wear the motley, the charade-clothes, of their present-tense in her brain. Her brother Alan suggests a first sketch of the character who was later to emerge as the mysterious Dr Görtler in *I Have Been Here Before*. He stands further from the action than Kay and, like

Görtler, seems to have an inner knowledge that is denied the others. He, like Görtler when we first meet the strange German, gives the impression of waiting for the inevitable, but Alan's main function is to provide the 'objective correlative' of Kay's puzzled sense of another dimension. His explanations to her are too explicit as statements to raise his status as a character much beyond that of spokesman, though a sensitive actor could well give him a wry presence.

For the rest, the characters are clearly and adequately created for their functions. The demands of one element of the plot do not require that they should be over-individualised. They remain examples of common types in an easily recognisable class. To this extent what is required of them is that they should represent the virtues and weaknesses of their class. It could be argued that the misfortunes that befall them are excessive, but insofar as they are representative so are their misfortunes. But the demands of the other element of the theme require that they should seem to be incomplete as individuals because they have no sense of the extra dimension which would give their misfortunes a longer context. It should be emphasised that Priestley is more concerned with the failure of the group to possess the extra dimension. Their gaieties, griefs, tribulations, jealousies, envies and cruelties have meaning in the play in direct proportion to their sense of being a closely-knit group. By the same token their 'ignorance' is a corporate one. 'One feels' as Hughes says, 'that the individuals must be rather less interesting when released from the close family atmosphere, A. V. Cookham's judgement that the point about *Time and the Conways* is not Time but the Conways, obscures the fact that it is only because they are shown to us from the vantage-point of the other dimension that they have any cogent reality. Uninteresting and pale though the Conways seem as individuals, their corporate existence has a rich human emotional context.

Priestley's own judgement of Act One is that it is 'fussy and clumsy', but it is weaker than that. It is tautological and slack emotionally; the family becomes boring and irritating in the *longueurs* of its thin gaiety, and the facts of its existence are related with thick-fingered obviousness:

HAZEL: Look at these! Could you believe people *ever* wore such ridiculous things?
CAROL: I can just remember mother in that, can't you?
HAZEL: Of course I can, infant!
CAROL (*more soberly, looking at man's old-fashioned shooting or Norfolk coat*): That was Daddy's, wasn't it?
HAZEL: Yes: I believe he wore it – that very holiday.
CAROL: Perhaps we ought to put it away.
HAZEL: I don't think mother would mind – now.

But, in Act Two, Priestley achieves the double-focus which he aimed at and, except intermittently, failed to achieve in *Eden End*. The undertones of opposed senses of value:

MADGE: I hope you're doing something besides this popular journalism now, Kay. Have you begun another book?
KAY: No.
MADGE: Pity, isn't it?
KAY (*after a pause, looking steadily at her*): What about you, Madge? Are you building Jerusalem – in England's green and pleasant land?

There is, too, the hastily smoothed surface hiding the danger beneath:

ALAN (*mildly*): I must grow a shaggy beard and drum on my chest and ro-o-ar!
JOAN (*doing her best*): When their Uncle Frank – you know, Freda's husband, they live in London – took the children to the Zoo for the first time, little Richard was only five – and there was an enormous monkey – what Alan said reminded me of it – and –
MRS C (*cutting this ruthlessly*): Would anyone like a glass of port? Kay? What about you, Madge? It's a scholarly wine. You remember what Meredith wrote about it in *The Egoist*. . . .

And the pathetic ironies:

KAY: Oh, no, Alan, it's hideous and unbearable. Remember what we once were and what we thought we'd be. And now this. And it's all we have, Alan, it's *us*. Every step we've taken – every tick of the clock – making everything worse. If this is all life is, what's the use? Better to die, like Carol, before you find it out, before Time gets to work on you. I've felt it before, Alan, but never as I've done to-night. There's a great devil in the universe and we call it Time.

The dramatic skill of Act Two in which is built up a picture of the unsteady lodgement of love, affection, anger and grief, in this family, is theatrically underlined by the actual comings and goings of the characters. The quiet elegiac opening when Kay meets Alan hardens into rancour with the appearance of Joan, whose bright-eyed love of eight years ago has been destroyed by the shiftless deserting Robin; this personal rancour turns into a sour ideological cruelty, as Madge, tramping in with her intellectual socialism, comes face to face with Alan and Kay's puzzled quietism. The appearance of the chipper and flighty Hazel, now cowed in an expensively dressed but pointless marriage, introduces a brittle bravery into the atmosphere. There is, too, the sudden calling up in memory of the ghost of the dead Carol, the solicitor's harsh news, and the final interrogatives of Alan and Kay. This act is a vindication of Priestley's poetry of people and action. All these moods and tensions appear and disappear as swift images of a relentless decay.

In Act Two the sense of dissolution is swift and definite, but Act Three, continuing the earlier revelations of Act One, takes us to the small beginnings of the decay. In the final act Priestley exploits a technique which dominated the whole of *Dangerous Corner*. He shows characters approaching certain crossroads of life, crossroads which we, in the audience, are already aware of, and which we know could so easily lead to different conclusions. The odd remark, the late answer, the intercepted look, the opportunity not taken. All this produces an irony for which the audience is put in the special position of foreknowledge. One marked quality is the extent of the sinister atmosphere which is generated by this foreknowledge. Episodes which in Act One were passed over with no more than a light touch, are now frightening. Our foreknowledge is exploited by Priestley even in the most apparently superficial situations. Robin's somewhat coy flirtation in Act One which results in his marriage to Joan, is now, because we know how it turns out, a kind of dark trap:

> ROBIN (*with satisfaction*): A-ha! (*Very quickly he closes the curtains but as he turns his back, Joan reaches out and turns off the switch of the standard lamp in her corner. The room is now almost in darkness.*) All right, Joan Helford. Where are you, Joan Helford. Where are you, Joan Helford, where are you? (*She is heard to laugh in the darkness.*) You can't escape, Joan Helford, you can't escape. No, no. No, no. No escape for little Joan. No escape.

The realities which lie behind the corners and which we are not to see until Act Two, are now given us again in their genesis. Sometimes the irony and pathos is too explicit in Act Three, when Priestley forgets the delicate balance of forces in personal relations, and remembers only the polemics of the background in which those forces have their reality:

> Under the League, we'll build up a new commonwealth of all the nations, so that they can live at peace for ever. And Imperialism will end. And so, in the end, of course, will Capitalism. There'll be no more booms and slumps and panics and strikes and lock-outs, because the people themselves, led by the best brains in their countries, will possess both the political and economic power. There'll be Socialism at last, a free, prosperous, happy people, all enjoying equal opportunities, living at peace with the whole world.

Admittedly this is a speech by Madge, the flag-waving revolutionary of the play, but its form steps neatly out of the human flux of the play, and its irony is not proved or even disproved. The force of its irony lies outside the terms of the play itself.

Far more telling and affecting is the pathos which emerges from our foreknowledge, incited by Kay's glimpses of the future in Act Two, of what will happen to the particular characters. Kay remains the central figure. The headlong rush around dangerous corners is occasionally halted for us by Kay's dim prevision of what lies around the next bend in the road:

> KAY: But there's nothing in simply writing. The point is to be *good* – to be sensitive and sincere. Hardly anybody's both, especially women who write. But I'm going to try and be. And whatever happens, I'm never, *never* going to write except what I want to write, what I feel is true to me, deep down. I won't write just to please silly people or just to make money. I'll . . .
>
> *But she suddenly breaks off. The rest wait and stare.*
>
> ALAN (*encouragingly*): Go on, Kay.
>
> KAY (*confusedly, dejectedly*): No . . . Alan . . . I'd finished really . . . or if I was going to say something else, I've forgotten what it was . . . nothing much. . . .

She has, for an instant, seen round the next bend in the road. Carol who in Act One is a centre of life and vitality, an unspoiled source of innocence and delight, is used in Act Three to produce one of the most touching pathetic ironies in the play. She has a long speech in which she describes what she is going to do with her life – the dresses, the travel, the friends, the cooking, the working. She ends her excited list with the words 'I'm *going to live*'. But Carol is, we know, already dead, gone young into the long darkness. Mrs Conway who responds to Carol's speech with a proud picture of what things will be like when her grown-up family has made its mark on the world, is interrupted by one word from Kay – the word is 'Don't'. Carol's mood immediately changes and she hurries across to Kay:

> CAROL: I won't bother with any of those things, Kay, really I won't. I'll come back and look after you wherever you go. I won't leave you ever if you don't want me to. I'll look after

you, darling. (*Kay stops crying, She looks–half-smiling–at Carol in a puzzled wistful fashion. Carol goes back to her mother's side.*)

Mrs Conway wants to know what is wrong, and Kay looks at Alan and says 'Alan . . . please tell me . . . I can't bear it . . . and there's something . . . something . . . you could tell me'.

It is in such moments that the best qualities of the play are shown. These are the moments when Priestley forgets the hard battles of the world that forms the context for the lives of the Conways, and sensitively explores the world of the family itself. The atmosphere he creates in these moments is not a tragic one, but a truly pathetic one. It may very well be, in fact, that Priestley, falling short of anything approaching high tragedy, has shown in this play that pathos is a mood amenable to dramatic communication. This can be claimed of very few English dramatists who so often mistake the irony of true pathos for the special indulgence of melodrama, where effect is more important than meaning. This play is meaningful in the sense that it shows the disparity between the thin conscious life that is lived from moment to moment, and the accruing reality of life when it is viewed from the vantage point of the future. In its evocative way, and despite its occasional compromises with unrelated explicitness of statement, it is an exercise in the emotional patterns of illusion and reality.

I HAVE BEEN HERE BEFORE

I Have Been Here Before, which had its first production at the Royalty Theatre in 1937 is, in some ways, Priestley's most attractively compelling time-play, and in others his most disappointing. Its attractiveness rests largely in the subtlety with which its theatrical tensions are maintained and the emotional excitement it generates, but it disappoints, in failing, in some respects, to follow through some of its own premises. There is an altogether different quality in its tone from the previous time-plays; it does not have the naturalistic clarity and contrived excitement of *Dangerous Corner*, nor the persistent wistfulness and irony of *Eden End* and *Time and the Conways*. Its note is harsher, and the play, overall, does not give the impression of easy transition in the writing from one scene to another. It seems to have been written with great difficulty.

Its difference from its predecessors is not merely due to the fact that this is the first occasion in which a time-theory is explicitly present on the surface of the play's action, nor because for the first time it is Ouspensky, rather than Dunne, who is the source of the theory. There is a new element which, though it is not altogether satisfactorily presented, nevertheless pervades the action – the element of Fate. In previous plays Fate is a very remote thing, hanging, like a mist, in the background; here it is nearer to being an actual presence which controls, and is in some measure recognised by the characters as controlling the actions of human beings. Its presence has three faces, the most significant is the exiled German professor (a character originally conceived of in supernatural terms); he becomes Fate the intervener. The second is the atmospheric suggestiveness of a harsh brooding fate in the thunderstorm which bursts over the action. The third is the insistent ticking of the clock – the reminder that Time will have its way with you.

The play parts company with its predecessors also in that all the characters are aware, to some degree, that they are involved in a mystery. They do not all have an equal understanding of what the mystery is, nor do they all respond to it in the same way. But there is no hint here that only the chosen are capable of catching glimpses (at the least) of something that lies behind the gritty present-tense in which they live.

Janet is perhaps most conscious of it, from her first entrance:

She enters the room with a slow indifference, then suddenly stiffens, frowns, looks incredulous, then examines it eagerly, without much movement. It is clear that there is some recognition, mixed with incredulity. The clock chimes at her. A sudden uprush of emotion makes her feel almost faint, and she sinks into a chair, exhausted, breathing heavily.

Sally, though unaware of the depths of the mystery, cannily

attaches it to the arrival of Görtler whom she immediately dislikes. She, Ormund, and Farrant are together:

> *This linking of the three of them together – for the first time – has its immediate effect, as if it chimed with some deep obscure feeling each of them knew. There is a pause before Sally resumes.* He comes here – looking about him – and when I tell him we've no rooms to spare because I'm expecting three visitors – he looks at me and asks if two of 'em are a married couple with the man older than his wife, and the other a younger man. And when I say No, we're expecting three ladies from Manchester, he seems disappointed and says something about it being the wrong year. So off he goes, and then the three ladies say they can't come, and you ring up for rooms, and when he comes back, there's a room for him too, and you're all here, and it's just what he expected.
>
> ORMUND: Oh – he was looking for somebody, and then gave it up.
>
> SALLY : And then upsetting you like that! He makes me feel right uneasy.

Even the come-what-may landlord, Sam, is involved:

> Nay, I just happened to say 'If I'd my time over again' – You know what you do? – and he seemed right taken up with it (*repeating it speculatively*) 'If I'd my time over again'. Nay it's a common enough saying.

The plot, on face value, is simple and rather obvious. A young rather querulous headmaster spending a holiday of recuperation in a remote moorland pub meets Janet, the wife of Ormund, who is a rich industrialist. Janet is out of love with her husband, and she senses a powerful affinity growing between her and the headmaster. The plot is basically that of the hoary old triangle. Will Janet go off with Farrant or stay with Ormund?

Into this conventional situation Görtler is introduced. He is studying time-recurrence, and his researches have led him to the pub in the expectation that he will witness a situation which he has witnessed before, and which, on its first happening, ended in catastrophe. He has calculated that it is all to happen again. His motive is to try and change the second course of the situation, to avoid the catastrophe, which resulted in the suicide of the industrialist, and the couple living in unhappiness.

Ouspensky enters the play with the Professor, and with him, too, a mystery and a moral force. Notwithstanding that when Janet meets Farrant she has some vague stirrings that they have met before, it cannot be too strongly emphasised that the whole of the play's dramatic, atmospheric and moral pattern is woven about and created by the intervention of the Professor. Priestley's stated theme was 'the depiction of a kind of Everyman of my own generation' who after undergoing 'the deep distrust of life felt by so many moderns', came to the conclusion, that, in the long run, 'the Universe was not hostile or indifferent to his deepest needs'. The Everyman of the play is Ormund the industrialist: 'Like a man who's suddenly born in to a strange new world eh? Well, that's not altogether fanciful, Görtler. I feel rather like a new-born creature. Rather cold, small, lonely'.

The play stands or falls by the extent to which it is able to reconcile the communication of this theme – generated by the personality of Ormund – and the 'interference' theme generated by the Professor. The initial difficulty for such a reconcilement is that Priestley's stated theme inevitably requires from the character in whom it mainly lies a quality of dignity and at least the illusion of choice, whereas the 'interference' theme suggests a manipulation of human kind which *ipso facto* tends to reduce the validity of individual thought, feeling and action.

What Ormund ultimately represents, is the ability of the individual to change his vantage point by experience and hence to change his conception of the relationships of man to society and to the universe. What the Professor, in part, represents is a theory of existence which declares that life is lived in a circle of time which we enter at a certain point at birth. After death we enter the circle again at the same point and unless something happens to create a change in the individual, either to deteriorate or improve him, he will for ever journey on in the same track. Interference or influence can cause the change, for good or evil, to occur, enabling the individual to move upward or downward in a spiral, but, in any case taking a different track. The contradiction which Priestley gave himself to solve was that between personal choice and outside interference. But the interference from the Professor does not solely involve the industrialist; it involves inevitably his wife and her lover, and, by implication, everyone who is within the orbit of Ormund. The typical Priestley vision of the interdependence of human beings is explicitly stated in the first act – we are in the familiar realm of the tightly knit group – not in this case a family group, but one held together by both personal and social ties, and by place:

GÖRTLER: There, you see, is more dependence.
SALLY (*distrusting this*): What's that?
JANET: It sounds like an insult, but it isn't. We've been discovering how much we depend on one another. You're in it because your boy's at Mr Farrant's school.
SALLY: And very lucky he is to be there too – with Mr Farrant looking after him.
JANET: And now you say you've money in Ormund's Limited.
FARRANT: And the school partly depends on Ormund's too. Which brings me in.
JANET: And I'm certainly one of the dependants. Walter, you're the only great one, the giant Atlas himself. We all depend upon you, but you don't depend upon anybody.
GÖRTLER (*quietly, but with startling effect*): *Nein!* (*They all stare at him.*) Mr Ormund depends very much upon somebody. (*To Janet*) He depends upon you – his wife.

The first act gives the growing triangle plot a due and direct share under the preternatural clouds that are gathering. Except for Sam and Görtler, each character is shown to be carrying his own particular grief or worry. Sally carries inside her the open wound of her son's death; Farrant, a nervous man, has an unease whose source we do not know; Ormund carries the weight of business cares and a questioning despair: 'Who or what are we?' 'What are we supposed to be doing here?' 'What the devil is it all about?' Janet has an air of puzzled despondency, but, less self-conscious than the rest, is more attuned to the atmosphere that is building up in this place:

> JANET: Have you been up here before, Dr Görtler?
> GÖRTLER (*watching her*): No. Have you?
> JANET (*frowning a little*): No – I haven't – really.
> GÖRTLER: You do not seem very certain.
> JANET (*slowly*): I've been wondering . . .

Görtler's part in the first act is not obtrusive but it is vital. He is established as a figure of some strangeness, not entirely likeable, though his tactlessness is carefully shown to be a measure of his direct apprehension of the truth rather than ill-will. After he has said that Ormund depends very much upon his wife, the reaction is swift:

> ORMUND (*quietly, with cold anger*): That's not the kind of remark we appreciate from a stranger in this country, my dear sir.
> JANET: Walter!
> GÖRTLER (*rising*): I am sorry. I am – as you say – a stranger – in a foreign country.
> JANET: It's all right, Dr Görtler.
> GÖRTLER (*as he moves towards door, to his room*): Good night.
> ORMUND (*crossing to him*): No, doctor. I shouldn't have spoken like that. Now don't be offended.

The first act very clearly establishes a tense situation which is unexceptionable in its credibility, but it hints strongly of a context beyond what we are given to see.

The balance between credible and incredible is achieved by the deployment of five elements which act contrapuntally. They are: the use of the clock, the stage-directions, the depiction of Görtler, the use of language, and Sam. Their use in this play represents a fair example of Priestley's meticulous and imaginative control of material, and his sometimes facile ability to achieve his desired effect.

The clock is used throughout the play, but more particularly in Act One where all its theatrical functions are established. Its most eerie effect is its accompaniment to the entrance of some of the characters. Priestley does not fall into the beguiling trap of opening the play with a ticking clock and making a Hitchcock assault on our nerves. The clock comes into our consciousness only with the appearance of Görtler, and it is significantly not mentioned in the preliminary stage-directions to Act One. No indication whatsoever is given that it is present until the arrival of Görtler: *Then there is a quiet knocking on the outer door and it opens slowly, and Dr Görtler enters. The clock chimes.*

The clock, subsequently, has its existence only in relation to character, and that this is a conscious intention by Priestley is strongly suggested at one point in Act One when the stage is left empty in a fading light, but there is no stage-direction that its ticking is heard. Its next appearance coincides with Janet's entrance when, as with Görtler, it chimes. But the stage-direction is notable: *The clock strikes at her.* Its third appearance is when Farrant meets Janet and *the clock joins in with its tick and chime, as if it had been expecting this.* Its final appearance in Act One is when Farrant casually says of Görtler 'I thought I'd met him somewhere before'. For the rest of the play it appears three times only – in Act Two when it strikes ten, when Farrant and Janet kiss, and as an opening chime to Act Three.

A reading of the play suggests that the clock represents a kind of Tiresias who observes now, and has observed it all before. It reacts to the appearance of an accustomed face, and the enaction of well-known situations. It is open to doubt, however, whether this minimal personalising of the clock which is reinforced by Priestley's direction that 'the clock chimes *at* her' and 'as if it had been expecting this' communicates itself on the stage. The ticking of a clock gives to an audience the expectation of mystery, even of the sinister; the chiming of a clock gives the sense of time passing and the implication that there is not much time left. It is these expectations which Priestley's clock satisfies, but it cannot add any other experience to the audience despite Priestley's conception of its function. The most to be said of the clock is that it concentrates the mind wonderfully upon the possibility of the supernatural.

The atmosphere of the natural, in a contrapuntal rhythm with the mysterious, is underlined by the stage-directions which give precise instructions for the pacing of the act, but which fulfil much more besides. The word 'pause' or the phrase 'after a pause' occurs very many times, and the pause is filled with instructions to the players. At the very beginning of Act One when Ormund and Janet have had their uneasy conversation about their bickering, and Ormund declares that he will try to make a go of things both with himself and with his wife, the audience is left wondering about the worth of his assurance:

ORMUND: No, no, I didn't mean it that way. I'm really doing my best. You're right. God knows you're right. It'll be something.
JANET: I'll do my very best.
ORMUND: And I'll do better still. You'll see. Nice. Easy. Friendly. All according to plan.

This is too pat, unconvincing, and it leaves a doubt about the nature of Ormund's feelings for his wife. But then there comes a pause and in that pause there is confirmation that though Ormund may be a puzzled and difficult man, he has a depth of feeling towards his wife: *He looks about him, whistling softly. She looks at him, and he breaks off and gives her a careful reassuring smile*. Without the pause, the audience's notion of their relationship would be very awry.

Later in the act when Görtler questions Janet about her feelings of having been here before there is an even more striking example of the use of the stage-direction. Without stage-directions the scene reads thus:

GÖRTLER: Mrs Ormund, what made you come here?
JANET: Oh – pure chance. We wanted to spend this week-end

somewhere in the country. A man at the hotel we dined at – to-night – not an hour ago – suggested this place. I'd never heard of it before.

GÖRTLER: It was all quite dull, ordinary?

JANET: Yes . . . until we were driving from Marlingset up here. . . .

GÖRTLER: Yes?

JANET: I find this – rather difficult – Quite suddenly I began to feel excited. . . . About nothing it seemed. . . . My heart was beating terribly . . . we stopped once . . . only a moment, to make sure about the way. . . . At the roadside there were some white harebells . . . just some white harebells. . . . Of course they looked lovely there . . . white and fragile and perfect at the edge of the great dark moor. . . . It must have been just that . . . anything else – is silly.

GÖRTLER: There has not been in your life so far a moment of crisis that you associate with these flowers?

JANET: No. But that's exactly the sort of feeling I had about them.

GÖRTLER: And then – you arrived here?

JANET: Yes.

GÖRTLER: You have met Mr Farrant?

JANET: Yes. But only for a few minutes.

GÖRTLER: He is very young for such a responsible post.

JANET: Yes.

GÖRTLER: But that does not matter, of course. He is fortunate, but he deserves to be. Very clever – and very charming, very good-hearted, too, I think. . . .

JANET: I'm sure he must be, Dr Görtler. Why do you stare at me like that?

GÖRTLER: I beg your pardon. I was thinking.

This is a conversation between a slightly inquisitive man and a younger woman who seems to have had a vaguely romantic experience which she cannot account for. As such, Görtler seems impertinent, and Janet somewhat fey. But add the stage-directions and another dimension enters:

GÖRTLER: Mrs Ormund, what made you come here?

JANET: Oh – pure chance. We wanted to spend this week-end somewhere in the country. A man at the hotel we dined at – to-night – not an hour ago – suggested this place. I'd never heard of it before.

GÖRTLER: It was all quite dull, ordinary?

JANET: Yes . . . until we were driving from Marlingset up here. . . .

GÖRTLER: Yes?

JANET: I find this rather difficult – (*She breaks off, and then, with urgency.*) Quite suddenly, I began to feel excited. . . . About nothing, it seemed. . . . My heart was beating terribly. . . . We stopped once . . . only a moment, to make sure about the way. . . . At the roadside there were some white harebells. . . . Of course they looked lovely there . . . white and fragile and perfect, at the edge of the great dark moor. . . . It must have been just that . . . anything else – is silly.

GÖRTLER (*slowly*): There has not been in your life so far a moment of crisis that you associate with these flowers?

JANET (*slowly and staring at him*): No. But that's exactly the feeling I had about them.

GÖRTLER (*prompting her*): And then – you arrived here?

JANET (*rather slowly*): Yes.

A distinct pause, during which Dr Görtler rises and goes nearer to her.

GÖRTLER: You have met Mr Farrant?

JANET: Yes. But only for a few minutes.

GÖRTLER: He is very young for such a responsible post.

JANET: Yes.

GÖRTLER: But that does not matter, of course. He is fortunate, but he deserves to be. Very clever – and very charming, very good-hearted too, I think. . . . *Looks at her questioningly*).

JANET (*rather stiffly*): I'm sure he must be, Dr Görtler. (*As he stares at her speculatively*) Why do you stare at me like that?

GÖRTLER: I beg your pardon. I was thinking (*pause*).

In the first place an urgency enters via the stage-directions into

Janet's words whose full force is not suggested by the words alone; secondly, there is much more of a suggestion of Janet's being led slowly and tensely in a certain direction by Görtler; and thirdly, there is conveyed the sense of magnetism in Görtler which he exploits by rising and going over to her. It is not enough to say that this is an example of Priestley's attempting to do the players' jobs for them. What these stage-directions do goes beyond the technicalities of where actors should stand or move, what tone they should adopt, what pauses they should make. In fact, the meaning of this short scene is incomplete without the stage-directions; they are a direct projection from a language which is not, in itself, capable of holding the full meaning. What is created here is of the same kind of dramatic poetry which informs some of the scenes in Pinter's *The Caretaker*, another play in which the word 'pause' is liberally used, and in which stage-directions are a projection of language and not a mere blueprint for puppet-actors.

The effect of this unity of language and stage-direction on the *reader* of Priestley's play is to establish with certainty those moments of engagement between characters in which the actualities of speech and action are set in a non-actual background. The translation of the *reader's* experience by players on the stage puts a great responsibility upon them, which is not lessened by the non-associativeness of Priestley's language. The associations are in the pauses between speech and what happens in these pauses. Priestley has this power to create the poetry of action and situation, but he does not relieve his actors of the task of trying to avoid the dangers of substituting a tight-lipped terseness of utterance, which fits the language as it stands, and a knowing glance to fit the pauses, for a more subtle rhythm between what is said and what is not said. Only truly poetic language can give the actor that aid which enables him to bridge the gap between the explicit and the implicit. Non-poetic language makes his task very difficult in the attempt to uncover nuances of characterisation and situation, and the actor is a prey to the temptation either to over-elocutionise in an attempt to convey 'otherness', or to reduce all to a flat naturalism, and thus diminish the play's meaning. Terse naturalistic acting comes nowhere near conveying the thematic rhythms that are intended in this scene between Janet and Görtler – rhythms which appear in other scenes of the play.

If the stage-directions increase the sense of mystery and otherness in one of their functions, there are other uses to which they are directed. On occasions here Priestley uses them to push the balance temporarily towards the credible, the normal, the expected. Immediately after the scene between Janet and Görtler, she is directed to assume '*a more social manner*', and the play returns for a period to the Inn and the triangle of human beings. Again, a little later, when Janet is preparing to go to her room Ormund is '*busy with his papers*', Farrant is '*going back to his book*' and he speaks '*casually*'. All this brings the natural atmosphere rushing back to prominence.

The third element in Priestley's deployment of his forces is irony. Görtler alone is completely conscious of the double meaning of a number of phrases uttered by others, although Janet is sensitive to respond to nuances:

JANET: Have you been here before, Dr Görtler?
GÖRTLER: No, have you?
JANET: No – I haven't – really.
GÖRTLER: You do not seem quite sure.

And there is Ormund's unknowing association of words – the clock ticks in them: 'Let me just keep ticking over – just ticking over – that'll do.' 'This is too small, too quiet. It throws us straight back on ourselves.'

And Farrant, without realising the full implications: 'That's how we try to teach it now. I show them how completely interdependent we are.'

All these phrases are spoken before the time theme has been mentioned in the play. Yet, in the long run, Priestley is careful not to throw it too heavily into the arena of the exceptional and the mysterious too early in the action, and he uses the otherwise minor character, Sam, to tip the scales just sufficiently in the direction of a norm to prevent that willing suspension of disbelief which a surfeit of the unknown invariably occasions in an audience. Sam is the natural man, a canny extrovert, who is less obviously concerned in the developing action than anyone. Sam becomes a resting-point for the beleaguered credibilities of an audience which is being gradually drawn into a mystery:

> SAM: Well, happen it's foreign style o' doing things. (*Begins to chuckle.*) Nay, what tickled me was him saying he must ha' come at wrong year. Now that's as good as aught I've heard o' some time. If he's going round asking for people – not friends of his, mind you – and he doesn't know where they are nor what year they'll be there – I reckon he's got his work cut out. I must tell that to some of 'em in t'bar.

By the end of Act One the audience's sensibilities are neatly strung between a bemused acceptance and a healthy scepticism. Görtler has emerged as mysterious but not, as yet, as completely incredible. Ormund has appeared fraught but hardly the repository of the problems of the modern Everyman. Janet is troubled but only dimly aware of the depths of the mystery. Farrant is querulous but not yet the selfish materialist that Priestley declares him to be in the preface to the play.

Act One is a brilliant setting of scene, situation and character, but Act Two belongs to Ormund. Audrey Williamson believes Priestley to have achieved his finest writing for the theatre in the creation of this character. 'For this is a figure that expresses something of modern questioning and spiritual unfulfilment, vainly balancing the pain of life, the cruelty of creation, against the glory of the cosmic pattern.'

The first part of the act does much to confirm this opinion. The long scene between Ormund and Görtler introduces and amplifies the moral core of the play. Ormund's problem is that of a man who outwardly has everything, but who feels cheated of self-determination:

> GÖRTLER: Ah! – you like power.

ORMUND: Well, you get some fun out of it. I don't mean bullying a lot of poor devils. But putting ideas into action. And not being at the end of somebody else's bit of string.

GÖRTLER: And yet this is what you always feel, and that is why you try to escape.

ORMUND (*sharply*): What do you mean?

GÖRTLER: That you are – as you say – at the end of a bit of string.

ORMUND (*as he rises and moves*): Nonsense! Do I look like – a puppet?

GÖRTLER (*calmly*): No. But I say you feel like one. (*Pauses, then with calm force.*) You are rich. You are successful. You have power. Yet all the time you try to escape, because deep down you feel that your part in this life is settled for you and that it is a tragic one. So all the time you are in despair. (*As Ormund does not reply.*) Is that not true?

ORMUND (*half-wondering and half-angry as he crosses to the sofa*): Yes – damn your impudence – it is.

GÖRTLER (*pressing him*): Now tell me please why you – who have so much – should feel this despair.

ORMUND (*after a pause, turning, speaking more freely than before*): I suppose – in the last resort – you trust life – or you don't. Well – I don't. There's something malicious . . . corrupt . . . cruel . . . at the heart of it. Nothing's on our side. We don't belong. We're a mistake.

GÖRTLER: But have you known – good things?

ORMUND (*looking down now at the sitting Görtler*): Yes. When you're young, you snatch at 'em and then find they're bait in a trap. Cheese for the mice. One nibble, you're caught and the wires are boring through your guts. I can feel 'em there.

GÖRTLER: No. It is something in yourself. Something that hates life.

ORMUND: All right, it's something in me. (*Almost muttering*) Something that's waiting to blot out the whole bloody business. *Moves restlessly, then finally speaks with more freedom, coming nearer and then sitting at the table across from Dr. Görtler.*

Görtler – when I was a boy I watched my mother die – of cancer. For two years she was tortured . . . she might as well have been put on the rack and broken on the wheel . . . and when she couldn't suffer any longer . . . when there was nothing left to feel any more devilish bloody torment . . . she was allowed to escape, to die. You see, there wasn't any more fun to be had out of her. Let her go.

GÖRTLER: Yes, that was bad. But did she complain?

ORMUND: No, she didn't complain much. She was a very brave woman. I remember – when she could bear it no longer and screamed in the night, she'd apologise next morning. (*With terrible irony.*) She was sorry if she'd disturbed us Görtler, she was sorry if she'd disturbed us . . . (*Pause*) No, *she* didn't complain – but – by God! – I complain.

GÖRTLER: Yes, I understand. (*Pause*) You feel too much and do not know enough.

ORMUND (*grimly*): I know too much.

GÖRTLER: No. You are like a child who thinks because it rains one morning, he will never play out of doors again. You believe we have only this one existence?

ORMUND: Of course.

Ormund's sense of being a puppet in the hands of a malevolent destiny is the colouring of his personality. Priestley carefully prevents Ormund's statement of his own feelings becoming sentimental or self-indulgent. His description of his mother's death introduces baffled grief and a sardonic acceptance of a belief that there is no individual control over individual destiny. The speech invites comparison with the scene in Osborne's *Look Back In Anger* in which Jimmy Porter describes the manner of death of his father. Here the anguish is totally self-indulgent; there is no relationship made between the experience of another man's death and any conception of what life is, or is not. Porter is an emotional hedonist, Ormund a sardonic philosopher:

JIMMY: . . . But I was the only one who cared! (*He moves L., behind the armchair.*)

Every time I sat on the edge of his bed, to listen to him talking or reading to me, I had to fight back my tears. At the end of twelve months, I was a veteran. (*He leans forward on the back of the armchair.*)
All that that feverish failure of a man had to listen to him was a small frightened boy. I spent hour upon hour in that tiny bedroom. He would talk to me for hours, pouring out all that was left of his life to one, lonely, bewildered little boy, who could barely understand half of what he said. All he could feel was the despair and the bitterness, the sweet, sickly smell of a dying man.

There is much that is inexplicable in Porter's anger, and it is largely because he is inexplicable, except in terms of an emotional self-indulgence that is all-consuming, that robs him of any stature and, more pertinently, any representative position. Ormund, the angry old man, not only has a personal sense of futility, but an ability to relate personal experience to what he takes to be the general nature of life itself. More than this he has an outgoing sensitivity which enables him to respond to the suffering of others without self-indulgence. There is, too, in the play, the hint of a cause for Ormund's bitter sense of futility – a built-in sense of doom, a self-destructive seed that, as he says, gets 'stronger all the time'. There are the makings of a tragic figure in the Ibsen mould in the character of Ormund, but while there is more justification for regarding him as a Modern Everyman than there is for regarding (as has been done) Porter as representative of a generation, Priestley does not develop the grief, loneliness, despair and curious courage which are part of the man's make-up. Having brought Ormund up to the point where these qualities are revealed Priestley is committed to the fatal necessity of explaining and resolving his problem by a more explicit statement of Ouspensky's time-theory. Regretfully, one sees the play and the character subjected to a mechanistic solution.

After the revelation to Görtler, Ormund goes out and we are left in little doubt that he has been very near to suicide. This is logical enough. But James Agate with his brutally correct prankishness places his finger upon the cause of the play's and this character's diminution of stature:

> Our author likes to play at the Game of Recurrence and Intervention because it gives people a second chance, and in the theatre people who are given second chances invariably lead better lives. But hold on a bit. The Game is only half of Mr Priestley's theme. The other half is pattern. All the people in the new play are as closely inter-related as the threads in a piece of cloth: you cannot alter the life of one without a corresponding change in the lives of others. Now let us see where this leads. I am a naughty little boy. My schoolmaster is a brutal fellow who likes using the rod. It makes me grow up into a good man, and I die a millionaire at the age of ninety. This happens thousands of times. Then one fine day my schoolmaster stops being a sadist, conceives a positive distaste for the rod, and so spoils me that I take to drink and die in the workhouse. And that, dear Mr Priestley, or dear Mr Ouspensky, just won't do.

The time-theory is, when detached thus from the play, palpably absurd, and when involved in a dramatic action which has developed with such sensitivity as is revealed in the first two acts of *I Have Been Here Before*, its effect is to diminish the human complexity, the values of human emotion and belief, which that very sensitivity has created.

After the middle of Act Two the time-theme begins to obtrude explicitly. It is stated awkwardly by Janet: 'Is it true, Dr Görtler, that time is curved? I read somewhere the other day that it is.' Clumsily mentioned by Ormund: 'But does he seriously think we all just go on and on with the same life.'

These remarks are like deliberately planted clues in a paper chase. Dr Görtler is no man to neglect clues, and by the end of the act his various explanations have reduced the atmosphere of the play to that of a half-occult charade. The end of Act Two is superbly managed theatrically, when the characters realise fully, for the first time, that Görtler has some special knowledge and purpose which terrifies them, but their terror is, by now, seen not against the human tensions which the characters revealed in Act One and in the first half of Act Two, but against the blankly mechanistic statements that Görtler has made about time. They have become figures in a thriller waiting for the 'thing' to happen.

There is some redemption in Act Three, but now the play is in the inevitable position of having to be forced into a conclusion. There are some moments in which Priestley's characteristic sensitivity to the nuances of human feeling and behaviour is shown. Sally's embarrassment at having given a cold shoulder to Görtler is expressed with a touching economy:

SALLY (*holding up notebook*): Is this it?
GÖRTLER (*taking it eagerly*): Yes. Thank you. That is all I want.
He glances at the notebook, then looks up at Sally, and gives her a smiling nod of dismissal. She looks at him hesitantly, then turns and goes.

The possibility of a tragic outcome for Janet and Farrant prevents the play from rushing headlong into a happy ending. But it is, in the final analysis, shackled to Ouspensky. Ormund's 'conversion' to a less self-destructive state is too swiftly achieved. The evidence of a man moving from a state in which he cannot believe that there is any self-determination to a state where he 'learns' the values of human life is expressed in language which is an uneasy mixture of quasi-theory and emotional vibrancy:

GÖRTLER: We do not go round a circle. That is an illusion, just as the circling of the planets and stars is an illusion. We move along a spiral track. It is not quite the same journey from the cradle to the grave each time. Sometimes the differences are small, sometimes they are very important. We must set out each time on the same road but along that road we have a choice of adventures.
ORMUND: I wish I could believe that, Görtler.

And a minute later Ormund utters this speech:

(*After a pause, staring at Dr Görtler, then with a certain breadth and nobility of manner*): New life! I wish I could believe that. You've never told me yet about a God so generous and noble and wise that he won't allow a few decisions that we make in our ignorance, haste and bewilderment to settle our fate for ever. Why should this poor improvisation be our whole existence? Why should this great theatre of suns and moons and starlight have been created for the first pitiful charade we can contrive?

Ormund becomes too glib, as Priestley hastens him towards a status of noble sacrifice and towards a kind of evening sunset, content with his lot. We get only the emotional overtones, the sentiments of re-birth, the actuality is unconvincing:

JANET: Yes. You're suddenly quite different. And yet – as you always ought to have been. I know you – you're bigger than I am – bigger than Oliver. I think – now – you'll be a great man, Walter.

The subtle theatrical skill remains throughout the play, an emotional and atmospheric tension remains throughout the play, the characters are constantly interesting, and their relationships are shown with a shrewd sense of changes of mood and posture. But the play diminishes as it goes along because the demands of the theory force Priestley's hand. Thrill and ingenuity, explicit statement, replace the powerful sense of truth and depth with which the play begins. But, like so many others of Priestley's plays, it haunts the imagination and in no other play has he created a character who steps out so firmly along the tragic path (only to lose his way) as Ormund. He does not seem at any point to be a modern Everyman, but he might well have been a modern Hamlet, had his creator shown the faith in him that he displays in the first act and the first part of the second act. The spiral reduces Ormund and confounds Priestley.

JOHNSON OVER JORDAN

In the critical notices and reviews of *Johnson Over Jordan*, the word that was most bandied about was 'expressionism' used pejoratively or admiringly according to the predilections of the critic. Few descriptive terms have been more bent to the whim, mood, theory, opinion, prejudice, and even age, of the critic than this word. It has been employed to describe types of play, film, acting techniques, painting techniques and even the nature of the imagination of certain writers. In the realm of drama it has been used to describe plays as different from one another as *On the Frontier*, *The Silver Tassie*, *Man and the Masses* and *Gas*. Playwrights as different from one another as Strindberg, Toller, O'Neill and Capek have been lashed to its lumbering shifts of meaning and association. Its spiritual home was Germany in the 1920s, but it emigrated to the United States when Orson Welles produced his early experimental films, and has recently made an appearance in critical descriptions of the work of Pinter and Ionesco.

Insofar as it is possible to give the word a definition precise enough to have any meaning at all, it may be said to describe works of art whose intention is not to present the outer forms of things, but their inner reality. In so doing the expressionist artist is inclined to one degree or another to annihilate the natural expectations of the way things look and seem. Natural appearance and environment become secondary to an inner reality, and form, in expressionistic art, becomes the invention of the artist, and is not likely to bear any relationship to orthodox forms. The expressionist dramatist, therefore, always bears the marks of an experimenter with both material and form, and what he communicates, since its source has little contact with the contours of the natural, lacks familiarity and often has a quality of mystery. Moreover, since the expressionist dramatist annihilates the expectations of human behaviour and natural form, the conventions of time and place are also placed in jeopardy. Ernest Short has summarised some of the particular characteristics and paraphernalia of the expressionist dramatist. He writes: 'Allusiveness is what arises most directly from expressionism'; 'expressionism telescopes images'; 'expressionism suggests rapid passages of thought, emotion and sensation'; 'it places emphasis upon emotion as opposed to intellectuality'; 'it exploits doubt and despair as opposed to faith'; it uses 'masks, megaphones, "modern" costume'. It is against this background that Short views Priestley.

Faced with this formidable assembly of characteristics it is easy to see why the word has been so variously applied. Different combinations of the characteristics could well be used to apply to almost any kind of artistic work. Shakespeare would not escape, neither would Dürer, nor indeed would Dickens. Yet it is nevertheless true that the first three decades of the twentieth century have witnessed a concentration, particularly by dramatists, upon an extreme form of communication of these characteristics. Certainly in Germany it might justifiably be claimed that, in the twenties, the major impetus for dramatic writing came from those playwrights who consciously embraced this disturbing creed. It is arguable whether, in fact, the combination of the characteristics outlined above inevitably means that the emphasis of an expressionist play is on doubt and despair as opposed to faith. There does not seem, on the face of it, any reason why the exploration of the hidden reality is bound to disclose a dark landscape. The most likely explanation of the darkness of most modern expressionist plays is that they took their cue from the tones of the German dramatists whose work was coloured by the instability and doubt of the social environment of the period immediately following the first world war in Germany. The interesting paradox about expressionist drama is that though it eschews the natural and expected contours of social and human environment, it seems particularly sensitive to the effects of that environment upon the inner reality which the dramatist seeks to concentrate upon. Toller, Auden and Isherwood, in particular, are, however expressionistic their plays might be, indexes, in a sense, to the social and political environment of the times.

Short places *Johnson Over Jordan* squarely in the tradition of expressionist drama. He says that Johnson is a 'typical Briton', an 'English Everyman'. He regards the play as an imaginative presentation of the mind of a man who has just died. But, he adds,

Priestley is more interested in Johnson living than in Johnson dead. In this the play is expressionist in its approach to theme. But it is also so in its use of unfamiliar devices – the use of masks, the rejection of the three or four act lay-out of plot. And, finally, he points to the way in which Johnson moves quite freely in and out of chronological time.

There are two major respects in which *Johnson Over Jordan* does not fit the characteristic pattern of expressionism. The first is its obstinate optimism; in David Hughes's words it is a play 'which disintegrates out of the sharp black shadows of a powerfully imagined hell of dreams into the cosy and, yes, somewhat jolly sunlight of the last act'. The second is its curious lack of connection with the prevailing realities of the society in which it was written. It is not necessarily a criticism of the play to remember that it did not in any way reflect the dark doubts and apprehensions of 1938, but the fact that it does not might partly explain its general failure to catch the attention which it deserved at the time. It remains true, however, that the play has haunted many people – its own reality perhaps, being remote from the harsh facts of 1938 has only impinged upon those who saw it, by hindsight. All the indications demand a revival; it came, originally, at the wrong time. Society was making a headlong dash towards annihilation, while Johnson moved towards Nirvanah.

Priestley himself is bewildered by the expressionist label attached to the play. He calls it an experiment, and for him, the play was an experiment in that, for the first time, he was attempting to use the maximum number of the resources of theatre – dance, mime, ballet, music. His intention was not to write a play about life-after-death, and the play is in essence a biographical-morality. In it a man's life is examined in a context in which time is annihilated, and the concentration of the action is not upon the development of characterisation but rather upon the assembly of evidence as to the nature of the characters, with the emphasis on Johnson. The state in which Johnson 'exists' in the play has obvious affinities with the Tibetan conception of the condition of the soul immediately after death: 'a prolonged dream-like state, in what may be called the fourth dimension of space filled with hallucinatory visions directly resultant from the mental content of the percipient.' This is a precise description of the state of Johnson in the play. In it his personality and his past actions exist in a flux which he observes much as a man observes in a dream. Time is not present in this play as a kind of dramatic agent, nor as a means by which Priestley can play subtle theatrical tricks. In a sense it may be said not to be present at all. In this timeless examination of the nature of Johnson the biographical and the moral intentions are held in equal balance. It is the story of an apparently ordinary man's life, but the hidden complexes which are revealed give the sense of an extraordinary man. The poetry of the ordinary man's deeply hidden emotions is revealed, the jealousies, envies, hatreds, loves – all of which lie below the surface in the natural life of the ordinary man – are brought to the surface with a kind of violence. Nevertheless we never lose sight of the 'little' man. It is the bowler hat and the mackintosh which, in the long run, constitute the most pervasive image of the nature of Johnson. Like Wells before him, in *Mr Polly*, and like Chaplin, Priestley never lets go of the image of the little man. Whatever volcanic eruptions we are allowed to see, the brave little figure chases across our emotions and demands sympathetic hearing.

Its morality is simple. Certain actions can lead to damnation, other actions can lead to peace and happiness. The damnation which Priestley implies has no theological context or implications. It resides in the tortured awareness of the individual that his actions have hurt others – it is a self-condemnation and is therefore a conscience. But there is no sense in which Johnson is made to seem accountable to any supernatural power. The universe that surrounds him does not contain a godhead, and the persona of death appears as a theatrical agent rather than as a projection of a supernatural truth. Similarly, the happiness which awaits the man who has accounted his faults is not embodied in a theological pattern. We do not witness heaven in this play any more than we witness hell. We are left, like Johnson himself, with a question: 'Is it a long way?' The terms of the play are secular in the sense that moral right and wrong are met by solutions which are expressed in terms which have nothing to do with an external and supernatural set of rules. The solutions are romantic not theological since they are based upon what man can imagine and not upon what may be imposed upon him outside his control. Thus happiness is a kind of self-satisfaction which comes out of a glow of having done something right; thus damnation is the conscience which says 'I was wrong to do that and I will never do it again'.

Priestley wastes no time in taking the audience into the suspended condition in which Johnson lives. There is no careful preparation in this play, as in the other time-plays, of the audience's reactions. He does not gently lead us from natural to non-natural. Within five minutes of the start, where we witness the arrival of the mourners at Johnson's funeral, we are at Johnson's side as he comes into speech 'like a man in a delirium'. The language which precedes this is flat and naturalistic, but the change is announced by a monologue from Johnson which is clipped – a 'stream of consciousness':

> They can say what they like, but I've a high old temperature. . . . Look at the way things bend and waver and then go floating about. . . . That's not normal . . . and corridors . . . long corridors . . . far too many long corridors . . . I noticed some corridors when they brought me in – you can't have a big nursing-home without corridors – but not as many as all that – and not so long. . . . And a pretty penny this'll cost us before I'm out again. . . . Fifteen guineas a week for the room at least . . . then the doctors . . . and extras – all sorts of nonsense – and charge you the earth for 'em. . . .

A stream of consciousness certainly, but very contrived to 'place' the state of Johnson. It is at this point that Priestley begins to use the resources of theatre as opposed to the resources of the dramatist. He relies almost entirely upon the usages of mime, lighting and music to convey the idea that we, with Johnson, have departed from a norm of experience and have entered into another world of experience. The visual effect is non-natural: secretaries have 'blank faces', quick movements are made 'in a stylised fashion'. The set is 'lit from below' so that it is not easy to see the action properly, but easy to note the big shadows which are thrown. This is followed by a 'hard white light'. The office into which Johnson enters is furnished 'expressionalistically' with a very modern desk 'efficient and opulent, and quite inhuman'. At one point Johnson is to be discovered 'only about half the size he was at the beginning of this duet'. But what is presented abnormally in visual terms is not matched by the language and what the language conveys. It is as if Priestley had built a fair-ground House of Horror and peopled it with traffic policemen. The movements of the secretaries and the old financiers conjure up memories of the Ballet Joos and *The Green Table*, the insistent badgering of Johnson as he fails to fill in his forms properly conjures up Kafka, but in essence, what is expressed in language is ordinary and naturalistic. Visually we are taken beyond the appearances of things, verbally we stay on the naturalistic prose level:

FIRST OLD MAN: We all want our money, don't we? Come, come, don't be childish, my dear sir.

JOHNSON (*apologetically*): Sorry! But you see – I can't remember. I was ill, y'know – really ill. I overheard the doctor. . . .

FIRST OLD MAN: Don't bother me with doctors. Plenty here if you want one.

SECOND OLD MAN: Wonderful medical staff here. But they won't get you your money, will they?

FIRST OLD MAN (*willing to stop for a chat about money*): How much are you expecting?

JOHNSON (*who cannot help feeling that this is pretty good*): Oh – well – several thousands, y'know.

FIRST OLD MAN (*contemptuously*): Several thousands!

SECOND OLD MAN (*perhaps the worse of the two, sniggering*): One thousand, two thousand, three thousand!

The two ancient and desiccated monsters cackle together and point contemptuously at poor Johnson, who watches them spread themselves in their chairs now.

JOHNSON: I don't see anything particularly funny about it.

FIRST OLD MAN: I cleared two hundred and fifty thousand on Consolidated Copper.

SECOND OLD MAN: I made a cool three hundred and fifty thousand out of National Nickel.

FIRST OLD MAN: I netted four hundred and fifty thousand out of International Iron.

SECOND OLD MAN: I cashed in for five hundred and fifty thousand out of Standard Steel.

The somewhat obvious incantation at the end of this extract is the only concession to a conception of communication which takes what is being said beyond the prosaic. But what is said in the first part of the first act is indeed prosaic. The iniquities of high finance, the pettiness of minor and major officialdom, the way in which the citizen is badgered by the machine of bureaucracy, the reduction of the human being to the status of a numeral. This is the country in which Johnson spends the first part of his 'suspended animation'. It fixes his world for us, but what troubles is that the technical means employed to project the image of this world seem disproportionate to what is revealed. It is only in the second part of the act when we are given a closer look at the character of Johnson himself that we begin to have suggestions that Priestley is attempting to reveal more than is explicitly stated in his language, and when we begin to feel that theatrical device is being justified. When Johnson's 'inner and deeper self is talking' in monologue Priestley switches to an associative prose, which is heralded by music:

That music doesn't belong to this place. But then neither do I. Who does? I've lived in the world where that music was, but not for long – no, never for long. Not my fault. It comes and goes so quickly, just gleams and fades, that other world, like the light at sunset on distant hills. . . .

The music goes on, high and trailing, but now a girl's voice sings with it, high and trailing too. He listens a moment before speaking.

But perhaps that is real – that, somewhere outside – and this only a dream. I've had dreams like this – with everything at first solid as rock – though they tell us now rocks aren't solid, only shifting shapes – but afterwards it all melted away, all the stone walls and iron bars. . . . (*This reminds him of something as he repeats it*) . . . Stone walls – iron bars. . . .

Up to this point what we have learnt of Johnson is hardly flattering. The prosaic world we have seen is an unpleasant world, and in it Johnson has been an equivocal and expedient man. Even his wife admits this: 'Don't Jill me, Robert Johnson. I wish to God I'd never set eyes on you – and wish those poor children of mine – had never – never – been born.'

But the deeper Johnson is not like this. The music that he hears tells him of a reality and a truth that are not to be measured by the lean actions of the world we call real, but which is really the dream. There is no mistaking a characteristic Priestley theme here. What must be recognised is that this theme is taken a step forward at the end of Act One by the introduction of the Figure in the Mask. The figure represents Death and corruption, and embodies all Johnson's fears about what another world will be like. It is only when he takes a closer look behind the mask of death that Johnson discovers that there is another reality to death just as there is another reality to living: '*Johnson hesitates, then, making up his mind, he suddenly steps forward, as the music makes a queer high tremulo, and plucks off the mask, revealing behind it the face of a calm, wise-looking person, at whom Johnson stares in bewilderment.*'

The significant thing about the features that are revealed is that they are, for Johnson, an amalgam of the features of all those people who have meant most to him in his earthly life. Here, the secular romantic in Priestley steps to the front of the stage. The reality behind the world is good and wise and beneficent, but it is compounded of all those elements of goodness and wisdom and beneficence which have flitted across the corrupt landscape of life. God lies in the world, if we choose to see him there, and he is of our own clay, and heaven lies in our response to him.

But Johnson at the end of Act One has not learnt the moral lesson. The recognition of the true reality has been fugitive, 'the awful daring of a moment's surrender', but it is not enough to pull him away from a fatal attraction to the corrupt face of the world.

At the beginning of Act Two Priestley provides another very swift point of reference in naturalistic terms. We are once more for a few minutes in the world of time, but he wastes little time before taking us back to Johnson's preternatural state. This is again presented in the form and colouring of dream. In fine, Act Two is really a recapitulation of the main theme of Act One. Johnson is again displaying his baser self. The sophisticated decadence of the club/cocktail/material world dominates the act, and the other reality, announced intermittently in Act One, still has to rely upon a fugitive appearance. Johnson's daughter, Freda, is responsible for one of its appearances. She has had a dream in which she has been frighteningly aware that she had to find her husband.

> '. . . I was – half asleep. Then I had a hateful sort of dream. Frightening, horrible. I suppose it was really a nightmare. I dreamt I was trying to find your father. I knew I had to find him. And I had to look in the strangest places – all vague – but – frightening.'

And Johnson himself, in the second of his monologues in which he detaches himself from the action ruminates on his state:

> 'Here I sit waiting – a fool. I know I am a fool, yet I know too I am no fool. All this has always been folly before, but now perhaps, just for once, the miracle may happen. . . . They say I am half-animal, half-god. . . . Yet I do not think it is entirely the animal in me that is waiting here, for the animal must be a simple creature, with a few sharp needs, easily satisfied. . . . But this is not simple, this lighted and scented jungle, where everything has been so carefully devised to taste bitter-sweet, half-rotten. . . . Even if the animal in me is fed and tickled, it is to arouse the god, grumbling in his sleep. . . .'

Freda's speech echoes a familiar Priestley theme – we are involved in one another, no man is an island; Johnson's speech merely reiterates that man is not flesh alone – that the glory of his existence lies in a reality (the godhead of man) which cannot be measured alone by the baser facts of his everyday existence.

These intermittent visitations from another dimension of reality are hedged in by an inchoate reiteration of the snares and vices of the self-indulgent life. In the club scene there is a clumsy attempt to allegorise the iniquities of the selfish life. Mr Rat, Mr Scorpion and Mr Slug whom Johnson meets are little more than fantasticated embodiments of the kind of attitude which is revealed by the financiers of Act One. What is added is the decadence of lust, the thirst for possession. There follows an episode in which Johnson unknowingly stabs his own son, and tries to 'make' his own daughter. Here, the implication is clear. All men, perhaps by the unknowingness of their actions, kill the things they love. The falsities of their hearts, and their blindness to the true realities of human behaviour make them treacherous to those whom they have least desire to betray. We tell our love too late:

JOHNSON (*distressed*): Didn't you see? My own daughter – my son – were here – and I – and I – oh! horrible, horrible!

THE FIGURE (*going over to him*): There are no human instruments created solely for our satisfaction, Robert. There are only persons. They are all sons and daughters, you see.

JOHNSON: I see that – and a thousand other things – now. But too late! My own children. . . .

Johnson is not allowed to suffer too much anguish. He is whisked to a comforting proposition:

JOHNSON (*agitated*): And there they are – Jill, Freda, Richard – unhappy. And I'm here. Oh – horrible! What a swine I am!

THE FIGURE (*cheerfully, but gently*): No, no. A fool perhaps, an average sort of fool. (*Pauses, considering him.*) Robert, I think you'd better go on to the Inn now.

JOHNSON (*sharply*): I want to go back to my home, to tell them I'm not really dead – to try and comfort them.

He is refused permission to return, but told that he can go on to the Inn, where he will need no money. The strong implication at the end of Act Two is that he who recognises his sins will be able to go to the Inn – will be able, in fact, to fare forward unpunished.

At the end of Act Two Johnson asks the Figure what he is likely to find at the Inn. The reply is that the Figure does not know 'what things have illuminated your mind and touched your heart'. Act Three makes clear what things have illuminated and touched Johnson's heart. The Inn is a sort of clearing house where the resident discovers what it is that, beneath the coruscating surface of the world, has really been the reality that meant most but which went unregarded. The Inn is a sort of super trust house – a repository of the good things for which no payment is asked but the recognition of the good things, the realities which bind person to person. In Johnson's case they are glaringly clear. The simple pleasures, like cricket, and the noble pint. The deeper relationships with parents and wife and children. The ennobling simplicities of the popular theatre, the half-forgotten but beneficent influences of sporadic reading. His parents, his acquaintances, his heroes, parade before him with an insistent benevolence which expunges for him, and indeed for the audience, all memory of the harsher personages and actions that have shown themselves previously. Wisdom and honesty appear in the guise of his old schoolmaster; Love emerges in the evocation of his marriage and the coming of his children. This ordinary man goes through a process of romantic annunciation as the true realities pass in parade before him, and he sits, as it were, upon an emotional throne purged and made happy:

JOHNSON (*with mounting excitement*): Look – there's good old George. It was he who did the trick for us that night. . . . Why, there's Tom . . . was he there? He might have been, though. . . . And Mr Clayton . . . he wasn't there, of course. . . . And old Morrison from my school . . . glorious idea

> bringing him in. . . . Look, Jill – your mother, having a roaring good time . . . do you remember how suspicious of me she was at first? . . . I'll bet Don Quixote's somewhere about . . . I had a talk to him. . . . And look – Richard – *our* Richard – that's cheek, if you like, coming to dance at the party where his mother met his father!

In this one speech Priestley underlines the way in which he throws away this play. Johnson has it too easy. The average man triumphs despite his iniquities. He goes out in a blaze of glory to an unknown but promised land. He has suffered little in the course of the action, though he has experienced the pangs of the unthinking and the selfish. In a sense the happy ending is plotted throughout the entire course of the play. If this is a modern Everyman then he is an Everyman certain of comfort not of damnation. He accepts a too easy punishment (the recognition of his faults) too easily. He is less, as Priestley claims, 'an ordinary middle-class citizen of our time' than a romanticised man who has to win through because the initial concept of the average man can have no meaning unless it is glorified by some kind of triumph. In a way Johnson is an irritating character because there is no fight in him. He questions nothing, and accepts everything that comes his way be it good or bad. The most potent emotion he displays is, as David Hughes emphasises, the emotion of bewilderment. He is, in short, not big enough to house or react to the issues which the play creates around him. There is a strong impression created in this play that Priestley has tried to utilise all the cards in his pack. Thematically, he has exploited his familiar themes of the twin-dimensioned nature of life, the oneness of humanity, the binding and valid realities of kinship. Technically, he has exploited the familiar processes of his own flexible conception of the nature of time, and has brought to the play all the craft of economy in characterisation, and the skill with action, that he possesses. In the language he has tried to indicate the sense of 'something far more deeply interfused', by the use of a rhythmic and associative prose and, at the very end of the play, a flexible verse-form. But the play falls far short of the triumph it should have been. It fails because, yet again, Priestley seems unable to trust himself and his audience with too much or too rich a diet of the non-naturalistic; the theme, the technique employed, cry out for a wholehearted plunge into symbolic drama. David Hughes says that Johnson presents 'the odd spectacle of a character who is too down to earth but hardly rooted in life at all'. Like the play itself, he is neither one thing nor the other. One of the results of this is to make the more obviously 'expressionistic' scenes, in which masks are used, seem oddly dissociated from everything. Johnson cavorts through the scenes but his dramatic significance bears no relationship to their theatrical presence. He remains relatively untouched by everything – he is like a man in a funfair who knows a good tea awaits him at home so long as he has patience.

Yet there can be no doubt that the disappointment that the play engenders is mixed with a sense of excitement. The play haunts. It cannot be dismissed simply as an 'expressionist' failure. The truth is that whereas one becomes not over-concerned with matters of life and death in the play, not over-stirred by Johnson's state, one is excited by the simple expectation of what is going to happen next. Once more the cunning hand of Priestley has fashioned something in the nature of an intriguing story. At the end of Act One he leaves us wondering what will happen to Johnson in the Night Club, at the end of Act Two we are told that Johnson will go to the Inn and we wonder where this is and what it is. And, throughout the play, certain episodes in which parts of Johnson's life are re-enacted have a strong narrative quality. This is one reason for the play's hold on the imagination. The second reason is its often brilliant evocation of atmosphere and mood:

FREDA: And we had a marvellous day, except that you weren't with us. (*Pauses*) What's the matter?

JOHNSON (*who has just gone closer*): I'm sorry. I was just thinking – you're a fine pair – just what. . . .

RICHARD: Now Dad, stop it.

FREDA: Daddy, no teasing.

JOHNSON (*as it dawns*): You're my children?

FREDA: Of course we are.

JOHNSON (*hastily*): Yes, yes, of course you must be. Oh – this is great isn't it? I'm sorry I was so stupid.

FREDA: Don't you want us?

JOHNSON: Of course I do. I tell you, it's – tremendous. Come inside, come in at once and talk to me.

RICHARD: No, Dad.

FREDA: We both agreed that wouldn't do, not to-night.

RICHARD: You don't want us here to-night.

JOHNSON (*bewildered*): I don't. How do you know I don't?

FREDA: We know the pair of you, when you're together, won't want us.

JOHNSON: The pair of us?

FREDA (*enthusiastically*): Yes. But to-morrow we'll all have an enormous day. And you're not to be lazy.

RICHARD (*also with enthusiasm*): We'll start just after breakfast, and climb everything there is.

JOHNSON (*dubiously*): To-morrow . . .?

RICHARD (*confidently*): Yes, to-morrow. Don't you believe in to-morrow?

FREDA (*laughing*): To-morrow and to-morrow and to-morrow. . . . (*Breaks off because she sees something in his face. Concerned now.*) What's the matter, father?

Priestley is typically at his best in those moments of closeness between members of a tightly-knit group, when love and need are dominant, but are at the mercy of ironies not one member of the group can really fathom. Freda's gay 'to-morrow and to-morrow and to-morrow' injects an irony and a depth of association into the scene which might have convinced Priestley that the play as it stands largely lacks the benediction of a rich enough language.

The third reason for the play's haunting quality is its insistent optimism – direct or implied. It cannot be too strongly emphasised that there seems to be in human nature a factor which responds to the depiction of happy events or the implication of a happy conclusion, irrespective of any evidence from experience to the contrary. When the happy conclusion involves a character or characters who seem to represent the average man then the effect has a double power. And if the average character achieves his happy end via a process which implies that there is something after all extraordinary about being average, then the power is trebled. The 'transubstantiation' of Johnson from ordinary man to 'hero' is given a theatrical crown in the very last moments of the play when, still with his uniform of the ordinary citizen, he walks towards the stars. He seems to have conquered time, and there is not one of us who would not wish to do that. The trouble is that there is so much else in the play he might have conquered, or taken up arms against. It is not so much Priestley's imagination that has failed him, but perhaps his courage – he does not give Johnson the means by which to prove himself human.

MUSIC AT NIGHT

In the brochure to the Malvern Festival for 1938 Priestley contributed a short essay which he called *A Note From the Workshop*. He had been asked to write a new play for the festival and the result was *Music At Night* which is the last of the time-plays published in volume one of the collected works. In the essay he wrote:

> You might as well be told at once that *Music At Night* is an odd and experimental sort of piece. I shall be most happily surprised – if I still know how to be happily surprised – to find more than half the audience liking the play. But even if everybody at Malvern heartily dislikes it, I shall not apologise. . . . I'd still walk about the town as bold as brass. This is not because I do not enjoy success or think there is something rather fine about failure. . . . No, I shall be unrepentant because I shall feel that I have done my duty. A dramatic festival should be, among other things, a laboratory for the dramatist who wishes to make experiments. The people who attend such a festival should be the very last persons to take into the Theatre with them some conventional cut-and-dried notions of what a play

should be. They should be on the side of the dramatist who is trying something new.

. . . In this play I attempt to dramatise the mental adventures of a group of persons listening to the first performance of a piece of music. It is assumed that the mood of the music more or less controls their moods. The progress throughout the play is from the surface of the mind to deeper and deeper levels of consciousness. The strange happenings in Act Three arise from my belief that at these depths we are not the separate beings we imagine ourselves to be. There is very little sheer whimsicality in the play, and I think that if pressed I could put up a fairly stout intellectual defence of everything done and said.

As usual with Priestley this is a precise description of the play, and the claim that there is no whimsicality in the piece is justified. Also justifiable is the claim that it is experimental – in some senses it is more experimental than *Johnson Over Jordan*. It did not, however, escape the fate of that play; it suffered bad notices, and has been rarely performed since the first production at Malvern.

The kind of experiment that Priestley is engaged upon in this play is what he calls 'the range and flexibility and sensitiveness of the instrument itself' – the form and the communication. Some critics thought he was engaged in what Priestley would call the first type of experiment, which is to try and introduce into the play and the theatre 'great lumps of life unknown to it before'. There is nothing extraordinary about the material of *Music At Night*, but the form deceives the eye and mind into believing that Priestley has embarked upon a somewhat *outré* examination of the odd corners of the individual psyche.

The material of the play is dug from familiar seams. The groups of people who are assembled to hear the new piece of music are a gossip-writer, a hostess, an old cabinet minister, a business man, a society woman, and the two players of the music. Each one stands for a particular element in society which, at first, is revealed in its grosser forms. The gossip-writer, with his reedy intelligence, pricks at situations to find the corruption inside them – he is a pandar to the immense appetites of the sensational press. The society woman is no more nor less than a sophisticated whore, ministering to a class that requires even its lusts to be well turned out and intelligent. The cabinet minister is carrying with him to his grave (he dies in the course of the play) the heavy weight of the equivocations of thought, speech and actions which the professional politician carries about with him. The assembly of people adds up to a microcosm of a society whose face is frustrated, deceitful, anguished. But the effect of the music is to release each person's inner self, to show the deeper reality that lies beneath the face that is carefully built for the world. Their outward relationships to one another are shown, but the inner truth of those relationships gradually emerges, forming a different pattern, and one that is more valid and unpolluted by the expediencies of the conventional stance, the unreal pose. As the inner reality replaces the outward show, so time is annihilated in its chronological terms to reveal past actions in a different light from that in which they first appeared. The framework of the play is naturalistic. The action takes place during the performance of the piece of music, but within this framework – the one hour's traffic of the music – time is expunged. Sometimes we see a character's memory acted out again, sometimes we see actions which have taken place in the past which lead up to the present-tense, sometimes we witness an action as a character would have wished it to proceed, so that for a time the character becomes a sort of impressario responsible for the manipulation of other characters in his own desired action. Priestley's problem in experimentation was to make characters who are established naturalistically at the outset remain credible when they passed not only into another time-dimension but, in a sense, into another psychological dimension. Priestley's attempts to solve the problem is twofold. First, at times, individual characters step forward to act as choruses to the action that is about to be presented, and in the course of their 'introduction', persuade us to accept a different view of certain characters than we have had before:

> When I went to California four years ago with the Shirly-Wilsons, we made a trip into the Painted Desert and the

Navajo Indian Reservation in Northern Arizona. The sky was pure turquoise and the colossal sandstone cliffs were like burnished copper, and it was all far away, far away, and very peaceful. The Navajo Indians have song-prayers and they used to invoke the Four Winds – the Black Wind, the Blue Wind, the Yellow Wind and the Iridescent wind – and they used to cry 'That it may be peaceful before me, That it may be peaceful behind me. All is peace, all is peace'. And nobody understood or believed me when I said that I wished that I'd been born a Navajo woman . . . to wander with my sheep in those lost canyons . . . under a burning empty sky . . . crying to the Blue and Yellow Winds . . . they wouldn't believe me . . . yet it was true . . . it was true.

Second, there is a sense of swiftness in the play which impersonates the swiftness of the incisively cut cinema film. The impression is of a quick series of images on a screen, and we are not allowed thereby to dwell too much on any one revelation of character or interpretation of incident, but are pushed to accept a cumulative view, into which the swiftly moving pieces fit, not as a jig-saw but as a kaleidoscope. The danger of too inchoate a picture is avoided by Priestley's careful designation of the role that each act has to play in the creation of the eventual pattern. In Act One we see, as indeed we do with Johnson, these people trapped in the time-bound stances of the present-tense. They are at their worst when they are unconscious of any dimensions behind their present-tense consciousness. In Act Two, Time begins to dissolve and we see them as the victims of their own lack of a sense of dimension, and victims therefore of lost opportunities, regrets, and a sense of failure in human relationships. Act Two shows the penalty of remaining unconscious of the fact that there is more to life than the living of it on the surface of the present-tense. In Act Three, as Priestley tells us in his essay, quoted above, his belief in the oneness of humanity, the interdependence of living in all its facets, comes to the surface. We are taken far from the view of these people that we got in Act One. The kaleidoscope's pattern is complete – the oneness is achieved.

The experimental nature of this play lies in its attempt to reveal credibly the oneness of the human condition, and all that this implies in terms of the relationship between the unconscious and the conscious, not only of the individual mind, but of separate individuals' minds. What happens during the course of the play is that the characters gradually lose their identity as individuals until they are *intended* at the end to be a composite image of the human condition. Priestley believes himself to have been defeated by this attempt in the last act: 'The chief weakness of the play is that when I reached the third act I was trying to show that personality, the separate self is an illusion – a hopeless task in the theatre'. It may be speculated upon whether the task is itself a hopeless one or whether the means adopted by Priestley make it hopeless. There can be no question that, in a sense, this play is the nearest approximation to a poem that Priestley has written. The characters are metaphors which are intended to create a total image, but their metaphorical nature is at the mercy of Priestley's insistent refusal to allow them to leave the earth. They become theatrically schizophrenic because part of them seems utterly bound to the 'actualities' of the present-tense while another part becomes intermittently conscious of a deeper 'reality'. There is too much of a gap between remarks like: 'If Bendrex likes the concerto tonight and then I go and die next week, he might be able to get Katherine awarded a Civil List pension of Fifty Pounds a Year', with the reply:

> 'What – fifty pounds of good government money – and they could have bought a nice bomb with it',

and the kind of romantic rhythmics such as are shown in the speech about the Navajo Indians. Once more the fundamental mistake is made of establishing the characters in too firm, not to say hard, a naturalistic context, and then expecting the audience, lured by prose rhythms, to accept another dimension of reality. What he is immensely successful in achieving in this play is the sense of human beings wandering in thought and feeling under the influence of music. The quick cutting from one character to another enables him to body forth the unknown directions which the mind takes as it is stimulated:

DAVID: . . . Why are you crying?
KATH (*urgently*): Oh – David – David. . . .
DAVID (*who has stepped further back in the dim light and can hardly be seen. In far away voice*): Why are you crying? (*Still further away.*) Why are you crying?
KATH (*in terrible alarm*): David, David, come back. Everything – come back.
She drops down, sobbing quietly. The music comes in softly. The speeches that follow can come through it, but now Katherine stops sobbing but remains seated in the same attitude in front of the others.
SIR J (*seated but looking towards audience, quietly*): I don't understand why the music should be so sad. I don't understand this elaborate sadness. I believe it's a kind of affectation, like finger bowls after dinner or going to dance in white kid gloves and that sort of nonsense. What really gets a fellow down is staleness, feeling weary and half-dead. I suppose you can't get that into music, but that's the real thing. Staleness. Feeling that nothing's worth the bloody great effort you have to make. I'm stale half the time nowadays. But not sad – no – that's all my eye.
LADY S: You are sad after you have made love.
SIR J: No. But I know what you mean. And I'll tell you what that is, now. It's a feeling I have there's a catch in this love-making business. It's like a lot of other things – it's a let-down. There's something about a good-looking woman that makes you feel, if she'll treat you right, that at last you'll get clean out of yourself, like a door suddenly opening into another sort of life. But – afterwards – you see that it hasn't worked – it's just another let-down. Nearly everything's a let-down.

Priestley is also successful in conveying the mixed nature of human beings: greys, not black or white being the right colourings. As in *Eden End* his sharp eye for the way in which happiness can quickly shade into grief, how grief can be momentarily salved by love and affection, how love can be ruptured by deceit, deceit mitigated by confession. But, in the long run, despite the smooth skill of the transitions, despite the scenes that strike home, one cannot but be irritated by these people. It is not that one agrees with Ashley Dukes that 'an evening in their company on the plane of realist convention would be just terrible', because Priestley is not fundamentally concerned with them on the plane of realist convention, but that their unpleasing qualities are too firmly established in the beginning of the play, and the deeper realities which should mitigate our judgement of them later fail to do so. 'Once again' as Hughes says 'Priestley is confronted with a language he cannot persuade to leave the ground.' In point of fact Priestley seems to be doing everything in his power to make his language leave the ground, but he is far more successful with grounded speech than with speech that tries to soar. There are several language patterns in the play. In Act One he relies largely on a bare prose-style which has little associative quality, and whose main characteristic function is informative. It builds up a formidable picture of the day-to-day lives of these people, and it is only slightly personalised:

LADY S (*loudly to Chilham*): Is it true Verity Astley-Uppingham is still bouncing all round Germany shouting *Heil Hitler* in shorts and showing the storm troopers her very Nordic legs?

KATH: And I hope you're fond of music.

SIR J: Some.

CHILHAM (*the knowing one*): It's worse than that, our Berlin man says. You see—

SIR J: I don't know much about it, but I'm trying. Can't say fairer than that, can I?

LADY S: Who's doing Mercy Beaufort's publicity now – do you know?

CHILHAM: A boy who's just started. No good.

LADY S: Definitely lousy.

CHILHAM: She's trying to get it on the cheap.

LADY S: Mercy always tried to get everything on the cheap. She thinks life's one great bargain basement.

In Act Two Priestley introduces, in those monologues where the regrets, the lost opportunities, the long-lost happinesses and verities are revealed, an emotive prose:

> Years ago, when Rupert was about five, we used to go in Spring and stay in a little village in Hereford, not far from the Welsh border, and there it was all white with apple-blossom, and when the wind blew through the orchards it would snow apple-blossom, and little Rupert, who was a lovely happy child, would run among the trees and sometimes hide and then come dancing out, and laugh as the white petals were shaken down . . . a little boy . . . in an orchard . . . years ago . . . I've been back since, but it isn't the same . . . there doesn't seem as much apple-blossom now . . . it's changed . . . it's changed.

Also in Act Two Priestley gives Lengel a rhetorical emotive speech:

> . . . Once I thought, all this love, a senseless cruel thing, but I did not know then what the face of the world looked like without it, what a vast weary face it wears . . . a face rather like yours, you dull rich fool, rather like yours. And now its reflection fills my sky, and not four times a year do I see the sun, moon and stars. (*Angrily to them all*) You sit there like lumps of clay. By God, I'll fiddle the dead out of their graves – the dead men and women, the great hours that are dead but once were alive – and full of magic. Look out, you clods, the earth's stirring. . . .

In the same act Katherine and David are given a clipped prose recitative:

KATH: I should think so. When do we start?
DAVID (*thundering*): To-morrow, woman, to-morrow!

KATH: David, we *can't possibly*.
DAVID: To-morrow as ever was.
KATH: Darling, it simply can't be done.
DAVID: Have I to take some other woman, then?
KATH: I'd kill her.
DAVID: Then to-morrow it'll have to be.
KATH: I'll have to stay up half the night, there's so much to do.
DAVID: I've known you stay up half the night when—
KATH: I haven't time to listen to your foul remarks.
DAVID: There was nothing foul—
KATH: Millions of things to do. . . .

In Act Three Priestley, in the choric section where the characters group themselves according to the stage direction: '*The whole effect should suggest humanity itself outside time*', gives them a rhyming speech which graduates to prose incantation.

SIR J (*agitatedly*): I had a friend once – he was drowned.
TOM (*cool, far away*): A fool in a dream was all I found.
SHIEL (*calling*): Master, this music we seem to make. How does it come our way?
DR E (*the last of the dead*): The spirit stirs the depth of the lake, and we are the fountains that play.
The dead have faded out now, and the living make a close group as if they were one creature.
ANN (*in wondering tone*): I have gone down, down, and I am alive and awake, but I do not know who I am, and it does not seem to matter, for I am alive, awake, and have no sorrow.
PETER: I am remembering. . . . To crouch in the cave and see the great deer in the knobs and hollows of the stone and then to paint the great deer and the other creatures on the walls of the cave. . . .
KATH: It was hard at first to come down from the bare hills into the thick forests, with the children afraid of the shadows . . . but afterwards it was better. . . .
LADY S: When the men with dark faces who came for the metal

> went back to their ship we went with them, and afterwards when it was calm on a blue sea we sat and combed our yellow hair which the dark men loved. . . .

In these ways Priestley attempts to wrestle with his problem of the multi-dimensioned form of the play. The most obvious characteristic of these various modes of communication is that, despite the facial differences, they are all in fact basically concerned with communicating the same kind of material. Emotive or not, rhythmic or not, rhymed or not, this language is fundamentally concerned with the conveyance of information. Whether it be apple-blossom in Hereford, the near self-indulgence of the angry man who wants to make music, the swift recitative or the incantations, the basic function is the same, and the language does not give the effect of being attached to character. The emotiveness of the more rhythmical prose lies merely upon the surface of the lines – the characters speak but do not seem to feel. In the final burst of poetry and incantation there is a strong impression that Priestley, in one final effort to convey the mystery of the oneness of his characters, has taken over from them and allotted them speeches which they pronounce like automatons. The flat prose which Priestley habitually gives to characters and which gives the actor tremendous elbow room to make associative is his dominant mode, and all his other experiments with language are too closely derived from this source. Thus his 'poetry' and his incantation have their roots in the ground and the wings do not grow naturally out of them but are stuck upon them.

Nevertheless, what he has attempted in this play is the immensely difficult task of widening the function of the naturalistic play. He has tried to make a poetic conception viable to theatrical communication. This task alone is daunting, but the task was increased in severity by his failure to discover a language which was flexible enough to withstand the sharp fluctuations of the play's movement and meaning. His language, obviously splintered as it is in this play, goes counter to the play's main direction: to show the oneness of the human condition. But the defeat Priestley has suffered here is a noble one.

Priestley's time-plays are a more remarkable body of writing than they have ever been given credit for. The list of their strengths and weaknesses is easily drawn up. On the credit side – the ingenuity with which the time-theories are juggled, the often brilliant manipulation of theatrical devices, the interest and frequent excitement of the narrative line of the plays, the sensitivity, at best, of the playwright's awareness of the nuances of human behaviour, and his apprehension of the flux of human emotions, the ability to convince us of the absence of chronological time, the diversity of setting and theme. On the debit side – the sometimes slavish catering for audience expectations, providing naturalism when it is not needed, flat prose when associative prose is needed, the tentative flirtations with 'poetic' writing, the occasional lapses into explicit statements when implicit statements are called for, the tendency for characters to illustrate rather than embody the theme, the compromises by which the dramatic logic is sometimes sacrificed to the contrived ending. Yet, to be aware of this balance sheet gives no more sense of the valid quality of these plays than a bank statement tells a human heart. These plays form one of the very few corporate bodies of dramatic writing, certainly in this country, in this century. Eliot alone rivals Priestley in this, and, in some degree, shares Priestley's faults. But both of them, in their plays, exhibit a unity of conception of the human scene. Neither Priestley nor Eliot gives the impression of jumping willy-nilly from one dramatic excercise to another. In his group of time-plays Priestley does not seem to be saying merely that now the time has come for another play, what shall it be about. There is a sense that the plays forced themselves upon him, though this is not to deny that many of his non-time-plays seem to have had him forced upon them. The plays are, therefore, a series of variations upon Priestley's abiding conception of the nature of man and his environment in place and time. To an extent he is perhaps too aware, for his own good, of the appetites of audiences. The visionary man is too much at the mercy of the theatre-man. He has not been wilful enough with audience expectation, persuading and cajoling when he might have hit them more forcefully. This weakness is most obviously exemplified in his use of language: the poet in him is allowed the faculty of seeing the ironic patterns of human behaviour, but is not allowed the grace, when it is required, of poetic communication in words. Many of the themes, situations and incidents in the time-plays lie below the surface of conventional naturalism and ask for language which itself would embody the texture of the world he is trying to communicate. There may not be enough of the verbal poet in Priestley for him to attempt this, but there is another possible explanation.

Priestley, like Eliot, is concerned with realities which lie behind the apparent actualities of the common world. For Eliot, those realities are spiritual and religious, for Priestley they are magical. Eliot's concern is to show how these realities are at work, if we could but surrender to them within the fabric of our so-called everyday world. Priestley's concern is very similar – to convince that the magic and the mystery swirls about us, that to be aware of it is to be aware of the oneness of humanity. What both dramatists face is the problem of translating the unknown into terms of the known, of translating the poetry of the world behind this world into a language which gives it a familiar currency. Eliot's reply is to diminish his poetic communication to such an extent that it becomes flatly out of key with its theme and its characters; Priestley's reply is to, rather obviously, hurl chunks of 'poetic' language into the plays. Neither will do to sustain what has to be said. At the same time, it is possible to apprehend that what is being said is important and worthwhile. The problem about both Eliot and Priestley is the problem of men who exist in a state of imbalance between the realities of the imagination and the facts of the everyday world.

PART THREE

CHAPTER FIVE

Comedy and Society

The great energy which Priestley has expended during his writing career is nowhere better represented than in the variety of modes and forms which he has employed. His most enduring work is to be found in no more than a handful of plays, but there are many others which show theatrical virtuosity of a high order and which entitle him, even without the claims made by the more considerable plays, to a place in the history of the twentieth century theatre. These other plays divide themselves into a large group of comedies, a smaller group of 'sociological' plays, and a number of entertainments whose main claim to notice is their efficiency as products for special occasions or for the commercial stage. With two exceptions – *Laburnum Grove*, and *When We Are Married*, the corpus of comic plays which is included in Volume Two of the Collected Plays lacks the thematic interest and dramatic depth of the plays from Volume One discussed in the last chapter. Priestley's choice of plays for inclusion in these volumes was careful – he did not include a number which, by any assessing standard, would only call for a cursory glance, though they will for years to come go the rounds in amateur drama festivals. *Laburnum Grove* and *When We Are Married* are the only plays in Volume Two which preserve the nostalgia which is associated with most of the plays in Volume One. Priestley is, in fact, less remembered as a comic dramatist, than as one who exploited unusual themes in an often unusual manner. This is surprising in the light of the output devoted to comedy, a fact noted by Ivor Brown: 'A considerable section of his dramatic writing has been deliberately aimed at the public who come for a good laugh.' It is also surprising in the light of his excellent critical assessments of humour and of the English Comic Characters, and, indeed, of the personality of the man. It is of humour, in the widest sense of the word, that one thinks in Priestley's company. The image of the angry old Yorkshireman, prickling with dissent and awkwardness, is only part of a larger canvas in which the surrounds are painted in less strident and lighter colours which are mutated constantly by sentiment and regretfulness. But the eyes that look out of the picture have a comic focus. They look for foibles that can be satirised, for rich character whose humours may be charted, for verbal wit that can be matched or remembered; and, most certainly, for the violent antic hay of tumbles and falls, of improbable actions and stupendous follies.

The variety of Priestley's response to comedy is best shown in some of his comments on Falstaff in *The English Comic Characters*. 'His character', he writes, 'is, as it were, a test of our sense of humour.' He sees Falstaff owing his predominant position among comic figures to the fact that, in him, the expanse and the extremes of the spectrum of comedy are to be found from 'the clown that delights the crowd' to the 'subtle character that engages the philosopher'. The catholic taste implied here finds its way into Priestley's plays. Indeed, all of them tend towards or explicitly arrive at the happy contented resolution contiguous to a comic view of life. Even in those scenes in which a pathetic event removes a character from the action, as in the case of Carol in *Time and the Conways*, there is a kind of justification for her death implied which turns any sense of waste or bitterness into a glow of sad-sweet regret; in the end all is worthwhile. The inclination towards the acceptable conclusion in a Priestley play too often takes the action through or towards a mere sentimentality when the dramatic logic suggests quite another destination. It is not that one eschews the happy ending, but that the happy ending does not always have to repose in the emotionally vibrant, the sentimental.

In his comedies Priestley attempts several different modes and, typically, often indulges in technical experiments at the same time. He has always found comedy more difficult to write than any other dramatic form. In his preface to Volume Two he distinguishes three types of comedy – High, Light, and Broad.

Although, as he rightly states, high comedy, by which he means intellectual comedy, has never been popular with English writers and audiences, he has written several plays in this manner. Some of his best writing (certainly in terms of language) is to be found in sophisticates like *Ever Since Paradise*, and the unpublished *The White Countess*, and *The Pavilion of Masks* which had its first production at Bristol in 1963, though written some years before. His version of Iris Murdoch's *A Severed Head*, prepared by them both, is perhaps the most extreme form of high comedy in Priestley's definition of the term as a playing of ideas. He is not precise, in defining, in the preface, the second category of comedy – light – except to say that it is a form which provides 'admirable vehicles for popular and highly skilled star performers, without whom these flimsy pieces are apt to look very thin indeed'. He dislikes the form because it lacks the strength of situation and character of the third type – broad comedy. It is a safe inference that he means the kind of comedy which hangs, with a dutiful nod to credibility, between farce and naturalism. Priestley declares that he has not included any of this type in his collected volume, but *Good Night Children*, a satirical comment on the establishment of Broadcasting, seems to be of this type, and hardly raises itself above the level of an idle entertainment. *Mr Kettle and Mrs Moon* is not, in his opinion, a light comedy. He declares it to be a broad comedy with quite serious ideas. It is not easy, in the absence of professional productions in this country, to test Priestley's claim for the play; a recent amateur production gave the impression that the 'seriousness' of the play was a minimal ingredient and that its overdrawn characters and exaggerated situations serve only to produce a somewhat humdrum inconsequentiality. The play, however, has been immensely popular both in Western Germany and in many of the Iron Curtain countries. But it is broad comedy which appeals to him most, and he believes this to be 'peculiarly suitable' to the English temperament, being less 'intellectually austere' than high comedy, and richer in character and situation than light comedy.

The plays in Volume Two in fact exhibit the mode of broad comedy in *When We Are Married* and *Laburnum Grove*, high comedy in *Ever Since Paradise* and satirical comedy in *Bees On the Boat Deck*, with some pretensions to it in *Good Night Children*. *The Golden Fleece* is best characterised as a sentimental social-comedy. Yet whatever the mode and label, and whatever the technical experimentation, there are several common factors to all these plays. Perhaps the most obvious is that Priestley is essentially a writer of purposeful comedy. It is one of the peculiarities of the English conception of drama that tragedy or the serious play (which in theatre jargon is often designated by the word 'drama') has automatically been associated with purpose. The assumption is frequently made that if a playwright has anything of moment to communicate, then it can only, and ought only, to be done through the medium of the 'serious' play. Catastrophe, gloom or deep speculativeness are, for many people, the only correlatives to serious intention. The history of the theatre in this country shows that even when, as in some Restoration drama, in Shaw, there has been, via comedy, a palpable assault made upon moral or social sensibilities with a serious purpose, the reception of the play by the majority of audiences has been confined to the top-dressing of 'fun'. The English are the most difficult people in the world to rouse to action or to speculation through the medium of creative art – the revelations of vicious satire, of social inequality, in writers of past and present hit a target, but it is nearly always the wrong target. The English do not require their laughter to be adulterated by other considerations. The great comic figures of English writing – Falstaff, Micawber, Doolittle, all of whom are, in a sense, exemplars of the commentating, judging 'serious' purpose of their creators, are generally regarded as 'wonderful comic types', and the matter is left at that. The English do not learn wisdom from their comedies, but their laughter is left to feed in a heedless isolation.

It is the more surprising that the well-springs of rich purposeful comedy in this country have never dried up, though, as in the drama of the 19th century the yield was low. Habitually, rich meaningful comedy has had to give first place in the affections of the English to farce or the frothy inconsequence of commercial light comedy. But the notion of comedy as a purposeful form, capable of expressing meanings of value beyond the reach of mere entertainment for the two-hours traffic of the stage has been relentlessly held on to by writers from Shakespeare onwards, and in the twentieth century has gushed into prominence in the work of Shaw, Fry, Pinter.

Priestley's comedies exhibit a purposefulness, a calculated design, upon the sensibilities of the audience. In this they take us nearer to the polemical social observer, and away from the visionary of the time-plays. In many of the comedies a steady gaze is directed at man's antics, not in the double-dimension of time now and time then, but in the society which he has inherited and to which his attitudes and behaviour will contribute for good or ill. The emphasis is on 'antics' since Priestley's view of man in society, particularly when he is engaged in selfish pursuits through materialistic and predatory means, is essentially that of the caricaturist. There remains a very strong impression that when Priestley looks at the iniquities of cupidity, class-distinction, pompous social climbing, materialism – his favourite comic themes – what he sees is comic human action, which is never very far from the sinister. He pushes his pen into bolder strokes which exaggerate and condemn by implication at the same time. Although he does not always see men as either black or white, there is little doubt that he tends to see them in terms in which the bad veers towards the monstrous in appearance and behaviour, and the good towards the small and reserved. In *Bees On the Boat Deck*, within two minutes of having arrived aboard ship Lord Cottingley, 'a robust, well-nourished, middle-aged man, with an easy genial manner' is in cahoots with a gullible scientist who has invented a new explosive:

> *Lord Cottingley and Fletherington, who have been talking quietly, can now be heard.*
>
> COTTINGLEY (*very genially*): Well, that's very interesting, very interesting indeed. I might be able to put your explosive on the market. That is, of course, if I were satisfied that it is all you think it is.
>
> FLETHERINGTON (*wistfully*): I'd like to try it on this ship—

COTTINGLEY (*thoughtfully*): Would you now, would you? On this ship.

FLETHERINGTON (*dreamily*): A beautiful test.

COTTINGLEY (*thoughtfully*): Oh, magnificent, of course! Just what you want.

FLETHERINGTON: Yes. And you'd see for yourself then.

COTTINGLEY: Exactly. And if it was *my* ship, you could do it. That is, of course, if the thing were done in such a way that the insurance people didn't object, but paid up afterwards....

Short of actually appearing in a black cloak, moustachio'd, and with a smoking bomb barely concealed in his crooked elbow, Lord Cottingley could not conceivably make a more villainous entrance.

Captain Mellock, another visitor to the ship is a '*trim, athletic looking man in his late thirties, not bad looking in a rather hard style. He has a romantic scar on his face. He wears no hat, a dark blue uniform shirt with a tiny Union Jack on one side and a number of military ribbons on the other, and neat dark trousers, with pockets big enough for a revolver. The whole effect is that of a Fascist uniform.*'

Here it might be urged that since Priestley was attempting to write 'political satire in terms of farcical comedy' there is every justification for the almost sensationally broad character like Cottingley and Mellock. Still, the contrast between these two and, say, an 'ordinary good bloke' like Bob Patch (even the nomenclature seems from a different country of the mind) or Hilda – 'a pleasant looking girl about twenty-five' – is startling; it gives the play an uneasy rhythm, so that it teeters between apparent naturalism and horny-handed satire. The play commits the sin, for satire, of not maintaining consistency of mood and characterisation.

Even in plays where there is little satire, like *When We Are Married* and *The Golden Fleece*, the tendency to divide mankind into the comically incredible and the reserved and quiescent, is at work. In the former play, Parker, the pompous small-town councillor, speaks to his wife:

Always reasonable – *and* reliable. But all the time, getting on, goin' up i' the world. Never satisfied with what 'ud do for most men – no, steadily moving on an' on, up an' up – cashier, manager, share in the business – councillor this year, alderman next, perhaps mayor soon – that's how it's been an' that's how it will be. Y'know, Annie, I've sometimes thought that right at first you didn't realise just what you'd picked out o't'lucky bag. Ay!

The wonderful swell of this monstrous ego dilates before us. Parker is sketched with a caricaturist's efficiency. But, in the same play, his wife is a decent reasonable woman who has always sacrificed her desires to the monumental pomposity of her husband. Her character, representing a goodness, a kindness and a shrewdness, is painted in light pastel shades. There is no exaggeration here. Again, in *The Golden Fleece*, the crushingly insufferable Lady Leadmill is caricatured with joyful abandon:

LADY L (*cutting in ruthlessly*): And the lantern slides were most peculiar. Some of them had nothing whatever to do with it. I distinctly recognised Market Harborough once – and another time Bury St Edmunds. Ridiculous of the Colonel to say I dozed off. How could I have recognised Bury St Edmunds if I'd dozed off? Eh, Miss Sell?
MISS SELL (*timidly*): Well, I did think once . . .
LADY L: Nonsense, you never thought at all.

And the decent 'norm' at the opposite end not only of the comic spectrum but of the social scale, is found in the buxom, motherly, kindly, Molly Crudden who, though she comes into money, is not altered by it, and knows instinctively how to make it work for good: 'Everything depends really just on how people treat each other. If people aren't willing, and kind, and hopeful, then it's all up. But if they are, then it's all right.'

Priestley's comedies sometimes therefore take on the aspect of a series of Rake's Progresses, whose reprehensible if comic activities are matched by and finally overcome by a decent ordinariness. It is not that the rakes and wrongdoers ever really strike one as being utterly and irredeemably vicious – there is no convincingly evil character in any of the comedies (though one sometimes feels that there ought to be). Priestley's fascist – Captain Mellor – is Ruritanian; upper-class selfishness and materialism (Lady Leadmill) is no more than ridiculous. No-one suffers very palpably before right overcomes wrong.

Though most of the comedies have their source in a sense of social injustice, its course is usually made to take a mellow direction; there is always the implied belief that all manner of things will turn out for the best. This, it may be argued, was always the way with comedy, but it may be pointed out that Priestley's social conscience is not allowed to take to their logical conclusions many of his own premises. Some might be prepared to condemn him for an unreal optimism in which the polemicist becomes the sentimentalist, but one cannot condemn him for his relentless pursuit of particular social injustices or malpractices. As Ivor Brown writes: 'It is a deplorably non-adult view of the theatre's function that rules out as non-theatrical any dramatic discussion of problems which are not purely personal.' At the same time it must be faced that the relentless pursuit often degenerates into a tender trot towards a roseate conclusion. Even *When We Are Married* which shows, with a great accuracy of mood, language and situation, the ridiculous illusions of small-town government, and in which the comic monstrosities are given full rein, relaxes too comfortably at the end:

PARKER: Well, that beats me. I've always seemed to myself an exciting sort of chap. (*To Annie*) Anyhow, stingy or whatever I am, I'm still your husband.

ANNIE: So it looks as if I'll have to make the best of you.

MARIA: We'll all have to make the best of each other. But then perhaps it's what we're here for.

HELLIWELL: That's right, love.

What has been, in parts, as trenchant as Molière, quite suddenly abandons its sharp consistency. It is not that we are left believing, in a hurried rush of reconciliation, that these pompous councillors with their contentious wives have learned humility, but that a happy tie-up is thrust upon them. They are bigger as characters when Priestley keeps them in his sharper mood, and what would have been entirely a rich comic indictment, slackens into 'entertainment'. Yet this is small criticism and, indeed, a careful producer might well preserve the play's early integrity by some ironic pointing of the last few lines.

There is, however, a more serious softening of movement and tone in *The Golden Fleece*. Priestley tells us that his intention was 'to tell the story of sudden vast gains' as a result of market speculations. The play leaves the reader in two minds about its intentions and its conclusions, and though Priestley may consider that it is pretty 'rough stuff', it is printed in the Collected Plays, and it is, despite its roughness, representative of the ways and means employed by Priestley in his comic writing. Is it an indictment of the misery, grief and cupidity created by the system of playing the markets? Or is it a modern fairy-story of an unexpected advance from rags to riches as a result of speculation? There is equal evidence for both possibilities. In the first category, the iniquities of speculation and gross materialism are shown in the gorged upper-class characters – notably Lady Leadmill and her sycophants, who are represented best by the ageing Dr Plumweather: 'He may look a harmless old pussycat, but he's really a pest and a menace. Instead of being a man of science, which he pretends to be, he's something between an old charlatan and a rich old woman's butler. He doesn't speak or even think the truth.'

Their iniquity is shown by such explicit condemnation as we get from the young Doctor Alec:

> It wouldn't matter if there was just one of her, but there are thousands and thousands of her – like – like stuffed old frogs – crocodiles – dinosaurs. This country's full of 'em. And there they are doing no good to anybody, not even to themselves – and because they have the money, demanding services all day long from other people.

The results of speculation are clearly stated:

> Well, it isn't just entering figures into a book and finding you've got lots and lots of money to spend. It's grabbing power, Molly. You're playing with people's lives – the lives of thousands and thousands of people you've never even seen. . . . People's savings disappear. They have to give up their houses, sell their furniture. Kids have to leave school. People can't take the holidays they planned. Fellows are sacked – middle-aged men turned out of jobs.

Its evils are represented by the chief character, Will, whom we first meet when he is a Night Porter. We learn that he has been a financier, has been in gaol, and now regards money thus: 'Now the first thing you have to do is to take most of the power away from money. In fact private money should be just pocket money. That's the only kind of money I believe in – pocket money.' But at the first whiff of an opportunity to re-involve himself in a big way in speculation on the market, the old vice grips him again and he becomes 'a changed man'. Molly, on whose behalf he is speculating, cries out: 'You're different already. Not half so nice. . . . I don't want any more.'

But throughout the play, the results of this evil in which all the characters are embroiled, because the charlady Molly comes into a vast sum, have no gripping reality. Perhaps the most pathetic creature, a victim of the cruel and demanding snobbery which money can create, is Miss Sell. She is a typed secretary companion to Lady Leadmill, she is the eternal fall-girl, mousy, tramped on, butted, scared and reviled. But she triumphs in the end. Molly, in love with Will, the now-substantiated Night Porter is also distressed by the effects of money on him. Nevertheless she gets over her difficulties with only a little more effort than that displayed by Miss Sell. She disappears for a while, then returns to the hotel, having spiked Will's guns effectively by revealing his identity to another speculator. Finally she gives a good deal of her money away, but retains enough 'pocket money' to initiate a number of good deeds. Her conscience is salved, her Will is saved from himself, and everyone is taken care of very nicely thank you – by 'pocket money'. Will is given the managership of a new kind of hotel, bought out of 'pocket money'. 'For people who've been working too hard and not just eating too much, for men who are some use in the world, for women who deserve to be waited on for a change – for real people.' Will's reaction to this is ominous: 'I'm the one man in England who could tackle this job for you. Good ideas! I've got thousands of 'em. Why look here . . .' and, with great zest, he produces a note-book. It looks very much as if it won't be long before he is on the rampage again.

The condemnation of money is not dramatically justified by the slack and unconvincing examples of its ill-effects and usages. But, ironically, even those like Molly Cudden and the young doctor who come out strongest against its evil usages benefit, in a fairy-tale way, from its powers. The young doctor, by Molly's generosity, finds himself with his own clinic. Truly the rewards of those who can talk like he can are great. In fact he receives a dividend which puts him morally right as well as getting him the right girl. Veronica, beloved by him, turns out, after all, not to be the snobby little rich girl he thought she was, but a hard-working underpaid secretary. Molly fixes it all. The young doctor, without stirring a finger, though admittedly having to make a few long speeches about the evil of our monetary system, becomes head of his own clinic, gets the girl and a well-turned-out moral system, to boot. On the other hand, the rather charming Lord Fleetfield, the arch-speculator, seems more rational, more credible, and certainly more attractive. His is a less opaque and static nobility than the young doctor's:

LORD F: In other words, you'll hand over your interest to the government, in the form of a public trust?

MOLLY: Yes, that's it.

LORD F: And do you suppose the government will manage these affairs any better than my friends and I would?

MOLLY: Well, if they don't, we can change the government, can't we?

LORD F (*smiling*): Possibly, though my friends and I generally have a hand in changing governments too.

So it seems, in short, that the arguments against speculative money repose in unbelievable characters, and they do so in such a dewy-eyed fashion that the play lacks clarity of purpose, and seems equivocal in its attitude. We come, in the end, to accept neither the arguments for nor the arguments against good, bad, or indifferent usage of money.

The blunting of the social criticism in *The Golden Fleece*, by the failure to maintain a consistent attitude towards the theme and the characterisation, is also manifest in *Bees On the Boat Deck*. It has already been noted how, in the characters of Cottingley and the fascist officer, the art of caricature is the dominant mode, whereas, in others, the mode is closer to flat naturalism. The conditions of the 1930s in which economic planning was based on expediency and human effort was grossly wasted, is the theme of the play. The fine vessel, *SS. Gloriana*, beached irrevocably up a backwater, may be said to represent England. She has a caretaker crew of two – Grindley and Patch who knew and sailed in her when she proudly breasted the high seas. Now she awaits the breaker or, if Cottingley has his way, she will be the victim of an experiment to test the efficacy of a new explosive with resultant profits to the same Cottingley. The several visitors to the ship are a cross section of population. The scientist, amiable enough, who has no moral control over his own inventiveness, the fascist politician, the small-time shopkeeper, who takes his truth and his values from the newspapers; the police sergeant, not sure who is guilty and who is innocent; the spoilt upper class young woman. Of the lot, only Gridley, Patch and Hilda (sought by the police for an act of mercy) have any unselfishness in them. It is, at face value, an attractive enough framework for satire, but as in *The Golden Fleece*, the dramatic movement becomes blurred. In the first place there is too much coming and going; in the second place there is a tremendous gap between the trio who are ranged on the 'good' side and the culpable ones. Once again indictment and satire become mixed with a fairy-tale quality, as in the scene where the champions of right roar in like heroes from the Boy's Own Paper:

> *Patch suddenly drops down on deck from some convenient part of the superstructure. He is extremely dirty and dishevelled and his clothes are torn, as if he had been crawling and climbing for the last hour. He has a stout iron bar with him, and is a very angry and formidable figure.*
>
> PATCH (*very menacingly*): Don't move, any of you. The first man who moves, I'll flatten him with this.
>
> FLETHERINGTON (*mildly*): But – Mr Patch –
>
> PATCH (*menacingly*): Don't talk either. I've been crawling and climbing for nearly an hour like a ruddy cockroach through the foulest holes in this ship, and I'm ready to kill somebody. So keep still and shut up, before I flatten you to the deck.

Hero number two arrives almost immediately, and his appearance and words take us, if possible, even nearer to those long-lost lads of our boyhood reading:

> *Gridley climbs out, very hot and dirty, in a furious rage, also holding a thick iron rod. He is a terrifying figure. At the sight of the three standing there, he gives a great roar of inarticulate rage.*
>
> GRIDLEY (*roaring*): Wa-a-ah! You bloody toads! You poxed-up rats! You red-eyed stinking weasels!

The result, as in *The Golden Fleece*, is to reduce the culpability of the exploiters and revolutionaries to the level of pantomime villains. Priestley who, in his articles and autobiographies, reveals a fierce, consistent and rational concern about social injustice, here leaves these qualities in abeyance, and the entertainer who loves a charade, and knows his audience to love a charade, takes over. To make this criticism is not to forget that in *The Golden Fleece* and *Bees On the Boat Deck* the intention is comic. But both plays pass that point where their meaningful themes are being exemplified and lived out in credible characterisation. The themes become exploited for ends which contradict them. They leave the impression that, bad as the villainy is, it is only so for the duration of the play. The gallery of the culpable in both plays, and in *Good Night Children* to which the same criticisms apply, seems to be playing a part into which it enters with great zest in the full knowledge that it is all a game. If Priestley had intended this merely, then he should not have been so insistent in his prefaces, and in many explicit speeches in the plays, on his concern for the iniquities represented by his chosen themes. Ben Jonson in *Volpone* does not cut the ties which bind his theme (a contiguous one to that of *The Golden Fleece*) to his characterisation. Satire and meaningful comedy fail when characters are pushed beyond the point where, however fantastic they may be, the audience is able to believe in them. It is perhaps a fault that Priestley inherited from his close reading of Dickens where so often the purposefulness of the comic spirit is blunted by the demands of the merely entertaining.

But there are three plays in the volume of comedies which show clearly that Priestley is capable of overriding these faults in a way which indicates that, when they are present, they may be due to hasty writing. He has stated that *The Golden Fleece* involved him in a good deal of work intermittently over long periods. Nevertheless *When We Are Married*, *Laburnum Grove*, and *Ever Since Paradise* are of a higher order of creativity than the rest. They are all purposeful comedies in the sense that their themes imply a social comment. *Laburnum Grove* is the earliest, and was produced soon after *Dangerous Corner*, in 1933. It has a similar taut precision of construction to the earlier play, though, because its characterisation is more highly developed, it does not seem as mechanically contrived as the later *The Golden Fleece*, the play has to do with money, but here the theme is not submerged, and the play consists of a series of well-constructed variations upon the way in which people react to the idea of wealth – both ill- and well-gotten.

Priestley writes that 'at the time I wrote it, when I was also gathering material for *English Journey*, I was very suspicious about our financial system, if only because the banks appeared to flourish when industry was failing'. The plot is simple in outline but neatly devious in its meanderings. In the comfortable suburbia of Shooters Green, at the house called Laburnum Grove, George Radfern's family lives in apparently typical suburban uneventfulness. It lives a life of mixed boredom, family tension, bickering, well-smoothed comfort, and it is heading towards a future which seems to hold exactly the same ingredients. Mrs Radfern is a kindly housewife, shrewd and not easily moved, but not too long-suffering. Her daughter, Elsie, is kicking against the pricks of suburban ordinariness. The 'guests' – Mr and Mrs Baxley – are relatives who have just come home from out East, where Baxley had a minor job which, by hindsight, seems to him very major. They are spongers. Mr Radfern is in the paper industry. He makes many journeys about the country for his firm. He is a wise, kind, gentle man, but he happens also to be a key figure in a gang of counterfeiters, and his friend Joe Fletter, with whom he spends many a happy evening hour in the greenhouse, is one of his contact men.

The play develops along the obvious line that it will be a shock to Laburnum Grove to discover the duplicity of Mr Radfern, and also along the line that if it be justifiable for banks and speculators to 'make' money then it is equally justifiable for the private citizen. Both these lines are present but they are cleverly entwined by a third line by whose influence a light morality finally emerges in which one person after another is put to the test and judged by his or her reaction to the idea of stolen money. In fact, on superficial evidence, they all emerge pretty well from their examination – even the most covetous like Mr Baxley. They will not touch tainted money. But Priestley has indulged in a neat double-take here. In the belief that they will all be tainted if Radfern's secret is discovered by the police, all his family, except for his wife, display, in varying degrees, a faithlessness. The greedy Baxley finds respectability more honourable than he thought, the daughter yearns for Laburnum Grove to return to its dull ordinariness, and her fiancé abandons her with rapidity when he concludes that they who touch pitch will be defiled.

Mrs Radfern alone accepts the situation with a simplicity which comes from her completely unselfish love for her husband. The comedy is purposeful about the pretensions of a middle-class attitude which aspires to, or fools itself into believing that it is a cut above its environment, but runs screaming back to its arid roots at the first onset of the extraordinary.

One's acceptance of this as something more meaningful than a cheap trick of the dramatist, by which characters are mercilessly placed because of their own innate decency into a situation where that decency seems petty, depends entirely on how far one accepts the premise that Radfern's illicit activity is no more illegitimate than the legal machinations of banks and speculators. Priestley succeeds completely in convincing us of the fundamental decency of Radfern, of his quiet wisdom, his sense of the absurd, and his dedication to this proposition:

> Well, a lot of people think this depression in trade is chiefly due to the fact that there isn't enough money in circulation. Like playing a game with counters and finding you haven't enough counters to go round. Our organisation – my associates and myself – have been quietly busy these last few years trying to remedy this unhappy state of things. It started in America – forging and counterfeiting bonds and notes – and then developed here, but just lately the American end has been doing badly, almost stopped. But we're doing quite nicely here, and sometimes I think that things in England would have been worse if it hadn't been for us. In fact you might say we've been doing our bit.

This is calm nonsense, acceptable roguery. Priestley has not made the mistake of stating his theme with seriousness only to turn his back on it, as in the plays discussed above. Here the irony makes its point. What increases the irony is that Laburnum Grove itself would have been the loser without his illicit operations:

> Tainted money. You've eaten it and drunk it and it's clothed and housed you and taken you to the pictures and sent you to

> the seaside. If I'd gone on trying to make an honest living, I don't know where you'd have been now, Elsie. As it is, look at us. So nicely off that Harold here – and your Uncle Bernard here – are both hoping I'll lend them several hundred pounds each, on very doubtful security.

Thus the holier-than-thou company which surrounds Radfern cannot kick against the pricks. They are already involved; in protesting their middle-class morality, they are not only biting the hand that feeds them, they are also refusing to face their own situation. We in the audience are convinced, and being thus convinced that Radfern not only has the whip hand but justifiably has it, we forget that a trick has been pulled. The family did not know that they were living on tainted money – how then can they be blamed for reacting so strongly against it? But Priestley is so successful in making Radfern attractively plausible, and some of his family so predatory that, emotionally, we accept that Radfern is right and the rest wrong. Priestley calls it an immoral comedy, and this is accurate because it supports the proposition that theft is justifiable. Its morality, however, lies in its revelation of the blindness, pettiness and timidity of those who have pretensions beyond their capabilities or courage.

When We Are Married, whose astonishing success has been a surprise to Priestley, is a richer exercise in the theme of pretentiousness. It is richer, not because it is subtler in theme than *Laburnum Grove*, but because the characterisation is more developed. *When We Are Married* is perhaps the only play of Priestley's which totally convinces one of the complete identification of character and language and situation. Even more, there is a self-sufficiency in the characterisation which is rare in the other plays. The characters here do not seem compromised between a life of their own and a role which the author has designed for them and which he is determined they should fulfil, whatever the cost in credibility. If it be true that Priestley has not created one completely memorable character, comic or otherwise, it is equally true that he has created memorable groups of characters, of which the group in *When We Are Married* is the most ineffaceable.

Singly observed (except for the photographer Ormonroyd) these characters do not have a strong presence; they flourish from the brilliant juxtapositions, from the fact of the group. *When We Are Married* is the comic proof of Priestley's incessant sense of the power and magic of the close circle of people. The clue to his success in this play is in his prefatory statement:

> I enjoyed writing this broadly farcical comedy because I had a lot of fun remembering and then using various aspects of West Riding life and manners known to my boyhood. The plot is nonsensical but the characters and their attitudes and their talk are all authentic.

The statement is strictly true. This is the only play of his in which there is a consistent absence of the flat language which elsewhere makes so many demands on the actor and reduces the sense of urgent reality of the character and the situation. The atmosphere grows into the broadly farcical but, except at the very end of the play where, as has been suggested, there is some compromise, Priestley never allows us to forget the purposefulness of the comedy. So magnetic is the tremendous self-deluding of the majority of this group gathered together to celebrate a joint wedding anniversary, that it is easy to escape other sharp purposes in the play. Self-deception, pomposity, expediency, indecisiveness, snobbery – all these flaws, comically displayed – emerge from the simple equation that none of the couples is really married at all. The great balloons of their pride begin to wrinkle into smallness by this one well-aimed pin: 'Joe, Herbert, they mustn't know. Nobody must know. Why – we'd be laughed right out o' town. What – Alderman Helliwell – Councillor Albert Parker – Herbert Soppitt – all big men at chapel too! I tell you, if this leaks out – we're done!'

But again, as in *Laburnum Grove*, Priestley does not merely write a variation upon one given theme. Other tunes, some of them wistful, are played. The long-hidden shynesses of youth, for example, which threw Soppitt and Annie away from their mutual love into others' arms, are beguilingly heard:

ANNIE: . . . D'you remember that time, just after you'd first come to Cleckleywyke, when we all went on that choir trip to Barnard Castle?

SOPPITT: I do, Annie. As a matter of fact, I fancy I was a bit sweet on you then.

ANNIE: You fancy you were! I know you were, Herbert Soppitt. Don't you remember coming back in the wagonette?

SOPPITT: Ay!

ANNIE: Those were the days!

SOPPITT: Ay!

ANNIE: Is that all you can say – Ay?

SOPPITT: No. But I might say too much.

ANNIE: I think I'd risk it for once, if I were you.

SOPPITT: And what does that mean, Annie?

ANNIE: Never you mind. But you haven't forgotten that wagonette, have you?

SOPPITT: Of course I haven't.

The covert affairs with which a respectable small-town dignitary gives piquancy to a life otherwise dedicated to the pursuit of the conventional are brought in to the open. As in *Clochemerle* the tightrope of respectability is thin and swaying: 'I'd known him here in Cleckleywyke, but it was at Blackpool we really got going. He said he was feeling lonely – and you know what men are, when they think they're feeling lonely, specially at Blackpool.'

The chicanery of small-town power complexes, basing their judgements upon prejudice, is revealed: 'No, as soon as they told me he's a southerner and his name's Gerald, I said: "We don't want him" I said.'

The realities of personal relationships held for so long beneath an iron lid of conventional activity and gesture, explode to the surface when the one convention that keeps the lid in place – the marriage bond – flies in their faces:

MARIA: But, Joe, you're not going to tell me that you feel different – just because of – this accident?

JOE (*solemnly*): I won't tell a lie, love. I can't help it, but ever since I've known I'm not married I've felt *most peculiar*.

When We Are Married is epic on a small comic scale, for it encompasses a world, and though we witness its present tense, its history is implicit, and the dim map of its future can be discerned. The play is not satirical in the sense in which satire makes a comic assault upon turpitude with a moral intent. Rather it has more of that spirit, typical of Chaucer, in which character is given the freedom to reveal uninhibitedly how, if at all, he fouls his own nest. 'Every time he opens his mouth at the Town Hall, he puts his foot in it.'

Ever Since Paradise is the most sophisticated of Priestley's comedies. It has élan of style and a graceful and extrovert theatricality. Priestley's claim that if properly produced it should have 'the air of a gay charade' is very supportable. It makes little attempt at naturalistic verisimilitude. All that is needed for presentation is two grand pianos on each side of an acting area, backed by a recessed or curtained area, in front of which are two chairs for the commentators. The method used is similar to that of Thornton Wilder's *Our Town*, in which actors engage in direct talk to the audience out of character, and certain sketches are played to demonstrate in action what has been said. Priestley has said that he would like to work with a non-proscenium flexible stage, and he is much attracted by theatre-in-the-round. This play gives evidence of his ability to write in a form suitable to a non-formalised stage, in which there is no slavish quest for illusion. The prefatory note refers to the play as a Discursive Entertainment, chiefly referring to Love and Marriage. To some extent it has that Shavian quality in which the relationships between men and women seem to be conducted in the spirit of a military campaign of wit and intelligence. As in *Candida*, the sexes here are embattled. But Priestley, unlike Shaw, is not concerned with driving home one, or several, particular points of view. Priestley is more concerned with showing us the broader panorama of the campaign by which men and women come together, part, and (in this case because it is a comedy) come together again. Whereas Shaw proceeds from generalities to particularities in his depictions of the campaigns of love and marriage, Priestley remains always in the realm of generalisation, and allows both sides to emerge without inflicting a certain moral or social or sexual direction on the play. The fact that it has a happy ending should come as no surprise, for the whole affair is conducted very much in the spirit of the game. Each set of three couples is both observer and participant, and one, Philip and Joyce, act as commentators by the unusual and engaging method of accompanying the various moods of the piece with piano music.

To call the piece purposeful might seem too heavy-handed a description since its touch is deliberately light and gives no hint of the social reformer. Irony rather than satire is its main weapon, and it is employed with great variety of effect. Most notably Priestley uses it to prise out the realities behind human postures and gestures. In Act Two there are three permutations on the same situation:

> *Curtains open to disclose inner set, as corner of a sitting-room. Paul is buried in the evening paper, while Rosemary is fidgeting between writing a letter, doing a little sewing and reading a book. . . .*
>
> ROSEMARY (*after pause*): I saw Diana Ferguson this morning.
>
> PAUL (*muttering*): Don't know her.
>
> ROSEMARY: Yes, you do know her. She says she's expecting her husband back from India at the end of the month.
>
> *Paul merely grunts. She looks at him in disgust, then tries again.*
>
> ROSEMARY: They're taking a house in South Devon for his leave. Then she wants to go back with him this time. And I must say I don't blame her. Do you? (*Pause. Waits for a reply and doesn't receive one, keeping her temper with some difficulty*) Is there anything particularly interesting in that paper, dear?
>
> PAUL (*blankly, looking up*): What? – no.

Variation number two introduces a false brittle relationship – too sweet to be true. It is what the commentator William believes Rosemary to want:

ROSEMARY (*sitting eating chocolates*): I saw Diana Ferguson this morning.

PAUL (*putting aside paper at once*): Did you, darling? When's her husband coming on leave from India?

ROSEMARY: At the end of the month.

PAUL (*brightly astonished*): No!

ROSEMARY: Yes. She's awfully excited.

PAUL: Of course. He must be too. I know *I'd* be almost off my head with excitement if we'd been separated so long. They ought to take a furnished house somewhere for his leave.

ROSEMARY (*triumphantly*): That's just what they have done. In South Devon.

PAUL: In South Devon? Oh, they ought to have a grand time there. I know we should. (*They lean to each other and smile.*)

ROSEMARY: She wants to go back with him this time. And I must say I don't blame her. Do you?

PAUL: No, I don't. Just imagine if it were us. How lucky we are to be able to be together without either of us making any sacrifices. (*Blows kiss to her.*)

ROSEMARY: Yes, darling. (*After smiling at him.*) But I'm keeping you from your newspaper.

PAUL: Oh no (*throws newspaper over his shoulder*). I'd much rather have a good talk about *us*, and especially about you. (*Leans forward, regarding her lovingly and kisses her.*)

In these two permutations the irony between what matters usually are like, and what they might be wished to be, is delightfully established, and the slight over-writing of the second version introduces a gentle mocking which preserves the comic focus of the whole. But yet a third permutation emerges:

Curtains open to same scene. Rosemary is reading a book this time.

ROSEMARY: And I must say I don't blame her. Do you? (*Pause as before.*) Is there anything particularly interesting in that paper, dear?

PAUL (*looking up blankly*): What? No. (*Half stifles a yawn and returns to reading.*)

ROSEMARY (*after another pause*): Did anything amusing happen at the office today, Paul?

PAUL (*indifferently*): No, can't remember anything.

She looks at him despairingly but he doesn't even see it. After another pause, to establish atmosphere of boredom, Helen marches in, looking very trim and gay.

HELEN (*briskly*): Hello, Rosemary. 'Lo, Paul. Just looked in to ask you about Saturday.

PAUL: Saturday, by all means, Helen. By the way, a most amusing thing happened at the office this morning. We've got a new client, a Mrs Dowson, who's actually very rich, but looks a queer, shabby old thing. We've also got a new charlady whose name happens to be Mrs Rowston. (*Laughs.*) Well, this morning this Mrs Rowston comes in for the first time, and of course the clerk thinks the name she gives is Mrs Dowson, treats her with enormous politeness, can't understand why she keeps mumbling something about cleaning and keeps apologising abjectly because my partner and I aren't about. *He laughs, so does Helen. Rosemary does not laugh.*

This permutation takes us back to the situation as it 'very often does happen'. The truth of observation here is acute, and despite the fact that the situation is theatrically hackneyed in form, the comment implied in the situation is sharp and amusing. The dramatic timing is immaculate, and yet another irony is introduced by the fact that what Paul relates as being a funny thing that happened at the office is not funny at all.

Priestley also uses irony in *Ever Since Paradise* with a telling pathos when he lays bare the reality behind the gracious military devotion of Major Spanner to a woman young enough to be his daughter, but married to another. His dog-like devotion has been life-long, and the major has hugged it like a perpetual Christmas present to his heart. But when he is pushed into the position of revealing his devotion by deeds rather than words or gestures, it is all too clear that, for him, the name without the reality is enough – to be a worshipper from afar is all-sufficient. He is alone with Rosemary in a hotel bedroom:

ROSEMARY: . . . We'll have to have dinner up here.

WILLIAM (*rather disconcerted*): Oh – will we? Oh, I say, I've just commandeered a good table down there. Slipped down for a short drink before feeding. (*Sneezes, then sniffs a little.*) Fact is, that bathroom's damned draughty and I didn't notice it in time. Have to be careful after all these years in a hot climate.

ROSEMARY (*vaguely*): Yes, of course. Well, you'd better slip down again and tell them we'll dine up here.

WILLIAM: You don't think it would look odd, do you? I mean, you know what these people are. (*Pointing to the door.*)

ROSEMARY (*rather impatiently*): Well, if you like you can dine down there by yourself and I'll just have something on a tray up here. I'm not very hungry anyhow.

WILLIAM: Oh, aren't you? Oh, I say, that's rather a shame. Food here's pretty good, too. That's how I remembered the name of the place.

ROSEMARY: I don't care. I didn't come here for *food*.

WILLIAM (*rather embarrassed at this*): No, of course not. Neither did I, of course. Happy, little girl?

ROSEMARY: Yes, of course, darling. I've been enjoying the lovely peace of it. To be quiet – with peace all around – lovely.

WILLIAM (*dubiously*): Yes, quite. Mayn't last, though.

ROSEMARY (*startled*): Why?

WILLIAM: Got a big table all laid out down below (*leaning towards her*) and the head waiter told me it's for a crowd of Air Force blokes who make a night of it here every Friday. Probably won't be much peace and quiet when those lads get started. Ho – Ho!

ROSEMARY: Yes, but I didn't mean *that*.

WILLIAM: No, of course not. Quite understand what you mean.

ROSEMARY (*after a pause, wistfully*): George, do you really love me?

WILLIAM: Why, Rosemary, little girl, you know I do. Haven't I carried that photograph of you with me everywhere for years? Got it here now, matter of fact. (*Pats his back pocket.*)

ROSEMARY: You don't want it now because you've got me. (*After staring at him speculatively.*) You know, George, darling, I hope you realise that a photograph is one thing and a real live person is quite a different thing. I mean, are you quite sure it's me – me myself – you really want?

WILLIAM: Why of course, Rosemary darling. I tell you I've dreamed of this for years.

ROSEMARY (*stifling all doubts*): Darling! (*holding up her face*) Kiss me!

WILLIAM (*moving to her*): By Jove, yes. Just a second. (*Suddenly stops and turns away, then violently sneezes.*) Oh – damn! Sorry! (*Sniffs and blows his nose hard.*)

And the poor Major's attack of defence mechanism gets worse and worse, and it becomes even clearer that he does not want the reality. The final touch of comic pathos comes at the end of the scene when Rosemary asks him what name he put on the hotel register:

WILLIAM (*almost off, still trying to sneeze*): All I could think of was the name of an old C.O. of mine – terrible old stickler (*sneezes*) Smith.

The protective anonymity of an old stickler with the name of Smith, together with the illusion of love, is what the Major wants. In this character Priestley has brilliantly sketched with delicacy of comic pathos (the sneeze is both a comment and a source of amusement) what Terence Rattigan later developed in the character of the military man in *Separate Tables*. The underlying note of the play is the unpredictability of the human species. Priestley does not make the mistake of adopting the hoary notion that man is always the exasperated victim of woman's fickleness. At certain points in the play he neatly turns the tables on the conventional idea – the man wallows in an infuriating flux of emotional responses and the woman is left in cold exasperated rage.

The strength of the play, as in *Laburnum Grove* and *When We Are Married*, is in the impact of the group rather than the single character. The intertwining of the various arguments for and against man and woman binds these three couples into a microcosm of human attitudes and follies. It may be remarked that in all three plays, too, the groups are closely socially identifiable – lower middle-class in *Laburnum Grove*, provincial middle-class in *When We Are Married*, and upper middle-class in *Ever Since Paradise*. When Priestley tries to straddle social groupings as in *Bees On the Boat Deck* and *The Golden Fleece* he seems to lose a sense of identity with his characters, and hence loses something that he needs to preserve a unity of vision and communication.

Priestley's comedy is essentially based upon his concepts of the 'groupings' of society. In the middle-class group which he knows well, his aim is usually straight and the target is neatly patterned with shots. But it may be a matter for regret that, except for the character of the photographer Ormonroyd in *When We Are Married*, he has not created a comic character whose impact is the result of some alchemy within its personality, rather than in the mixing process of class status. It is surprising that Priestley, one of whose best critical essays is on Falstaff, should not have engaged himself, as a dramatist, with the kind of comic figure represented by the fat knight. Falstaff grinds beneath his feet the pettinesses of the patterned society of his world, and his comedy comes from a personality whose gigantic conceit of mood, statement and belief seems self-generated. He is not tied, except at the very end, to the 'rules' of society, of class; he straddles all, entirely himself. Ormonroyd the photographer shows, in little, something of this self-generating sufficiency and, as a result, he is, apart from seeming to be of a richer depth than the rest, quite literally more funny than the rest. Priestley's comedy of class inhibits the full-throated laugh. There is always a qualification around the corner, and the most that it is possible to expect is a succession of momentary chuckles interspersed with ironies, fantasies, and social polemics that put a guard rail around laughter.

It might be suggested that Priestley does not have that ability to be ruthless in the exploitation of the comic in the individual figure which characterises the creators of the great comic figures we remember – the ruthlessness which Shakespeare shows in his creation of Malvolio and Falstaff. Shakespeare's magnanimity lies in his extraordinary weighing of forces. His comic figures have their good and bad qualities, but he is relentless in pursuing both, while magnanimous in giving both the correct place. Priestley's temperament always tips the scales in the direction of giving the benefit of the doubt – even his despicable upper-class layabouts are unbelievable because, in the long run, he cannot bring himself to accept that any man is really bad and irredeemable. His whole cast of thinking and feeling about individuals is optimistic though it is pessimistic about the organisation in which those individuals imprison themselves and call society.

He looks straight, and with a compassion that too often creates sentimentality, or unreality, at what is virtuous, but his stare at vice is sidelong, and one senses at times that he tries to compensate for his own awareness of his weakness with vice by putting on the mask of caricaturist. His comedy is, in the end, always aspiring towards the artificial reconciliations of the forest of Arden.

THE SOCIOLOGICAL PLAYS

Priestley is regarded as a stern and unrelenting and often furious critic of modern society. His bolts, slings and arrows of criticism are to be found scattered throughout the entire body of his work – in plays, novels, articles, published lectures and speeches. He has never seemed to let up on a consistent pressure he has exerted, or tried to exert, on the conscience of a society which has seemed to him to be heading towards destruction as a result of its own folly, and not as the result of some malevolent intervention from beyond the stars. Society to him does not mean British society alone, although he has reserved a good proportion of his polemic prognoses for it. He implies the whole organisation of Western man, and he is one of the few modern writers to have looked with any clarity at American society and to have produced a diagnosis which many Americans themselves agree with. What he finds wrong with the contemporary world may be easily and quickly categorised. Class distinction, whatever its source and its nature, is a rotting cancer in society, and one of its symptoms is the exploitation of what he calls always 'the people'. For Priestley, who has a genius for the descriptive and associative label (his coinage of 'admass' appears – unacknowledged – in the new Oxford Dictionary of Current English), the exploitation which turns 'the people' into the 'mass' is characterised by 'organisation' and 'quantity'. These are the two gods which dominate the structure of modern industrial societies. He saw, a long time before most others, in Hitler, Goebbels, Göring and what they created by organisation, 'our worst selves with the lid off'. He is particularly angered and bitter about the grim results of the industrial revolution 'where money and machines are of more importance than men and women'. His imagination rises to his gorge, and in article after article he has painted a picture of people turning into mass as they disappear into satanic mills 'slogging away in the dark, ignored, forgotten'. The agents of exploitation and their weapons are self-seeking politicians, unscrupulous international bankers, press-lords, a monetary system which propagates itself and becomes the monopoly of those who acquire thereby the means of power with a minimum of effort and work. His view of modern society is essentially pessimistic, because he cannot find much in mitigation of the grimness which he sees. In *Topside* he writes:

> . . . ten more years of national self-deception of Topside religion, Topside royalty, Topside politics, Topside culture, Topside journalism; ten more years when originality, inventiveness, and creative enthusiasm will be smothered to death by men and minutes, and the nation's energy will run down for ever . . . Topside, once you see it for what it really is, a power organism that stands for everything and believes in nothing, a huge conspiracy of ambition without talent, you will realise offers the country nothing but decay and ultimate ruin.

The pessimism which is implicit here is underlined when it is understood that Priestley does not absolve from blame or responsibility those who are exploited and 'organised'. It is too often assumed that Priestley is always a sort of cheery Sancho Panza to the 'idea' of 'the people' – advocating a return to a sentimental earthiness, revelling in the folksy comfort of the simple pleasures, bringing back a vague maypole dance in which all are equal, all are tolerant, all are bright-eyed and uncaring of material wealth. This is not so. 'Britain is simply another territory in which there exist large docile masses, ready to work all day and be mechanically and profitably entertained each night. . . .' People as such have 'roots' but they too easily allow themselves to be turned into a mass.

Priestley's analysis in *Topside* was published in 1958, and since he wrote the words very little has happened in this country to prove him wrong. Priestley is that kind of writer who pushes you into a corner in which you have to make the clear decision whether you are with him or against him. It would be easy to forecast who, after reading *Topside*, would be against him, but it is impossible to believe that anyone who is not utterly trapped by the net of *Topside* could honestly move away from his side. His evidence is in the wasteful expenditure of money on inefficient rocketry, the indications of equivocation in the inner councils of government, the phantasmagoric situation in which two girls of easy virtue dominate, exploit and are exploited by a ravening press and public appetite; the monotonous reappearances of economic crises, and the hurried and, by now, pathetic expediencies to obliterate those crises; the unhappy spiritual heart of the Church, bolstered by large coffers; the manner in which, so often, small talent is inflated into an image of monumental genius by the ignorant armies of press agents who clash by night and emerge with a new god every morning. To align oneself alongside Priestley only for a moment is to allow these images and memories to embed themselves in one's mind and emotions. He is so clear and certain in his indictments that the first inclination is to counter pessimism with the response that such things have always been, and that our misfortune is merely that we now become more quickly and intimately aware of them. Then comes the quick realisation that, for Priestley, this response is only proving his point. That we should be so aware of them, accept them greedily, and be content that they represent a status quo of a highly organised society is, for him, a symptom of the decay he rails against. It is infuriating to be so convinced by a man that the only response that one can make is to wriggle in the mind and the emotions. Priestley has infuriated many people, but there still comes the point when one has to ask the question: 'is he, on the evidence, more likely to be right or wrong?' Every day the evidence piles up, and so much of it supports him, that one becomes infuriated again, and the process begins anew. It is a kind of education by correct intimidation.

Although Priestley exhibits a good deal of pessimism in the articles he has written about the sickness of society, he has not confined himself to gloomy prognostication. The solutions which it is possible to deduce from his writings take one, however, out of the arena of the political social world, and into that more private personal area inside the human heart. The Priestley solution depends very much upon a kind of salvation process which is to take place, not under the organised banner of a complex society, but in the mysterious reaches of personality. It is because perhaps this kind of solution does not, and cannot offer formalisations, and because mankind is likely to become suspicious these days at the mention of the 'spirit', the 'heart', the 'soul', that it has gone unnoticed by many people that Priestley has never said that the process of disintegration in society is irredeemable. The difficulty is that his strictures and diagnoses seem far more certain, and amenable to examination and proof, than his prescription. And so he seems to be merely a prickly prophet of doom.

Basically, Priestley's prescription has little reference to the actual organisation of man in society. He does not believe in the mystique of institutions and political organisations. The sum total of human beings in a society is far more important. Many have believed that Priestley has advocated a marxist solution to the problem of the distribution of wealth but, in point of fact, his strictures of marxism in action have been as severe as his condemnations of unbridled capitalism. He refers in *Literature and Western Man* to communism as involving a 'hasty substitution of what is irreligious, not belonging to the spirit, for what should be profoundly religious'. He believes that it is not the political and economic structure of its society that makes communism so 'gravely menacing' but its denial of anything that suggests any other dimension to man beyond the beliefs of dialectical materialism. He believes that such things as transport, fuel, power should be taken over by the community, and he believes that the community is best served by a small number of what he calls 'statesmen' as opposed to 'politicians', but he has never issued a really practical plan for the kind of society that he wants. This society in fact lies in the realm of desire and the ideal, and it cannot be really formulated or subjected to organisation because the individual human heart has still a long way to go to be in the receptive state for proper organisation. What is required is an abandonment of selfishness, greed, exploitation, and their replacement by tolerance, kindness, and work. Each man must give and work according to his capabilities. The easy label for such a view is 'romantic' and Priestley would himself perhaps not deny the validity of the label if its user assumed that it implied a worthwhile ideal rather than what it sometimes implies, an idle dream. The truth of the matter is that Priestley hates organisation because he feels its dangers to be potentially much greater than its advantages. It is this which has so often left him open to the accusations 'nihilist', 'bolshie' and revolutionary, and it is this which has made British socialists no less than British tories suspicious of him. And, indeed, because no Christian God figures in his ideal, he is suspected by orthodoxy of a rampant atheism. But Priestley has his own idea of God:

> We must wait.... But while we are waiting, we can try to feel and think *as if* our society were already beginning to be contained by religion, as if we were certain that Man cannot even remain Man unless he looks beyond himself, as if we were finding our way home again in the universe.... We may need much more to establish order, justice, real community, in the

> outer world, and may not ourselves find the right healing symbols for the inner world, but just as a first step, we can at least believe that Man lives, under God, in a great mystery.

And what is this God? '. . . Man is a god-worshipping creature, and if he doesn't choose to worship a mysterious universal power of goodness and love, then he'll find something else – and much worse – to adore.'

This 'universal power of goodness' can only be characterised by the extent to which its operations become manifest on earth, as it were; it has no existence except in terms of what it does to man, and in terms of man's consciousness of it. Priestley's ideal is that it should sweep

> Through the dull dense world, compelling there
> All new successions to the form they wear;
> Torturing th'unwilling dross that checks its flight
> To its own likeness.

Although Priestley intermittently gives this spirit the name of God, its source lies deep in the human being: 'Spirituality does not mean some tepid ghostly business round the corner, but the light in the mind, and the flame in the heart'. He concludes in *Literature and Western Man* that 'it is doubtful if our society can last much longer without religion'. What he means is – this particular religion.

This, then, is the solution which the rampaging admonisher, the lasher of Topside and admass, proposes. The solution seems, in spirit, so far from the problem as to be the emotional whistlings in the dark of another man. One does not have to believe in original sin to reject the solution; it is easy to reject it for oneself on the grounds that it poses a superficial and sentimental remedy to a problem that is hard, vicious and amenable only to the ruthless therapeutics of political, moral and social re-organisation. But the extraordinary fact is that, just as it is impossible to deny the correctness of much of Priestley's analysis of the ills of our society, it is impossible also to deny that there comes, day after day, intermittent proof of the efficacy of selflessness, which is what Priestley's goodness and love really means. The evidence of the iniquity and evil of a society is always more readily available, and of grander proportions than the evidence of the contrary.

Quite simply, Priestley has faith in the quality rather than the quantity of evidence of 'goodness and love' in the world. His pessimism is balanced by a tremendous act of faith in small things, and it is significant that so often he finds the true 'spirit' in 'small' people – those who have a kind of guts not to be turned into mass, those who naturally accept that there is a mystery whose power can bind humanity together were not humanity drossed with its own blindness. The sociological Priestley has no unique analysis to make of our ills, though his vision of them is vivid, and his therapy is vague and to some perhaps simply disingenuous – how can a man so tough believe in what is so softly emotional? His own answer would be:

> I see Man as both an intellectual and an emotional creature, and so I dislike any theory of life that treats him as being entirely one or the other. . . . I have always been equally repelled by the idealism that denies matter and the materialism that denies mind,

and

> I believe that the very grooves in which our lives run are created by our feeling, imaginations and will. If we know and then make the effort, we can change our lives. We are not going round and round in hell. And we can help each other.

The time-plays are by way of being explorations of the order of mystery and magic which lies behind our individual lives, many of the comedies are explorations of the ways in which either an affirmation or a denial of the processes of feeling, imagination and will, affect us. The 'sociological' plays which form Volume Three of the Collected Works examine two aspects of man in society – organised society and the 'theoretical' society which emerges from the reality of 'goodness and love' in action. They can, therefore, be divided generally into those plays which deal with the present-tense actuality of society and those which contain visions of an ideal society or a society which is in the condition of reaching toward an ideal state. In *Cornelius* the theme is the harshness of the commercial world and its effects upon the individual who is a cog in its machine. *People At Sea* exploits the well-tried idea of placing together a diversity of people in a particular and critical situation; the result is a 'cross-sectioned' society which demands from each individual part an exercise of co-operation and tolerance in a situation in which wealth and class give none of them an advantage over the others. *They Came To a City* is called, by Priestley, a play of 'symbolic action'. The idea behind its movement is that of Utopia, but what Priestley is most interested in is not the City, but the respective attitudes of the characters towards it. It must not be taken, as some critics have taken it, as futuristic, but literally 'symbolically' – the symbolic city is merely a catalyst to start the reactive processes of hearts and minds. Although *An Inspector Calls* is, technically, a return to the taut 'thriller' method of *Dangerous Corner*, the play, in theme, is perhaps the clearest expression made by Priestley of his belief that 'no man is an island' – the theme is guilt and social responsibility. *Home Is Tomorrow*, written during the early days of the setting-up of the various agencies of the United Nations Organisation, is concerned with the dangers, weaknesses and virtues of Internationalism, and *Summer Day's Dream* is futuristic. It takes us beyond the United Nations, in the sense we know it, and beyond the present tense, to an England which has barely survived a third world war. In its materially denuded condition, its inhabitants, or those whom Priestley chooses to represent its inhabitants, have re-discovered the old lost values of co-operation based on mutual trust, on barter, on want served by possession. The moral rather than the material power generated is sufficient to prevent the exploitation of the country by the U.S.S.R. and the U.S.A. aided, in a technical capacity, by India. They are co-operating only on a basis of mutual cupidity, but their representatives are made to see the evil of this, and learn, by a kind of infection, the ways of simplicity and love.

Cornelius is at one and the same time one of the most technically weak of Priestley's plays, and one of the most attractive. In Act One Priestley shows an astonishing gaucherie in the handling of characters. The setting is an office – one of those nondescript and untidy rooms which stare at one out of Galsworthy, and which Priestley no doubt saw, in reality, in his early days in the wool trade. Through this office in Act One there pass a bewildering number of people whom we see once and never again, among them a man selling rugs, one selling paper towels, and a young woman selling shaving soap. The reason for their appearance is only too plain. Priestley wishes to emphasise the degrading and depersonalising effects of the commercial world. These people trot in and out like ghosts, but the effect on the audience is less to convince us of their plight than to make us wonder that Priestley could not have found a more skilful and economic way of introducing them. Again, later in the play, there is a most uncharacteristic awkwardness in the handling of a particular situation. In Act Two the creditors of the firm are meeting, and are awaiting the arrival of the senior partner from a business-trip, in the hope that he has been able to restore the firm's fortunes. When he arrives he is palpably distraught, and on the edge of, at least, a nervous breakdown. His peculiar condition causes one of the characters to leave. She does not re-appear until Act Three when she suddenly emerges to ask '. . . I've been wondering what happened after that meeting. . . .' She has not hitherto shown herself, in any case, to be the sort of person to leave anything at a moment of crisis; she is merely being used as an agent by which Priestley can provide his audience with information, and his use of her as such is painfully obvious.

Nevertheless, there is much in the play which attracts, most notably the character of Cornelius himself. He is one of the most personable and likeable of Priestley's gallery of puzzled men, for the simple reason that the situation which occasions his state of mind and feelings is not over-explicitly communicated as a factor in itself, insulated from the characters whom it influences, but is embodied by the characters. The reason for Cornelius's wry state is quite simply that he has come to realise that so much of the world of commerce is a rat-race, and that while running that race a man may waste much of what is really life. The predatory creditors, the ambitious young men just about to begin the race, the hangers-on – these are the surrounds to his realisation of his wasted life. But what colours the realisation vividly is, first of all, his conclusion of the heartless illogicality of the commercial world:

> Look what happened. The pound sterling was worth twenty shillings here and only twelve shillings somewhere else. Some countries you couldn't get money into. Some countries you couldn't get money out of. You could send goods in a ship with a blue flag but not in a ship with a red flag. It wasn't business any more. It was a game of snakes and ladders – but without the ladders.

> I've never got much fun out of selling aluminium. And whether Briggs and Murrison of Birdcage Street, Holborn, ever sold any aluminium to anybody couldn't be of any real importance to the world. . . . And what's it all about? If we've to live by private trade, then let it be private trade. Why have they made it like a lunatic's obstacle race? Why are we condemned to scheme and scratch in these cubby-holes?

And, secondly, the fact that his senior partner and friend is driven to suicide by the rat-race. Cornelius's adjustment to his awareness of both these experiences is communicated very much on a personal level. Unlike the character of Ormund, his persona does not have to suffer the compromise of being seen through the dark glass of a theory or through the author's polemics. Thus, for example, his relationship to a young secretary who joins the firm in its last days becomes a very moving and telling image of the vital life he has missed through being involved for so many years in the function of buying and selling. The scene when his love for her is made apparent, with its implications of lost opportunity are worth all Priestley's characteristic over-statements of theme:

> COR: Not much happened then, perhaps. But afterwards – only a day or two – just before we had the meeting here – and I came in and you were singing.
>
> JUDY: I remember. You were very nice about that.
>
> COR (*almost to himself*): It's as if it's been dark here ever since then – and you carried a little light with you. When you came in it wasn't so dark. There was a light round your head. And the song has never stopped. It's a long time since I felt like this, a long long time. That's why I can't tell you properly. It's a good record but the gramophone's old and rusty. I'm sorry. I'm sorry.
>
> JUDY (*putting out a hand*): I'm sorry too.
>
> COR (*eagerly*): Are you? How small and clear you are – like the flame of a candle! (*Pauses, then laughs shortly and harshly.*)
>
> JUDY: What does that mean?
>
> COR (*eagerly*): I was thinking – here's the good old situation they're so fond of in the magazine stories and the comic papers. The business man keeps the typist in the office after hours to make love to her.

The tone of this keeps it away from the sentimental statement of the meaning of Judy as the repository of 'the light in the mind and the flame in the heart'; there is a self-mocking quality that underlines the irony of the eventual disclosure that Judy is in love with someone else and that Cornelius is too late. This irony is doubled when it emerges that her affianced is a young man whom Cornelius has earlier detected in dishonest commercial dealing. Thus the progression of Cornelius out of the rat-race to a realisation of its organised meaninglessness is not attended by that softening process which mars, for example, Johnson's progress from the material cupidities of the world to a refined sense of happiness. Judy is doomed to spend her life with a man who is a citizen of the waste land – she knows it and Cornelius knows it. All that seems left for him is suicide. His decision to kill himself is halted by the appearance of the char, Mrs Roberts.

She introduces the over-simplified proposition that some people don't know when they are lucky: 'Why, you're not going to start grumbling now are you – just because you've spent a few years sitting here in a nice office, with other people waiting on you, and three good meals a day and anything else you liked? Gertcha – you don't know you're born.'

Because Cornelius has been presented throughout not as a sentimentalised sacrifice to a great machine, but as a wry individual, half-mocking himself, it is easier to accept this over-contrived effect, and even to accept Cornelius's final rejection of death, as he walks through the door shouting that he will seek the lost city of the Incas – the romantic vision of the man who has realised that an adding-machine existence is not enough. One accepts both these theatricalities, but only just. Their cosy emotionalism adds nothing to the knowledge we already have of Cornelius – they are, no more and no less, concessions to a happy ending for which Priestley seems to have an obsession.

It is not only in the depiction of his major character that Priestley is, in the main, successful in this play. Miss Porrin, the dutiful secretary to the firm, is a professional horn-rimmed virgin who falls completely in love with Cornelius. She is of the same breed as the mousy Miss Sell in *The Golden Fleece*, but is presented in a much more convincing manner. She is also a victim of the commercial world which Cornelius turns his back upon, and she has a dim comprehension that he has notions of a life outside the rat-race. She cannot express herself, except in terms of her quite hopeless love. The scene between her and Judy – the one who loves and cannot have, and the one who does not love but is wanted – is one of controlled irony:

MISS P (*in low tense voice*): I wish I didn't hate you so much. I've never hated anybody like this before.
JUDY: And you've no right to hate me. What have I done?
MISS P: Lots of things.
JUDY: What things?
MISS P: That isn't it.
JUDY: Please tell me why. I don't hate you. I don't hate any-

body. As a matter of fact, I don't even dislike you, although you've been unfriendly to me ever since I came here. I've been – rather sorry for you.

MISS P: Why should you be sorry for me? You're only a child yet, a silly child. You don't really know anything.

JUDY: That's stupid you know, Miss Porrin. I may be years younger than you are, but I'm not a child. I believe I'm more a grown-up person than you are.

MISS P (*wildly*): Because you're young and pretty now – you think it's going to be always like this. It isn't – (*Breaking down*) – it isn't, it isn't.

The effect of *Cornelius* is that of a Galsworthy novel. Though set in 1935 it reeks of Edwardianism despite the appearances of the rug-merchants, shaving-soap travellers, and other paraphernalia of modern commerce. The office itself seems a left-over from the nineteenth century, the staff, with its lugubrious office-boy, and its faithful old and trusted chief clerk, seem to exist in a world that disappeared with the first world war. Perhaps this is why the firm is bankrupt, but certainly this is why the play, however sympathetically Cornelius is drawn, does not support its implied indictment of the ruthless machinations of the rat-race. Priestley himself admits that it would 'have to be done as a period piece because it does not belong to our post-War world'. But the world it belongs to does not seem to be that of the thirties either. It has the charm and attractiveness of the period-piece fiction of the early part of the century and in the long run is less a play about the iniquities of the rat-race than a kind of biography of a gentle man who woke up to find himself in a hard world.

Priestley calls the characters in his play *People At Sea* 'rather a shop-soiled lot'. This does them an injustice since they are not really characters. They are really representatives of certain attitudes, and their function is not to embody the action but to speak for the author. The action, which takes place in the veranda café of the *SS. Zillah*, a ship carrying passengers and cargo to Central America, only has the purpose of underlining the attitudes represented by the characters, and has no vital dramatic interest.

The situation is simply that the ship is in grave danger of foundering as a result of a fire, and its survival depends to a very large extent on each passenger doing his best. The play is blatantly an attempt to show the way in which common danger demands the qualities of co-operation, sympathy and effort. The implication for society is obvious.

The play, however, is curiously negative in its effect. In the first place it is difficult to believe in the danger to which these people are subjected, and, in the second place, it is difficult to accept the reality of the people involved. Everybody on board seems to be playing in some kind of charade, and it would seem that Priestley is so intent on making the play have a general application that he has forgotten that the agents of representation still have to be credible. Thus Myricks, a Wall Street financier, sets himself up as ship's cook and revels in the simplicities of it after the harsh actualities of the world of money. Myrick does not have ambitions to find the city of the Incas – he 'finds' himself making scrambled eggs: 'For the last twelve hours the ether must be getting jammed with messages for me from those boys in Wall Street . . . and here I am, and for the first time for over thirty years, I don't give a darn. No, sir. I'm busy cooking eggs, not balance sheets.'

This has all the ham-fisted social morality of scores of Hollywood films in which the gnarled and twisted old veteran of commerce, soured by years in the jungle of money, stumbles upon a little clearing, and finds, if only for a short time, the good and simple life. Everyone feels happy for him, even those whom he has exploited for years, and he feels no end restored. Priestley is not so overtly cynical as that, but his characterisation is of the same breed, and its morality is as shallow. This is true not only of this end of the social scale, but also of the nether end. The stoker, Boyne, who is angrily conscious of belonging to an exploited class, is completely unconvincing as one of the chief irritants in this little fellowship which is trying the experiment of living together and perhaps dying together. Boyne is as unconvincing as O'Neill's Hairy Ape – both of them stumble out of their creator's imaginations half made-up to look like violent men of the dirt; all they succeed in being is the mouthpiece for a point of view which, in fact, they never convince us they are real enough or bright enough to conceive. He responds to a speech by Miriam, a ladies' maid, with the words 'You've got the right ideas'. The speech itself is a masterly example of dissociation of dialogue and character:

> Now just listen to me a minute. There's two sorts of people on this ship. There's the people who've had it all their own way up to now. Then there's people like us, who've never had a chance. What happens to us when they come and rescue us? Are we going to be petted and made a fuss of? No fear! We're going to get even worse than we've had already. And I've had enough of it. These others, the lucky ones, they don't care a damn what happens to me or any of you. Very well, then, I don't care a damn what happens to them. You hear? I don't care what happens to them.

Boyne has already made one of his many violent little speeches asserting his rights and the rights of his class: '... Well, they're not going to do it to Paddy Boyne – see? 'Ere. I say a man's got his rights. Let's 'ave turn and turn about. I've done my flamin' share 'aven't I....'

Between the two extremes of the rich man who finds the answer and the self-consciously exploited man whose only answer is talk and violence, there are varying shades of representation of attitude. There is the Professor who, for years, has been writing a vast tome entitled 'Prolegomena to a Philosophy of Conditioned Values', but, of course, he learns that theoretical knowledge without experience is meaningless. At first he 'explicates':

> PROF: Exactly. Now, like the rest of us, you can't help feeling that your *real* self is behind this appearance, that you too have a *something*. But the immediate effect of your appearance is so astonishing, the reaction to it is so strong, that the real self behind – with its *something* – always appears

inadequate. Therefore you feel that nobody really knows you, understands you, or really cares about you.

DIANA: I say – go on.

PROF: Therefore you find it impossible to live in a real world of persons. So you live in a world of sensations. But a world of sensations – without persons and their relationships – is a false world, and one that is for ever shrinking.

And then, at the end, he destroys his book.

There are, also, Valentine and Diana, formerly lovers who went their separate ways – she to a loveless drugged existence, he to a superficial fame and a reliance on alcohol. They both recognise each other's weakness, they are both on the verge of desperate remedies. Priestley chooses to plant in these two his characteristically emotive hints about a new world around the next corner:

DIANA: Is it true that everything's changing, that we'll soon be in a different kind of world that won't want us – at least me – all ungracious and busy and hard – like – like so many of the boys and girls one meets nowadays?

VAL: I've said something like that to you, myself, Diana, almost thrown it in your face, but when you say it, something – I don't know what it is – a deep fellow-feeling – affection – perhaps real love – begins to stir in me. I'm all on your side, and I want to say 'Damn your new world, this is mine'. Meaning – you.

In a totally unconvincing scene these two re-discover one another. He crunches her pep-pills under his feet and she says 'But God help the first whisky bottle I catch near you'. This is wholly unworthy of Priestley's deeply held belief in the efficacy of love, the reality which lies behind the surface compromises of the world. The poetry of this conception which informs *Eden End* is here reduced to a tremulous mechanistic and prosaic melodrama. Two other passengers – a displaced man with no passport named Velburg and the disenchanted ladies' maid Miriam decide to end it all and throw themselves overboard, but they do it with such dewey-eyed romanticism that it is very difficult to accept what is presumably implied by their action – that, in Miriam's words, 'you might walk straight into another sort of life, like this – with people and houses and all that – but different, like it is when you dream sometimes'. The whole effect is that of 'Marie Rose Goes To Sea'. Indeed the automatic ways in which the various passengers on board find their levels is one of the worst features of this bad play. It is yet one more example of Priestley's failure to keep control over his material and his craft when he attempts to straddle 'class' – the result is a confusion between allegory and representation. When he forgets to write both, and attempts to achieve one or the other, his hand is surer, and his impact is more telling.

They Came To a City is one of Priestley's most popular plays, surprisingly so because it is, unashamedly, one which has a calculated design upon an audience. Its popularity is probably the result of its completely frank and unabashed vision of Utopia, and because it has no pretensions to being anything else but a piece of sincere propaganda for Priestley's belief in the perfectability of man. But the sheer simplicity of its message is not enough to account for its attractiveness; its technique is more cunning than the smooth passage of its action might reveal. Priestley does not repeat the mistake he made in *People At Sea* when he tried to force a message out of a group of people. In *They Came To a City* the handling of character is surer, and the deployment of thematic material less chaotic and frantic.

Nine people, as a result of some unexplained shock which is described in various ways (one believes he has been felled by a golf ball, another remembers a gas explosion) find themselves outside the walls of a mysterious city. Their bewilderment about how they arrived there gives place to curiosity as to what lies behind the huge gate which seems the only entrance and exit of the city. Most of the characters have been met with before in Priestley's plays: the self-indulgent aristocrats – male and female – the vulgar speculator, the shrewd homely char, the belligerent workers, the young upper-class girl with a heart of gold beneath the tinsel, the depressed middle-class wife clinging to convention and full of fears and inhibitions – while her husband secretly has his dreams of something better.

These people are put to the test of the City. What reactions will they make to it? At the end of Act One the gate opens and they enter. At the beginning of Act Two, as dusk falls, they begin to return from the City. The financier has not been touched at all, except by frustration, by what he has found there – his main concern had been to find a post-office from which he can communicate with his financial friends. He has been reviled and mocked for attempting to engage in a fast property deal in the City. Sir George has found it all a little trying – all he wants is to get back to his golf and duck-hunting. Lady Loxfield has found it all a little outré, perhaps dangerous, and is anxious to return to her normal pursuits. Mrs Stritton has been angrily disturbed by what she has seen – her conscience and her fears seem to have been touched. She cannot understand why her husband has been captivated by it and wants to remain there. He has made quite a hit as a comedian – in his explanation of our banking system. His desire to stay in the place is shared by Joe, Alice and Philippa, Lady Loxfield's daughter, and by Mrs Batley, the charlady. The characters line up to what the City has to offer in the accustomed manner. There are no surprises in the sociological pattern of the play – some wish to stay in the Utopia, some, not understanding, do not.

The total effect is one of a simple clarity of conception and a downright honesty of theme, and the unexceptionable ideas of the play strike home with much more credibility than in *People At Sea* and *The Golden Fleece*, in which Priestley has gathered together the same mixture of humanity for an experiment in human behaviour and for an exploration into the hinterland between society as it is and society as it might be.

The acceptability of the play is due, in the first instance, to the manner in which the City itself is presented. It is never described in detail, and its nature is communicated through the eyes of different characters. It is not each individual's conception of Utopia, for it obviously has certain fixed values which would not be subscribed to by all the characters. These values are spaciousness, beauty and gaiety and, in its inhabitants, friendliness, honesty and happiness. But Priestley does not make the mistake of going beyond these generalisations. We have swift glimpses of these qualities as they impinge upon, and are interpreted by, the visitors – the society inside the City is an ideal democracy, but of this we have only hints.

As it is, the sweetness of the place may be too sugary for some tastes. It must, however, be remembered that Priestley makes no pretence that it is anything more than an ideally sweet place to be in. The important point is that Priestley is not saying that such a place exists, but that its perfection is a quality to be aimed at. It is beside the point that not everyone would, with all the will in the world, find the particular kind of perfection depicted to their liking, but Priestley is not saying 'thus it will be' but that 'the fulfilment of the ideal is possible'. In any case it may be suggested that there are two features of the play which mitigate its sweet conclusions. The first is the dextrous maintenance of mystery; throughout the first act, for example, there are few clues to what is happening and to what the City is – audience and characters are kept in a state of mystified anticipation. The simplicity of the great gate and the changes of light throughout the play, in themselves, help to woo the audience's minds away from too contemplative a criticism of the over-sweet City. More, the changes of light and the inexplicable opening and closing of the gates give an illusion of action in a play in which there is very little actual action. The second feature which mitigates the sweetness of the City and introduces zest and a sense of movement, is humour. Apart from *When We Are Married*, Priestley has rarely shown such sharpness of tongue in his characters – a sharpness whose result is to show a healthy scepticism about the City and about all convention and pretence.

There is Sir George clinging manfully to the conditioned reflexes of his existence and steadfastly refusing to compromise his 'values' with anything different. Sir George, slightly caricatured, goes marching through the play with the banner of upper-class snobbery nailed to his masthead:

SIR G: Oh – look here – can you tell me how far I am from the clubhouse?

MRS B: What club 'ouse?

SIR G (*surprised*): Why the West Windlesham Golf Club, of course.

MRS B: I'm sorry, but I never 'eard of it. I live out Walthamstow way meself.

SIR G (*horrified*): Walthamstow! Good God – this isn't Walthamstow, is it?

MRS B: No, it isn't. Nothing like it. So maybe it's what you said – West What's-it——.

SIR G: West Windlesham? Ought to be, because I was playing on the course there. But it doesn't look like it to me. D'you play golf? – no, I don't suppose you do——.

MRS B (*much amused*): Me – play golf! (*Laughs.*) Well, nobody ever asked me that before. I 'ad to come 'ere to be asked that.

SIR G: Yes, very amusin'. Well, I was playing on the course there at West Windlesham – and I think one of those two young idiots behind – I told 'em they were too close – must have knocked me out with a long drive or something. Then I must have been somewhere deep in the rough – or rolled into a bunker – unconscious and so on, y'know – and then started wanderin' about. That's all I can think.

MRS B: I dare say that was it. I was doin' a bit o' shoppin' meself. . . .

SIR G (*ignoring her remark*): Look here, if anybody should ask for me, I'm Sir George Gedney. Sir George Gedney.

MRS B (*without irony*): Fancy!

The broad ridiculousness of Sir George is in sharp contrast to the shrewd perkiness of the humour generated by Mrs Batley:

' "D'you play golf?" 'e says. "No, I don't suppose you do", 'e says. "Me play golf", I says. "Well, nobody asked me that before", I says. . . .'

In Joe and Alice, Priestley has caught something of cockney humour, in which swift scepticism and irreverence mix with an unexpected sentimentality:

JOE: Ever called yourself a mug?
ALICE: Yes, but don't try calling me one.
JOE: Okay. I've been calling myself one for – oh – fifteen years. No, longer.
ALICE: Steady. You're not that old.
JOE: I'm nearly thirty-five.
ALICE: Well, what's that?
JOE: Nothing – yet.

Alice is consistently presented as a mixture of hard and soft sentiment, and she, in particular, is given the role of presenting the facts of the material world. Her remarks about what a struggle life is come naturally out of her nature – she complains with a wry sense of humour. Through this character Priestley is able to avoid what is so often his undoing – an over-explicit and over-drawn picture of the iniquities of our society:

ALICE: That's life. I'm telling you. Talk about your feet! I've felt sometimes mine must be as big as footballs. And it's a mean life too. My God – it's *mean*. You wouldn't believe! Most of the time the management's trying to cheat the customers, and half the time the customers are trying to cheat the management. Proper monkey-house. The men aren't so bad – except of course half of 'em's got their pig's eyes sticking out of their head trying to imagine what you've got under your uniform. And some of 'em pinch you, of course.
MRS B: That's right. One pinched me once. Upper Clapton Road it was, outside a greengrocer's.

Joe is an extrovert, and a little over-exposed to the temptation to make speeches about the evils of class and the monetary system. But even here there is a consistency, since Joe is persistently represented as being a natural rabble-rouser. He speaks always with the sense of an audience before him: '. . . But where you people made the mistake was in ganging up with these money boys. You ought to have ganged up with us – the crowd, the mob, the people without any money. I once read a piece by Disraeli where he said that. But you didn't. And it's too late now.'

The least satisfactorily presented character is Philippa who seems to have no clear motivation for her determination to go and live in the City. On the one hand Priestley reposes in her that dim half-knowledge of, and attention to, otherness which he displays so often in his women characters (notably in Kay in *Time and the Conways*), but, on the other hand, one is led to suspect that she goes to the City for the most negative of reasons – to get away from her mother.

The foursquare character, Mrs Batley, is one of the sturdiest branches of a lineage that stretches back in the plays – the serving-class woman, the overworked drudge, the exploited martyr of the bucket and mop. This type grasps, time and again, the cockles of Priestley's warm heart, whether he finds it in the kitchen, the office-block or the below-stairs of the swish hotel. The type is possessed of a set of characteristics which vary only slightly though the emphasis may change from one to another. Their constant sense of faithful duty to their menial work is always implied or stated; their cheerful acceptance of hard work is often placed in marked contrast (as in *The Golden Fleece*) to those who have achieved material prosperity and position by the minimum of effort, and whose life is tainted with the unhappiness of a futility they hardly dare acknowledge; they have no sense of defeat in their hard lot, again in marked contrast to the fortunate-unfortunate in whom material cupidity has drowned human sensibility. In a sense these women are victorious, and often become an external conscience to the more materially lucky. In their work they display a militant bravery which usually expresses itself in a persistent cheerfulness and verbal shrewdness – a spry ability to keep their ends up whatever the company. They may be servants but they are never servile and, finally, they often have a quietude, a certainty which is born of an intuitive sense that, in the long run, all will be well.

In the raw jungle of the material world they often have an apprehension of the truth of another dimension of reality in which the world and men are better than they seem. They are essentially romantic in the way they are characterised and in what they represent, they are the happy conscience of the world, and they seem always to avoid the real hardness, the tragedy which their way of life could so easily encompass. They are half-theatrical creatures, unreal in their undiminished rightness of attitude, and, to a contemporary world, quite unbelievable – their heirs now arrive to char in cars, and present type-written bills. But they are cheerful agents of an essentially cheerful philosophy – something will turn up. Such a one is Mrs Batley. She is not really surprised at finding herself outside the gates of the City. She goes and has a look at it, runs an approving eye over it, and comes back outside the gates only for her basket. She knowingly sees the truth in the relationships of the others, what makes them all tick, and the City is only an expected affirmation she has secretly always known would happen. Her moment has come:

MRS S: Did they tell you the way to get back?
MRS B: No. I never asked 'em.
MRS S: You'll have to come along with us then.
MRS B: Thank yer for the invitation, Mrs Stritton. But, yer see, I'm not going that way. I'm staying here. I only came to get my basket. I might as well 'ave it.
JOE (*with enthusiasm*): That's the girl.
MRS S: Mrs Batley, I'm surprised at you.
MRS B: 'Ows that?
MRS S: I thought you said you had a lot of responsibilities – looking after people – keeping your home together – going out cleaning——
MRS B (*going for her basket*): That's it. 'Ad years and years of it. Could 'ave done with 'alf a dozen pairs of 'ands sometimes.
MRS S: Well then, you can't leave it all – to stay here——
MRS B: 'Ooo says I can't? (*She has now taken the basket and returns to go, but stops just in front of doorway.*) As long as I can remember, they've been telling me what I can do an' what I can't do. An' no thanks for it neither when I did what I could do. Well, some of 'em can look after themselves for a change. It'll do 'em good.

Mrs and Mr Stritton also have a lineage in the plays. They come from that line whose strongest branch is found in *Music At Night*. They are middle-class failures in marriage, growing apart because of their inability to know each other, to love, to understand, to make allowances. Priestley is most successful in giving Mrs Stritton a quality of pathos. She rejects viciously everything that the City represents to her husband, not because she finds it ridiculous or unreal or frightening, but because it brings to the surface all her fears and inhibitions which have tightened round both their lives. He, in his love for her, agrees reluctantly to return 'home', but her pathetic promises that everything will be different ring with a brave falsity. After the event she promises a new start – what can her husband resent?

The attraction of the play lies in its variety of humour, its precise indications of what the characters stand for, its suggestions of mystery. When the play was first produced British society still had in its hands the ration books of a diminished material and spiritual existence and the play owed part of its popularity, one suspects, to its unequivocal promise of better things; hungry hearts and minds do not always find golden promises naïve. But since then it may be that the obese slaking of material thirsts and hungers has produced a cynicism in hearts and minds which produces only a sneer at the emphatic simplicities of *They Came To a City*. But it is a matter for speculation whether the new heroes of drama who have, it is alleged, looked at our society with a harder, clearer and less damp eye than their forebears have, in fact, produced a picture which is any different, any truer. Wesker, the most overrated hero, may give us more of the ironies, the animal cries, the details of the dispossessed and the exploited, but, in him, the secret aspiration so often comes to the surface and it is found so often to be not old Priestley writ new, but Priestley plain:

> You don't know the half of it yet. Then there are all the smart boys – the kind I was – who've had to take plenty and know it's all rotten, but won't have it that you can see anything any better. They get big laughs at your expense. I know. I've

been one of them. And there are plenty of them, too. And that's not all, Alice. There'll be days – rainy days – dark days – when nobody wants to listen, when the butcher hasn't been paid and the grocer looks at you sideways and you've nothing to smoke and they're asking you when you're moving on to the next town – and *then* – we shan't be sure ourselves we were ever here. . . .

Joe, who speaks these words, finds his echo in Dave and Ronnie and Ada in Wesker's *I'm Talking About Jerusalem:*

RONNIE (*desperately*): Then where do we look for our new vision?

DAVE (*angrily*): Don't moan at me about visions. Don't you know they don't work? You child you – visions don't work.

RONNIE (*desperately*): They *do* work! And even if they don't work then for God's sake let's try and behave as though they do – or nothing else will work.

DAVE: Then nothing will work.

RONNIE (*too hastily*): That's cowardice!

Is it possible that the Jerusalem to which Wesker journeyed was Priestley's City?

After the urgent simplicities of *They Came To a City*, Priestley turned his dramatic attention to the aspirations of a post-war world that was trying desperately to put to work the usages of international co-operation. In *Home Is Tomorrow* he pictures, in effect, the work of a United Nations' team on a South Pacific island. He probably felt that he had to distance the play thus because of the frenetic 'yes and no' attitude towards international co-operation which characterised the early years of the United Nations Organisation. The play is an outright thesis play which poses the ideas first, that international co-operation is vital, and secondly, that it is difficult. The play aroused a great deal of critical dissension; some critics thought it a discussion-play, others a devious and inconclusive plot-play with, for Priestley, the unusual setting of a south sea island.

It is a lack-lustre piece in which the dramatist makes a personal entrance at far too many points. He telegraphs his plot-line, which bears little relation to the play's theme; this theme is pressed home without any real sense that characters and statements should be one flesh. Priestley, the urgent warner, steps in and takes the words out of his characters' mouths. As David Hughes says, 'One has the feeling that the action of *Home Is Tomorrow* is proceeding dimly behind a gauze curtain while the dramatist is himself standing illuminated by a spot, wearing workaday clothes and throwing off a few generalisations about world affairs'. In the play Priestley's time-complex, given such fruitful communication in his time-plays, stalks the action like a weary ghost:

> FORTROSE: . . . She seems to me the best of the other half of everything. She completes life and makes it whole. With her I'm not loving an extension or reflexion of myself, but somebody strange – from the mysterious other side – challenging. . . .

And there is much rhetoric which falls flat on its face as the characters struggle to be anything at all:

> And I tell you – that I am suspicious of talk of civilised persons that keeps out the masses and regards them with scorn. That is not true civilisation, which is rooted in pity and hope for the masses. This earth is the home of Man, all men, and not hotel-de-luxe for a few special persons.

The dream of the ideal round the corner – the city of the Incas – comes creeping in like a man too late for the charade: 'You see it sometimes in the corner of a picture . . . in a line of verse . . . hear it for a moment perhaps in a string quartet . . . the enchanted place on the other side. . . . And there has never been enough time to go through the door and wonder and admire. . . .'

The play is tired, as if Priestley is going through certain automatic responses to the world which he sees about him, but has no energy left to make those responses mean anything beyond verbiage. Yet, again, as Hughes says, 'One feels that these people might be excitingly alive if only Priestley would let them off duty for a spell'. Hughes's intuition seems true. It is as if the ingrained beliefs of Priestley have battened on to a chorus of characters whom he has not the energy to individualise and personalise, and so all that is left is to load them with the verbal alternatives to reality. There are hints here and there of the cunning pen – in the characterisation of Jill, the amoral but sensitive wife of the island's governor, and in the sharp cynical Riberac, a Frenchman on the governor's staff, who realises all along that the ideals of the internationalists are at the mercy of the human heart. But, all in all, the play is a desperate failure to realise that it is one thing to argue about the rights and wrongs of internationalism and another thing to give the arguments a human validity and energy.

By the autumn of 1949 Priestley recovered something of his sense of characterisation. *Summer Day's Dream* is an adventure into the future which deserved a better reception than it got by the evidence of a mere fifty performances at the St. Martin's Theatre. It is, in a sense, a play about those people who have seen the City in circumstances of harshness and deprivation, but who are trying to live by the example it has set. The play is set in 1975, but its atmosphere is timeless, since the lessons it seeks to draw are meant to have validity for the present as well as the future. England has been the victim of an atomic war and the survivors who are represented by the people in the play have had to return to a basic existence which they have discovered is more than mere existence; they have had to create entirely by their own efforts their food, their enjoyment. This representative group in the play is visited by a young Russian woman, a brash American, and a young Indian. It transpires that Russia and America have divided world power among themselves and have, as technical lackeys, the representatives of states like India. They are in a condition of peaceful exploitation of the world for material progress. So they arrive in the South Downs and immediately discover that the chalk deposits are a valuable raw material for synthetic products. Their duty is clear – it is to report on the deposits to their respective governments and to recommend that the area be developed. But they fall victims to the attractiveness of the simple life which is all that is left to England. The Russian girl, cool, dedicated, and a faithful scientist, falls in romantic love, the American is a victim of the quietude of the place and the people. They learn the simple lesson that it is a happier and more fruitful life which does not exploit but earns, which creates its own pleasures, which barters, and which equates its rhythm with that of the soil and the seasons. They do not stay, but they agree not to ruin this life they have, by accident, stumbled across.

The play's strength is in its atmosphere – in its evocation of values that are in danger of exploitation and in the excitement of its depiction of those who discover new values through the uninhibited operation of the senses and through a natural rationality. There is, too, a sense of careful design in the characterisation. The old man has gone through fire and come out with wisdom on the other side; the middle-aged widow, woman of two worlds, who remembers enough of the old world before the holocaust and is young enough to want to protect the new world being born; the two youngsters who have known nothing but the natural life. This is a new lineage which takes its strength from past, present and possible future, and owes its fidelity to a discovery that mankind does not only not live by bread alone but that it only really lives when that bread is baked by those who consume it.

There is a disarming simplicity in the play especially in the way in which the characters of this brave new world communicate their positive faith in the kind of existence they have had to forge for themselves. Their simplicity in contrast with the initial deviousness of argument of their visitors is what Priestley concentrates on. He succeeds well in showing the frantic aridity of the competitive world of power, represented by the Russian and the American, brought to a halt by the sheer naïve example of life lived by the rule of common sense, barter, kindness, forgiveness and love of beauty – the life of the civilised natural man.

It is perhaps the most avowedly idealistic play that Priestley has written. In it he celebrates rather than argues about the wonders of life when it is disengaged from the encumbrances of a world dominated by commerce, expediency and convention. He justifies, in this play, his often expressed idea that an audience has to be gradually wooed to an acceptance of 'heightened speech'. Here the language moves from a sinewy to a rhythmical and evocative prose. The impression that is produced is that of a vision being expressed as concretely as possible at first, achieving the status of a ritual in the end. First of all the message is acted out and then it is ritualised; the effect is not without emotional potency:

> 'What is it, Margaret? What do you see?'
> 'A thousand eyes narrowing to watch us here,
> Eyes that may never reach this time we show,
> But sees us as so many shadows on the wall. . . .'

It is at one and the same time therefore an idealistic play – he shows us, albeit in a devastated land, what a new world can be like: a warning play – the hold on the new world is tenuous – and a sad play – it is more of a dream that we see than a reality, and it is more of a dream that we are than a fact. It moves the feelings towards melancholy and the mind towards wry speculation, but it does not lodge itself as an indictment or a warning or an inspiration because it does not seem to make up its mind which it has most faith in.

Priestley's strength and weakness as a playwright can be characterised by the statement that he too often confuses the explicit with the implicit. The caring, angry man who looks on society and man and burns with the need to declare his position too often gets in the way of the artist who knows that art is not preaching, that the reality of human existence can only be embodied in character. His swift and restless mind and emotions cannon between the needs of the committed man and the intuitiveness of the observing artist. In play after play one witnesses the uneasy rhythm that this creates. The straight talk of naturalism has to give place to a contrived nuance; the evocative language of symbolism has to be proved by an equally contrived show of actuality. When he is over-conscious of the desire to achieve both extremes he loses his grip on his precise sense of dramatic and theatrical feasibility, and he succeeds in writing no-man's-land plays like *Home Is Tomorrow*. But there are two plays of Priestley's which show that he is capable of writing, on the one hand, the explicit play, in which he shows his hand, but in which he keeps a firm grasp on the content and the technique of the play and, on the other hand, that he can achieve the implicit drama of nuance of suggestion, where the hand is hidden but where the technique is equally fine. The first type is unique in his writings, the second type he had already shown himself a master of in the 1930s in *Eden End* and *Time and the Conways*. The two plays are placed in different volumes of the collected works, but they are both, in their very different ways, comments upon contemporary society. The first, *An Inspector Calls* is, in form, a throw-back to the technique of his first play *Dangerous Corner*, though it was written in 1946 and is included in Volume Three of the plays. It has the shape of a thriller, well-defined in plot, location and characterisation, and it moves with a fast pace. But like *Dangerous Corner* its theme implies depths beyond what is stated, and beyond the exciting mechanics of the unfolding story. The family depicted here are, like the assembled family in his first play, contented and a little smug in their contentment. The atmosphere of material well-being at a party to celebrate an engagement is destroyed by the entry of a police Inspector who, by insistent questioning, reveals the story of the death of a girl in which all those present appear to have been in one degree or another, implicated. Like the cigarette box in *Dangerous Corner*, the Inspector is a catalyst for truth. Under his stern influence a human jigsaw is created, and he shows how those present fit into the picture. The resultant picture is only too easily recognisable before the end – it is the degrees of responsibility for the girl's death in each of the members of the family. But the tension of the play centres on the revelation of these degrees of responsibility, and the effects which the revelations have on the existing relationships. The Inspector picks his relentless way towards truth, but this way becomes strewn with excuses, recriminations, denials, pomposities, assertions of innocence. Yet the evidence is completely and utterly undeniable. Then the Inspector leaves and a doubt sets in. Was he an Inspector or a practical joker, since none but two of these people are prepared to admit except under his pressure that a word of what he has revealed is true. A 'phone call to the police and to the local hospital where the girl is alleged to have died that night after a self-administered dose of poison reveals that neither girl nor Inspector is known.

An atmosphere of relief returns to the party, and with it the self-indulgence which existed at the beginning. But there is an irritant in the fact that the son and daughter have been disturbed by the revelations of the Inspector; they have learned a lesson and desperately try to persuade the others that there is a lesson to be learned. For these two the mysterious Inspector's revelations have a relentless truth – we are all responsible to and for one another: any man's death diminisheth me for I am part of mankind. The impression at the end of the play is that a sermon has been preached and been given graphic visual aids and has moved two of the chosen congregation, leaving the rest untouched except by relief that its truths were only theoretical and they are free to resume their tracks. As the play ends, with a minority battling against the smug self-indulgence of a majority, the 'phone rings to say that a girl has died at the hospital and that a police Inspector is on his way to make some enquiries. The neat twist becomes a kind of judgement on the majority: the unexpected has been shown first to be a nasty illusion and then to be a prophecy.

The play preserves to its very end the atmosphere of the thriller; the pieces of evidence brought forward by the Inspector slot neatly into a pattern, and each character's personality and reactions slots equally naturally into the pattern created. The play is a designed morality therefore, but it does not give a sense of the mechanistic. If it is taken on a naturalistic level certainly everything can be judged to be too coincidental and pat, but there are two features of the writing which force the mind away from such a judgement. The first is the Inspector himself. He creates from his first entrance a sense of mystery which ebbs and flows within a sense of actuality. At times he seems to know too much to be a mere Inspector, at others, he employs, with a ruthless efficiency, the methods of question and insinuation which suggest that he can be nothing else but an Inspector determined to hound his quarry. But the final impression left after he has gone is of the third who always walks beside you – not Christ, but conscience, which makes cowards, hypocrites, liars, bombasts and contrites out of this group.

Trewin calls him the representative of a 'celestial Watch Committee', but his celestial nature is created not so much by Priestley as by our own assumptions that what is inexplicable as a moral force must have a supernatural origin. But he creates nothing that is not already in existence in the group to whom he appears, and, in the end, he becomes less an inquisitor than a completely disinterested listener to confessions for which he has not asked. There is nothing celestial in Priestley's conception of him – he is, rather, an embodiment of a collective conscience, and his presence is harsh and secular; he promises no forgiveness, and names no punishment. He is the most neutral character created by Priestley, not committed like Görtler, to whom, as a presence, he has some resemblance. The second feature which takes the mind away from naturalism is the simple fact that what is revealed does not establish who is most guilty, for the evidence does not search out *the criminal*, but it reveals that they, and we, are all guilty and responsible for our fellows. There is a great deal of subtlety in the way in which the revelation of corporate guilt affects the relationships between the characters. The self-made confident father is seen by his children to be an equivocator, the fiancé is seen to be a man of secrets, and both he and his girl are left to relearn their love.

It is one of Priestley's most warning plays, but the warning is all the more acceptable because it is thrillingly communicated and because what it warns about emerges directly from the play's action and characterisation. It makes no large statements about the state of society, does not pronounce on class or the monetary system, it ignores the politicians and does not sentimentalise the exploited or caricature the exploiters. Perhaps because Priestley does not make the large statements in this play, some felt he was not making any statement at all. But the statement is here, less strident than ever before and more effective. The warning is 'we have to share something. If there's nothing else, we'll have to share our guilt'.

If *An Inspector Calls* is a return to the sharp focus and form of *Dangerous Corner*, then *The Linden Tree* is a return to the evocative mode of *Eden End*. It is included in the Collected Plays in the volume devoted to the time-plays but its theme is more apt to the plays of sociological comment. It was a great success and won critical acclaim. It is most certainly not of the same breed as the later plays, for unlike most of them, the surface of its action shivers from time to time and we are shown glimpses of the depths beneath statement, and situation. Nuance is as important as direct speech, the small gesture as significant as the obvious action. It gives an impression of existing in a timeless condition overall, but there are sharp reminders that it is intended to be an image of the contemporary world of 1947. In returning to the small family circle – to its magic and its symbolism – as an image of the larger complex of humanity, Priestley was returning to a source in which he has discovered his most assured manner and his most acceptable material. Indeed as the play opens, and we see the strange servant who lives in a half dream world of her own, and possessed of the dignity of service and a faith in a dim 'other world', we are in the familiar territory of *Time and the Conways* and *Eden End* where what is and what might be dance to a half nostalgic, half cynical rhythm. The Professor, too, throws us back to the double world of the early plays. He is of the lineage of the doctor in *Eden End* – wise, kindly, materially unfulfilled, but with a quietude which is partly a faith in well-tried principles of behaviour and partly a resignation. The Professor is about to be forcibly retired from his chair of history in a small provincial University, but he is preparing to fight the decision not because he does not feel that he has reached the time for retirement but because he cannot give up a struggle against what he feels to be a wrong and uncivilised trend in University policy and appointments. His specific fight is against what he believes to be wrong in the University – the Vice Chancellor represents this: 'He's been a very successful director of education in several cities. You might describe him as a high-pressure educationalist.'

The 'proof' of the validity of this particular fight is the implied old-fashioned nature of his own teaching – liberal, free-ranging, imaginative, untied to the wheel of vocation or the expediencies of passing examinations. But the particular struggle is only an element in the larger struggle which begins to surround his energies as his family gather around him, each one, apart from his youngest daughter, determined for the best possible reasons to persuade him to retire. He realises that what he is fighting is the brash overthrow of tradition and human value in the new world that is rapidly emerging, and that even his own wife is a victim. He becomes something of an emotional reactionary as well as an ageing and stubborn fighter. His ideals, his sense of peace and beauty, are rooted in the past – the historical past, and his own past in the Edwardian period. Very swiftly and economically Priestley provides the evidence for the validity of the battle he gives the Professor to fight. One daughter is a doctor but there is much in her that is callous technician: 'half the people we try to patch up might as well be dead – they're only half-alive——'.

Another daughter is smugly happy, finding in the Catholic Church protecting arms which release her from responsibility of her own: 'And the more I see of the rest of you – no, not you, Mother – and – of everything here – the more thankful I am that I am a Catholic – and – and have a Faith – and – and belong to a community that may be old-fashioned, as you call it, but is still civilised'.

The son is a smooth financier – money is his god, and he believes that 'before the bombs come again' the only thing to do is 'to earn some easy – and play'. The Professor's wife is disinclined to stay in the dingy house in the dingy provinces, and has no indication of the fact that her husband can only now stay because his roots of his being and belief are threatened by those he loves most and the only place to stay is where he is not wanted. His one ally is his youngest daughter, Dinah. She is of the lineage of the dead Carol in *Time and the Conways* – one of nature's children, unsullied by the world. It is she, whom the Professor describes in the words 'it is as if nature, which doesn't propose to give in, is now producing a new race, like Dinah, who can't be downed by anything', remains with him when all his family leave.

The final speech of the play which the Professor reads from a book which he has, for years, been writing, sums up what it is that the Professor feels he must fight for:

> The first pattern is that of man reproducing himself, finding food and shelter, tilling the land, building the cities, crossing the seas. It is the picture we understand now with ease, perhaps too easily. For the other pattern is still there, waiting to be interpreted. It is the record of man as a spiritual creature, with a whole world of unknown continents and strange seas, gardens of Paradise, and cities lit with hell-fire, within the depths of his own soul. History that ignores the god and the altar is as false as history that could forget the sword and the wheel.

Priestley's triumph in this play is that he has foregone the temptation to set one world against another, for the Professor's stubbornness and regret holds within it an understanding of why the new world is so inimical to all that he believes. He realises that it is not all inimical, but that much that is good is only hidden. More than this the Professor's complete faith in the efficacy of the past and its potency for the present tense is completely convincing. It is not merely stated but has to run the gauntlet of the scepticism of two students who come to the house for tutorials – his faith is proved in action, and becomes the more credible in that it is subjected to a wry uncomprehension by these two rather pathetic representatives of the new world who see history, in the Professor's words 'as a lot of dim staff in a book to be mugged up this week for old Linden. So did Fawcett. Didn't you, Fawcett? With real life roaring all around you'.

The two worlds which confront one another here are both passionately dedicated to their own principles, and though to the one, represented by the Professor, the other seems brash and strident, both have a quality of warmth in them, although in the case of the contemporary world the warmth seems generated too often by friction rather than by love. But, in the final analysis, what emerges is the ebb and flow of tolerance and intolerance, of understanding and misunderstanding, of stubbornness and temporisation. There are some scenes of most subtle truth to human nature, as when the tough Rex shows the young, pimply and bespectacled student that she can be pretty. Rex's ruthless but well-meant gesture is typical of him, and the girl's mixed reaction of pleasure and shock is typical of a puzzled inability to come to terms with the world:

> REX: . . . Now – suppose you take off your glasses. . . .
> *She does.*
> and then pull your hair back – and then up – let me take your cigarette – no, not quite like that – further back – then up——
> *He does, then, following his instructions, she pulls her hair back in a much more becoming fashion. She now looks quite different, quite attractive, and smiles at him uncertainly.*
> Makes a tremendous difference. You'd be surprised. Now any sensible young man would want to kiss you.
> *She does not react to this, but still holds her face up, smiling uncertainly.*
> I mean more or less – like this.
> *He bends down and kisses her, neatly and warmly but not passionately. When he steps back again, she releases her hair, gives a queer choking little sob, turns her face away, and fumbles for a handkerchief.*
> Oh I say. This is all wrong. I didn't mean——
> EDITH (*cutting in, chokingly*): No, it's not you. . . . I didn't mind. . . . It's something quite different . . . suddenly I felt so miserable . . . as if everything is so hopeless . . . oh where's my rotten handkerchief?

Thus, in this scene, and in others, a mood is created in the play which seems to embody without making over-explicit the point that Priestley is anxious to convey – that life without understanding and tolerance is no life worth living. Priestley offers no overtly happy ending here; the Professor and his daughter are left alone in their natural and accepting world. The family circle is broken, the magic has gone – all that is left is solitary determination to go on; perhaps the magic will come back one day.

Conclusion

Priestley's writing about theatre and drama has always been characterised by two qualities. The first is the constant impression of a man who has arrived at conclusions by experience involving work as opposed to imaginative speculation. The second is the self-knowledge which his writings display. Both these characteristics are shown in his precise ability to describe his own plays in prefaces and essays, and to describe in detail his own intellectual and emotional experience of theatre. His sometimes apparently peremptory summations of the nature of drama, of theatre, of the experience and work of the actor, of the audience, and the playwright are, nevertheless, projections of a hard-won knowledge of a chosen trade. He has written much, in essays and articles, about the world of theatre, but the essence of his conclusions is in an inaugural lecture which he gave, under the Hubert Nehry Davis fund, at the Old Vic, in 1956. In this lecture it is made clear that he feels that after twenty-five years of what he would call journey-man work in the theatre, he feels entitled to speak his mind. But behind this assurance there is the characteristic insecurity of a man to whom categorical statement and theory come with difficulty:

> As I write this I have behind me a quarter of a century's work in the theatre, and there are few tricks of the trade I do not know. With what result? I have to plan and plot far more carefully than I did twenty years ago; I write at about half the speed; I have to rewrite whole scenes where once I might not have changed a hundred words in a complete script; and even then I commit blunders and fall into traps I would have once avoided with ease.

Perhaps, indeed, this workman feels for the nature of his own workmanship too much, and does not allow its results the freedom of its own expression. However, he is one of few dramatists who have ever anatomised their craft with such deliberation. His starting-point is his own precise memory and deliberation about the problem of the dramatist, but the focal point for Priestley, in his estimate of the nature of his own writing, is the actor. The proof of this lies in the texts of the plays themselves, in two respects. First in the amount of elbow room allowed the player by the action of the play – the stage-directions, for example, do not tie the player to a precise definition of where he should move, and the indications of the tone of a speech are always, when they occur, put in general terms: '*He stares at her, perhaps having moved a little closer. She does not look at him at first, but then is compelled to meet his hard stare. There is something about this look that penetrates to the essential weakness of her character.*'

Secondly, particularly in those parts which were originally played by Ralph Richardson, one may catch, in the dialogue, the tones and pauses of the actor himself. Richardson, with his characteristically clipped speech, and his habit of unexpected verbal emphasis, is indelibly printed upon the words of the plays.

The presence of the actor is with Priestley from the very inception of a play, and each play is written upon the very fixed principle that: 'A man who wants to be read and not performed is not a dramatist. The dramatist keeps in mind not the printer, but a company of actors, not readers but playgoers. He is as closely tied to the Theatre as a chef to a kitchen.'

This principle has its main strength in that there is always an active connection in Priestley between the initial idea of the play, its working-out, and its eventual performance. But there are disadvantages. Although Priestley would not readily agree with the view that he writes particular parts for particular actors, there is some evidence that it is often difficult for him not to have the image of a particular actor in mind when he is in the process of creating a character. In *Bees on the Boat Deck*, for example, the Richardson tones are very noticeable in much of the dialogue of Sam Gridley.

> That's what I said. And don't be in such a hurry to laugh at it either. Suppose you get your revolution, what then? The first thing you'll want is a lot of people who can be relied on to do their duty – just that. And if you've laughed 'em all out of it before that, you'll find yourselves in a nice pickle. You'll be having to shoot managers and foremen in batches – Russian style.

> Most of 'em wouldn't know whether they were making a ship or a skating rink. And wouldn't care. All most of them think about is beer and football, and they don't even know so dam' much about them. I don't want a party, yours or anybody else's. I don't care about capitalists and proletarians, masses and bosses, red shirts, black shirts, brown shirts, green shirts. I want to see some men about, real men who know what sense is, and duty is, and order is. (*Shouting*) I'm getting on, my time's running out, and I'm tired of living among millions of howling monkeys. For God's sake show me some men.

Both these short speeches exhibit some of those qualities which have become the Richardson trade-mark. There is the alternation of ''ems' and 'thems' which makes his stage-speaking have a quality of moving between a sort of hail-fellow cheerfulness and a chilly precision of enunciation. There is, too, the alternation between the short phrase and the long. Richardson's speech characteristically creates a rhythm between short clipped phrasing and even flow. This is his strength in prose drama, for the rhythm comes, as it were, out of the actor and enters into the lines; it is also his weakness in poetic drama, since there is given the sense of an imposed rhythm which is sometimes at variance with the rhythm of the line. Priestley has caught Richardson's style, and has even given him the opportunity to indulge in his capacity for word-colouring. Richardson's open vowel-sounds, in which the vowel often seems to engulf the consonants, are reflected in 'masses', 'bosses', 'red', 'black', 'brown', 'howling'. But Johnson is the most notable example of the actor offering an image to the playwright. The acting persona of Richardson, at its most characteristic, is found in his ability to invest the ordinary, the apparently inconsequential, with a quality of inner passion, and to imply the hidden poetry of the prosaic and often-forgotten man. His acting persona often suggests the exciting mystery that lies behind the common man, and he meticulously makes the common unusual and unique:

> Here I sit waiting – a fool. I know I am a fool, yet I know too I am no fool. All this has always been folly before, but now perhaps, just for once, the miracle may happen. . . . They say I am half-animal, half-god. . . . Yet I do not think it is entirely the animal in me that is waiting here, for the animal must be a simple creature, with a few sharp needs easily satisfied. . . . But this is not simple, this lighted and scented jungle, where everything has been so carefully devised to taste bitter-sweet, half-rotten. . . . Even if the animal in me is fed and tickled, it is to arouse the god, grumbling in his sleep. . . . I make a beast of myself, but the beast is no simple animal, though it may have a shaggy hide and claws. . . . It has the god's head, like the Sphinx, which perhaps looks calm because once, years ago, in a night as big as our centuries, it slaked all its passion. . . . And even here and now, as I sit slavering, sweating and lustful as a cow-led bull, I know that I wish for peace. . . . Let a miracle be worked for me – the – beast, so that the beast shall be satisfied and I shall have peace. . . without regret . . . without regret.

The notations for pauses, and the vowel-tones here, are, it might be suggested, cast in the image of Richardson.

It is for Priestley, then, a first principle that dramatic experience is something that can only be achieved by an audience in the theatre, and that it is the playwright's task to minister to this and not to the literary demands of a reading audience. For him, dramatic experience is quite unlike any common experience, except that 'there are certain rare moments in our lives – perhaps when we are physically exhausted but alert in spirit, perhaps when we find ourselves in great danger – when reality itself suddenly turns into dramatic experience, as if the whole world were a giant theatre and all this life a drama, so much play-acting compared with some unknown deeper reality'. Dramatic experience, in essence has, for Priestley, little to do with conscious understanding or speculation, and it does not or should not put the spectator into the position of being educated or assaulted by anything other than the actuality of the play itself. It is, for him, something of the nature of mystical insight; the drama is close to religion because what it does is to enable the participator (audience) to enter into a state of mind and feelings in which the relationship between what is known, accepted, and what is unknown, strange, apparently unreal, is very close. The dramatic experience occurs at the point where two worlds meet: 'It is in the delicate relationship between belief and disbelief, between the dream life of the play and the real life in the play's presentation, that our true dramatic experience has its roots and its being'.

This has application to the actor in the sense that he is not merely the means by which this relationship is communicated, but is himself part of this dual world of reality and unreality, out of whose relationship the magic, the mysticism, the religion of theatre is created:

> Polly Brown, the actress, is playing Maggie Smith, the farmer's innocent daughter. If I go, for professional reasons, to observe Polly Brown, caring nothing about Maggie Smith and her misfortunes, I reject the dramatic experience. But if I entirely lose sight of Polly Brown and see and believe only in Maggie Smith, so that there is no actress but only a farmer's daughter, I am still outside dramatic experience. The genuine unique experience comes from Polly-Brown-playing-Maggie-Smith. The best actors and actresses . . . are always tremendously themselves and yet at the same time somebody else.

This notion is unexceptionable and, indeed, is hardly innovatory. Its chief merits are the clarity of its expression and its obvious truth to the nature of dramatic experience in the theatre. But Priestley's enunciation of it is important within the context of his own personality, and the personality of the time-plays which he wrote in the 1930s. The idea of the actor being, as it were, two people – one which plays the part, and one which is by nature of being an 'observer' – fits exactly into Priestley's conception of the nature of life, and that quality in life which excites a sense of mystery, awe and magic. The implication is that, for Priestley, drama is naturalistic in its presentation of adult perspective. Each action has its apparent 'reality', but behind it is a hinterland which seems unreal or is dimly perceived; each person has an apparent reality, behind which is a dim familiar who watches and, to an extent which is mystifying and indefinable, controls. The dramatic experience in the theatre is, therefore, for Priestley, an intensified, concentrated version of the dramatic experience of life itself. The glass which is held up to nature by the play is more in the nature of a microscope than a mirror. The microscope is naturalistic in its function, but it makes sharp what is otherwise indistinct, and can even show the apparently invisible:

> When, for example, in Act Four of *The Three Sisters*, we hear the regimental band in the distance, it is not there because regiments must have bands to play them out of a town and this is realism; it is there because the distant fading marching music at once deepens and widens the emptiness and desolation of the sisters' garden.

This kind of naturalism also demands that 'the dialogue must be spoken by characters of unusual quality too, and these characters must be involved in an action that seems to us significant, and that, if possible, and without obtrusive symbolism, makes us feel that it casts a "long shadow". The "long shadow" in which exciting dramatic experience is found also contains, for Priestley, the poetry of drama. He rejects the idea that in plays 'of our own time' in which 'ordinary business' is conducted in 'neat economical prose' that verse should be employed in moments of high tension. He does not reject poetry in its sense of language for contemporary plays, but most obviously is in favour of a definition which would allow the playwright elbow room. The kind of poetic contemporary drama which he finds most in tune with his own feeling is that which has 'a certain kind of sensibility' but does not necessarily have poetic language.

Chekhov's drama is, for Priestley, poetical because of what lies in the long shadows behind the action which we see. Priestley inexorably forces the conclusion that he thinks of poetic language as 'heightened speech' and cannot accept that moments of low tension are capable of communication in anything but prose. He explicitly states that the poetic dramatist tends to be laborious and pompous in unemotional scenes. This, he says, is true of Shakespeare. He quotes from a speech of the Archbishop of York:

> My friends and brethren in these great affairs,
> I must acquaint you that I have received
> New-dated letters from Northumberland;
> Their cold intent, tenour and substance, thus:
> Here doth he wish his person, with such powers
> As might hold sortance with his quality
> The which he could not levy; whereupon
> He is retired, to ripe his growing fortunes,
> To Scotland; and concludes in hearty prayers
> That your attempts may overlive the hazard
> And fearful meeting of their opposite.

He adds:

> Now this pedestrian stuff, containing no memorable beauties of verse, is merely saying in effect: 'Gentlemen, I've just heard from Northumberland, who couldn't raise enough men and has gone to Scotland. He wishes you luck but sounds a bit doubtful.'

It is easy to cavil at Priestley's prose version of the speech. The tone of his version does not have the pompous gravity of the original. He ignores the freezing effect of the line 'Their cold intent, tenour and substance, thus'. There is a considerable difference between 'He wishes you luck but sounds a bit doubtful', and the implied cynicism of the original lines.

Priestley is prepared to admit that it might theoretically be possible for a poetic style to be evolved which would not be too 'absurd' for these 'ordinary occasions' (although one baulks at the implications that York's speech is addressed on such an occasion), but he seems to be saying to any aspiring poetic dramatist: 'I wish you luck but I am a bit doubtful'. He is doubtful because he does not believe that a contemporary audience is capable of being wooed into a totally poetic medium. He believes that any new poetic medium which will cover ordinary occasions will have to be very different from most admired contemporary verse, for it cannot depend too much on 'telescoped images, elaborate associations of ideas, and the introvert's private symbolism', nor can it be 'too involved and obscure or nobody will know what the characters are talking about'.

Priestley believes, in fact, that the contemporary 'dialect of the tribe' – the flat language of the twentieth century makes it extremely difficult for a dramatist to think of writing in specifically poetic language:

> Nobody has worked harder than T.S. Eliot, and whatever the result we should commend him for it – but it is clear that he has been compelled to sacrifice most of his poetry and at the same time to over-simplify not only his own basic ideas, but both characters and action, denying us colour, variety, complexity; so that in the end we feel there is less essential *poetry* in his action and his people than we can find in some prose drama.

The record of attempts to write poetic drama in the twentieth century has done little to prove Priestley wrong. He puts his finger squarely upon an important but often ignored point when he declares that it is a mistake to suppose that 'the poet somehow involves the dramatist, that if we can push a poet somehow through the stage door he will begin to write great plays'. The lamentable history, in this context, of Coleridge, Byron, Shelley, Tennyson, Browning and Swinburne, ranges itself upon Priestley's side. His argument is an implicit recognition of the mistaken idea that Shakespeare was a prototype.

All this is irrefutably true, but one is constantly faced with the question as to why Priestley should, so persistently, have made these apologies on behalf of non-poetic drama in the twentieth century. He is surely right when he says that Shakespeare's context was fruitful for poetic writing, and right when he says that it is mistaken to believe that any poet can be a dramatist. And he is right about the twentieth century attempts to create poetic drama. But why does he go to these lengths? Is he trying to excuse his own lack of verbal poetry, or is he trying to denigrate attempts to write poetic drama because he does not so write himself?

Priestley is no shy violet, but, categorically, he does know his own limitations. One senses rather than knows that he would wish to be capable of poetic language, and therefore one assumes that his writing about language in the theatre has about it some element of self-justification. At the same time it must be remembered that his arguments on behalf of the modern play (like his own) are based on his actual and instinctive knowledge of what works with audiences and what does not. In a letter he writes:

> My plays are meant to be *acted* not read. They are not literary (as Eliot's plays are, in my opinion, and Fry's) but at their best intensely and triumphantly theatrical. They moved audiences to laughter and tears, which is what should happen in the theatre. Though my plays have ideas in them, I have never regarded the theatre as a medium for ideas – the plays and the actors are there to move people; and I wish to God you could have seen how often I did it. And fundamentally I don't think I have been 'sentimental', as many English dramatists have been; what you call 'sentimentality' is to my mind a kind of easy indulgence – I think you suggest it somewhere – that is part of my character. I am a poor hater of people, as distinct from ideas. This may be a weakness in me as an artist. I am not really sufficiently ruthless, either in life or work, to pass as a genius. (Something I have never claimed to be.)

There could perhaps be no more precise summation of the man and his plays than this statement. He claims no more than to be an accomplished workman, but it is extraordinary how so often we find ourselves expecting that we should get more than this from him. This is because the best of Priestley is so very often the best of anything that can be found of its time. He has the ironic quality of making us expect more from him than he can either give or even wish to give. But there is another reason why more is expected of him. He is, fundamentally, a visionary who seems too often to have turned the gold of his dreams into loose change so that it may have a wider currency. He cannot be condemned for this because he honestly believes in the beneficence of wide and popular circulation, but it may be regretted that he does not sometimes a little selfishly hoard his visions a little longer and spend them more judiciously. There is mortality in this, but there is a great deal that is immutable in Priestley's dedicated ability to fulfil an often underrated function of the dramatist – to entertain the heart and stir the mind.

BIBLIOGRAPHY

The plays of J. B. Priestley, with dates of first performance

The Good Companions (adapted from the novel), 1931
Dangerous Corner, 1932
Laburnum Grove, 1933
The Roundabout, 1933
Eden End, 1934
Duet In Floodlight, 1935
Bees On the Boat Deck, 1936
Spring Tide, 1936
I Have Been Here Before, 1937
Time and the Conways, 1937
People At Sea, 1937
Mystery at Greenfingers, 1938
Music At Night, 1938
When We Are Married, 1938
Johnson Over Jordan, 1939
The Long Mirror, 1940
Good Night Children, 1942
They Came to a City, 1943
Desert Highway, 1943
How They Are at Home, 1944
An Inspector Calls, 1946
Ever Since Paradise, 1947
The Linden Tree, 1947
The Rose and Crown, 1947
The Golden Fleece, 1948
Home is Tomorrow, 1948
The High Toby, 1948
Summer Day's Dream, 1949

Bright Shadow, 1950
Dragon's Mouth (with Jacquetta Hawkes), 1952
Treasure on Pelican, 1952
Private Rooms, 1953
Mother's Day, 1953
A Glass of Bitter, 1954
Mr Kettle and Mrs Moon, 1955
Take the Fool Away, 1956
The Glass Cage, 1958
A Severed Head (with Iris Murdoch), 1963
The Pavilion of Masks, 1963

Works by J. B. Priestley quoted in the text

The English Comic Characters. Lane, London, 1925.
The Art of the Dramatist, A Lecture. Heinemann, London, 1957.
Literature and Western Man. Heinemann, London, 1960.
English Journey. Heinemann & Gollancz, London, 1934.
Midnight on the Desert, A Chapter of Autobiography. Heinemann, London, 1939.
Thoughts in the Wilderness. Heinemann, London, 1957.
Topside, or The Future of England, A Dialogue. Heinemann, London, 1958.
Rain Upon Godshill, A Further Chapter of Autobiography. Heinemann, London, 1937.
Margin Released. Heinemann, London, 1962.
Faraway. Heinemann, London, 1932.

Selected Bibliography of works relating to J. B. Priestley

Gillett, Eric: *Introduction to J. B. Priestley: All About Ourselves and Other Essays*. Heinemann, London, 1956.
Hughes, David: *J. B. Priestley, An Informal Study of his Work*. Hart-Davis, London, 1958.
Lindsay, Jack: *J. B. Priestley*. In Baker, Denys Val, ed. Writers of To-day. Sidgwick and Jackson, London, 1946.
Löb, Ladislaus: *Mensch und Gesellschaft bei J. B. Priestley*. Francke Verlag, Bern, 1962.
Pogson, Rex: *J. B. Priestley and the Theatre*. Triangle Press, Clevedon, 1947.

Other Works Consulted

Abbott, E. A.: *Flatland, A Romance of Many Dimensions*. London, 1885.
Agate, James: *More First Nights*. London, 1937.
Red Letter Nights. London, 1944.
The Contemporary Theatre, 1944–1945. London, 1946.
The Ego Books.
Bentley, Eric: *In Search of Theatre*. London, 1954.
Dent, Alan: *Preludes and Studies*. London, 1942.
Dunne, J. W.: *An Experiment with Time*. London, 1927.
The Serial Universe. London, 1934.
The New Immortality. London, 1938.
Nothing Dies. London, 1940.
Guthrie, Tyrone: *A Life in The Theatre*. London, 1961.
Nicoll, Allardyce: *British Drama*. London, 1947.
Ouspensky, P. D.: *A New Model of the Universe*. London, 1931.
The Oxford Companion to the Theatre. London, 1951.
Short, Ernest: *Sixty Years of Theatre*. London.
Trewin, J. C.: *The English Theatre*. London, 1948.
We'll Hear a Play. London, 1949.
The Theatre since 1900. London, 1951.
Dramatists of Today. London, 1953.
The Turbulent Thirties. London, 1960.
Theatre Programme. London, 1955.
Williamson, Audrey: *Theatre of Two Decades*. London, 1947.
Theatre Arts Monthly: Nov. 1937; Jan. 1938; Feb. 1938; Dec. 1938; Dec. 1939.
And reviews and notices of Priestley's plays in *The Manchester Guardian, The Observer, The Sunday Times.*

Index